BEING EDDIE WARING

Being
Eddie Waring
The Life and Times
of a Sporting Icon

TONY HANNAN

MAINSTREAM
PUBLISHING

EDINBURGH AND LONDON

First published in Great Britain in 2008 by
MAINSTREAM PUBLISHING COMPANY
(EDINBURGH) LTD
7 Albany Street
Edinburgh EH1 3UG

ISBN 9781845963002

A catalogue record for this book is available
from the British Library

Typeset in Adobe Garamond Pro and Palatino

Printed in Great Britain by
William Clowes Ltd, Beccles, Suffolk

For Mally & Barbara

ACKNOWLEDGEMENTS

A number of people and organisations provided valuable assistance in the course of writing this book, and many are quoted within its pages. The author is grateful to them all.

Thanks are due especially to Tony and Harry Waring, without whose help and openness the book would have been trickier to write and a good deal less enlightening.

Brian Batty, Mike Latham, Harry Jepson, Dave Williams, John Ledger, Graham Morris, Richard de la Riviere, David Howes and Jack Williams all shared useful items of research, while Margaret Watson of the *Dewsbury Reporter* was particularly helpful in this regard, as were Jeff Walden and the team at the BBC's Written Archives Centre in Caversham Park, Reading.

Thanks are also due to Bill Campbell, Graeme Blaikie and Claire Rose at Mainstream; editor Claire Wingfield; Keith Bunker and Isobel Williams at the production company Bite Yer Legs Ltd; the staff and pupils of Eastborough Junior, Infant and Nursery School, Dewsbury; and Tony Collins for access to the Rugby Football League's historical records at Red Hall, Leeds.

Unless otherwise stated, all photographs are from the private collection of the Waring family.

Finally, a belated thank you to my own favourite trilby-wearing teacher at Southmere Primary School, Bradford, the late Mr Gargan, without whom I might never have discovered my love of the written word and Seabrook smokey bacon crisps.

CONTENTS

Introduction   11

PART I   FAITH
1   He Ain't Heavy . . .   19
2   Theatre of Dreams   41
3   Centre of Attention   59

PART II   HOPE
4   Expanding Horizons   89
5   A Man of Vision   113
6   The Court of King Eddie   147

PART III   CLARITY
7   Making a Splash   173
8   Send in the Clowns   209
9   Be Not Afraid   259

Postscript   281
Afterword by Harry Waring   285
Notes   287
Index   297

INTRODUCTION

Britain: Christmas Day, 1977. The annual pile of turkey remains, Brussels sprouts and semi-demolished Christmas pud has been cleared to the kitchen, and millions of overstuffed families settle down for another festive feast – eight or more hours in the company of BBC television.

Outside, the weather is unremarkable. As ever, there is no sign of snow, although many parts of the country will soon sit under six-foot drifts as blizzards continue on and off into early February. Inside, Dad is emptying his first bottle of Webster's Green Label – slogan: 'Drives out the Northern thirst' – of its stale and acrid contents. Mum and Grandma treat themselves to a rather more exotic drop of Warninks Advocaat or, perhaps, a Snowball. As for the goggle-box, this year the big day has fallen on a Sunday, so the BBC must find room in its schedules for a seasonal edition of *Songs of Praise*, and it is to that show that the honour of opening the evening's festivities falls, once Her Majesty the Queen ('Isn't she looking well?'), Billy Smart's Circus, *The Wizard of Oz*, Basil Brush and the early evening news are out of the way, of course.

A leaf through the Christmas and New Year double edition of the *Radio Times* (price 26p) reveals that *Songs of Praise* is to be followed by Bruce Forsyth's *The Generation Game*. Then comes Mike Yarwood, whose cosy impersonations of Ted Heath, Harold Wilson and Denis 'Silly Billy' Healey have become as familiar a Yuletide feature as untouched sticky dates. The programme that everyone is really looking forward to, however, does not come on until five to nine. Its name is *The Morecambe and Wise Christmas Show* and it is destined to attract a record-breaking audience of over 28 million – more than half the entire population of Great Britain.

This, then, is what many regard as the golden age of light entertainment, and Eric Morecambe and Ernie Wise are its kings. In 1977, Eric and Ernie are at the top of their game, firmly established as a year-round national institution. They are best known, however, for these lush and spectacular annual specials, which, since 1969, have been devoured like salted nuts. Though they are Northern comedians through and through, the appeal of Eric and Ernie's surreal and silly humour transcends all social and geographical boundaries – no mean feat in the class-conscious and economically troubled 1970s. 'What would you have been if you hadn't been comedians?' the quick-witted Eric Morecambe was once asked. 'Mike and Bernie Winters,' came the reply. In their own daft way, Morecambe and Wise united a nation. Queen Elizabeth herself was said to be a fan, even if Eric and Ernie's 1977 Christmas offering did attract some six million more viewers than her own.

No wonder, then, that many of the biggest names in show business and the arts scrambled to appear with Eric and Ernie. Among their guest stars, at one time or another, were actors of the calibre of Michael Redgrave, Robert Morley, Diana Rigg, Peter Cushing, Arthur Lowe and Glenda Jackson. From the high-culture worlds of music and ballet came Nana Mouskouri, André Previn, Shirley Bassey, Elton John, Yehudi Menuhin (whom Eric once told: 'Bring your banjo') and Rudolf Nureyev. Household telly names got in on the act too, with broadcasters and newsreaders such as Robin Day, Barry Norman and Angela Rippon taking an opportunity to reveal their less serious side (or, in the last case, legs). Into this mix, on TV's most important night of the year, dressed as a sailor and flanked by Frank Bough on one side and Richard Baker to the other, marched Eddie Waring, rugby league commentator extraordinaire and the best thing to come out of Dewsbury since the heavy woollen overcoat.

* * *

At least, that was how the vast majority of the population saw it. To many in Eddie Waring's Northern homelands, and particularly those who followed the sport in which he had made his broadcasting name, dear old 'Uncle Eddie' represented something else entirely.

To his critics, Eddie's comical on-screen persona was an embarrassing regional stereotype. The BBC, they claimed, wasn't laughing with Eddie, it was laughing at him and, by extension, the north of England and rugby league itself. So infatuated was the Corporation with rugby union, the Establishment code, that it took every opportunity to paint the 13-a-side game in an unfavourable light.

Today, around a quarter of a century after his death, the mere mention of Eddie Waring's name is guaranteed still, at one end of the country anyway, to spark fierce debate on the implications of England's so-called North–South divide. To what extent did the BBC's unwavering loyalty towards Eddie propagate the tired old cliché whereby Northerners are less intellectually complex than their Southern counterparts? And to what extent was all this just a reflection of rugby league's own insecurities and stubborn refusal to get to grips with reality?

As the *Guardian* television reviewer and resident league fan Martin Kelner rather wittily put it in April 2001:

> Thanks to the BBC, rugby league established a reputation it has still not quite shed, as a quaint northern pastime, like clog dancing, underlined by the presence for many years of Eddie Waring, as the 'voice of rugby league'. Waring was, of course, one of television's great 'characters' for whom we were supposed to be grateful; but I never remember the BBC asking Magnus Pike or the Two Ronnies to front the Five Nations.

Even those who sang Eddie Waring's praises had a tendency to do so in a somewhat backhanded fashion. A decade before Waring's appearance alongside Morecambe and Wise, in 1967, the soon-to-be legendary television interviewer Michael Parkinson, for example, wrote that:

> My definition of the good television sports commentator is that he should be the sort of man you would like to find yourself next to at a game, the companion whose knowledge and wit illuminate the spectacle. Which is why my favourite three are David Coleman, Eddie Waring and John Arlott.

Parkinson went on:

> Of the three, Waring is the one most closely identified with the sport he watches. For me, Waring's main asset is his uninhibited approach to commentating. He is blessed with neither a gift for fine words nor a deep insight of the game. What he does possess is the uncanny ability of saying exactly what the man on the terraces is thinking.[1]

It is easy to see why Michael Parkinson felt that way – yet, as the pages to come will hopefully reveal, there was much more going on under the trademark Waring trilby than that.

But what of the man himself? Away from the microphone, Eddie Waring – a deeply private and in many ways complicated individual – came to be viewed as something of a mystery figure, developing a mythical reputation that he was happy to encourage whenever it suited him to do so. Seldom would he discuss anything of a personal nature with his fellow journalists – staving off their attempts to pierce his armour with a cheery 'That's Eddie!' For several years, it was even rumoured that, though married with a son, he was a permanent resident at the Queens Hotel in Leeds city centre. On television, Waring spoke little of tactics and lots about players, telling stories designed to put the game into context for those who might otherwise be unfamiliar with it and popularising phrases like 'up and under' and 'early bath' as he went.

In his 2004 book *Up and Over*, the *Independent* journalist and broadcaster Dave Hadfield describes how he and his fellow walkers for charity, the former Great Britain internationals Mike 'Stevo' Stephenson and Phil Clarke, these days enjoying high-profile television commentary careers of their own, one day turned up at the Queens Hotel, reputed to be Waring's one-time home. 'It's a story of which I was vaguely aware,' writes Hadfield. 'I made a mental note to investigate further some day . . .'[2]

During the research for this book, at a media open day in June 2007, Dave Hadfield and I sat in the shiny red seats of the rebuilt Wembley stadium – the venue with which Eddie Waring was perhaps most closely associated by the nation at large – and discussed what, if anything, he had since unearthed about the story. 'I went back to the Queens,' said Hadfield, 'and first of all they denied all knowledge of him. Then, eventually, they managed to find somebody who had worked there at that time. I had this image in my mind of an isolated, reclusive figure living on the top floor, but, as usual, the truth was more intriguing than the fiction.'

So, just what is the intriguing truth behind the myth of Eddie Waring, exactly? Was he really just the incomprehensible comic Northerner of popular legend – part Establishment stooge, part music-hall turn – or was there a less well-known and more surprising side to the broadcaster who took an underappreciated sport into British homes like no one before or since? One thing is certain: in evaluating the legacy of this most iconic of sporting figures, the separation of fact and fiction is long overdue. It is time to go in search of the real Eddie Waring.

Part I

FAITH

One

HE AIN'T HEAVY . . .

'He'll be all right – I saw his eyelids flicker.'

On the face of it, there is nothing particularly extraordinary about Dewsbury. Boasting a total population of some 54,350 and nestled snug amidst the foothills of Earlsheaton, Thornhill and Grange Moor, amongst other windblown extremities, it resembles many another small West Yorkshire town whose diminutive stature belies the influential and even international punch it once packed back in the glory years of the nineteenth and early twentieth centuries.

Busy and bustling at its compact heart on the banks of the River Calder and blessed with rural outskirts that emerge dramatically from a bleak and seemingly interminable topography of craggy promontories and high open moorland, Dewsbury is a pleasant enough town when the sun shines. But when the dark clouds gather or the latest lashing of its 100 centimetres of rainfall per annum beats down upon its once-cobbled streets, it can be as dismal and uninviting a place as any on earth.

This, then, is the centre of what is still rather nostalgically referred to as the Heavy Woollen District. So named on account of that aforementioned mighty industrial past, this particular corner of Yorkshire's former West Riding has been a site of no little historical and geographical importance since Saxon times, maybe even before. In the modern era, Dewsbury's stock really began to rise with the completion of the Calder and Hebble Navigation Canal in 1770, through which it was linked to the crucial distribution centres of Manchester and Hull. Henceforth, the area would develop into one of the world's most important producers and exporters of textile goods, particularly when it came to the business of shoddy – i.e. the mixing of new wool with old, from which came the ideal material with which to make heavy blankets, coats and military uniforms. Stand in the right place, they said, and you could see 'upwards of 60 mill chimneys at a time'.[1] With the arrival of the railways in 1848, the influence of Dewsbury and its surrounding area grew until, as with many Northern towns and cities whose wealth and confidence were made and sustained on the back of the Industrial Revolution, the decline and fall of Victoria's all-powerful British Empire brought with it a descent into uncertainty and struggle.

Situated some eight or so miles equidistant from big-city rivals Leeds and Bradford to the north, Wakefield to the east and Huddersfield to the south-west, though no longer blessed with any real strategic industrial importance, the town nevertheless retains more than a spark of the pugnacious survival instincts that served it so well in years gone by. Handily close to the M1 and M62 motorways, and served by the TransPennine Express rail service, today Dewsbury is reinventing itself as a commuter town. The presence of a burgeoning Asian community has, since the 1950s, added another cosmopolitan ingredient to a place that has always looked outward by necessity and inward by nature. In short, behind Dewsbury's nondescript facade, and those of the Heavy Woollen neighbours with which its fortunes are so closely intertwined – Batley, Heckmondwike and Ossett complete the core quartet – there lies buried a depth of hidden character and an array of yarns unspun. As an outsider, you think you know Dewsbury, but, really, you do not.

Along with all that warp, weaving and weft, Dewsbury has also, in its time, been synonymous with at least two more examples of character-building social activity. One such is the town's century-old passion for the sport of rugby league and, more specifically, its very own club, which, thanks to the appendage of an unusually appropriate nickname, is known in these days of cheerleaders and razzmatazz as the Dewsbury Rams. With a home ground at Owl Lane, on the site of the old Saville and Shaw Cross colliery, where the club has been based since the old Crown Flatt stadium burned down in the late 1980s, this present-day Dewsbury side currently bumps along before crowds of a few hundred in the sport's semi-professional National Leagues. Glamorous it is not. Yet, as we shall soon see, things were not ever thus.

As is also the case with many other Northern towns and cities where their relationship with the local rugby league club is concerned, although on-field fortunes have fluctuated through the years, traditionally Dewsbury RLFC has been a source of enormous civic pride, not least because it allowed an otherwise unremarkable town, whose days of wider influence seemed firmly rooted in the past, to assert itself once again on a bigger stage. In an era before television and overseas travel, for the public of Dewsbury the trials and tribulations of its local rugby team meant more than might easily be comprehended in today's fast-moving world of unfettered global communication and Internet technology. In Dewsbury, the value of sport, in general, was easily understood. For one thing, it provided an affordable release from the daily drudgery of grind and toil. For another, whoever first set up shop among those hills was clearly unafraid of exercise. It is just about impossible to walk anywhere without crampons on your boots. You can develop a nosebleed nipping out for a loaf. And whether as amateur recreation or mass entertainment, in Dewsbury, as elsewhere among the communities of Yorkshire, Lancashire and Cumbria, the 13-a-side code was king.

More than just a simple social pleasure, the particularly working-class phenomenon that was rugby league was both a symbolic expression of personal identity and a crucial component in an entire way of life. Indeed, for many, it still is. Rugby league told of who you were and from where you came. Every grunt, tackle, bashed-up nose and spray of sweat told of the hopes, dreams, limitations, frustrations and aspirations of those who watched the game and stepped out into its arenas. Rugby league stadiums were temples in which semi-mythological ideas of just what it meant to be masculine, gladiatorial and Northern were rehearsed time and time again. With its unfussy, no-nonsense rules and democratic off-field constitution, league was a game which prided itself on what were commonly held to be honest working-class values. It promoted qualities like truth, courage and the benefits of hard work. For those with the physical aptitude to meet its demands of speed, skill and raw-boned strength – not to mention quick-witted mental toughness – the playing or coaching of rugby league might provide a pathway to local fame and, most importantly, greater financial security. It encouraged camaraderie and loyalty, and it engendered team spirit. It was fun, too, of course, and, unlike its middle-class 15-a-side cousin, it belonged to the people, giving it an appeal to those with a socially dissenting voice. On a Saturday afternoon, the bosses could kick and clap to their hearts' content. Rugby league was 'our game'.

In the opinion of Harry Jepson, a one-time rugby league administrator in nearby Hunslet and now a sprightly 87 years old, the 1920s, in particular, were dreadful times in which to live. 'There was the Depression towards the end of the decade and times were tough,' he recalled, 'so there was a lot of incentive to play rugby league football and be good at it. At a lot of clubs – Featherstone, for example – players could receive about 45 shillings for a win and 25 shillings for a loss. When you think that the average wage in the country was less than two quid, if you played rugby league you could do a lot for your family. Times were hard and so that made the game hard. Those lads wanted to win. It wasn't a question of a few pounds' pocket money – this was money that made a big difference to their lives. As a smaller club, Dewsbury was always a great producer of talent. It was always difficult for an away team to win there.'[2]

If the personality of the Heavy Woollen District was shaped by sport and the industry from which it took its name, then in the region's religious traditions, we find one more explanation for its robust singularity of character. From the Middle Ages onwards, the established Church – whether Roman Catholic or Anglican – was as much an instrument of social control in Yorkshire as anywhere else. Yet in Dewsbury and its environs there was a more independent spirit abroad, amidst all the established fire and brimstone. That great religious evangelist the Reverend John Wesley, for example, is said to have visited the town at least five times during the mid-eighteenth century and, in 1746, that evangelical zeal paid off when Dewsbury's Methodist Society was first established in his name. The tradition Wesley inspired remains much in evidence to this day.

Another strand of Nonconformist local worshippers were the Congregationalists, a breakaway sect of Christianity for whom democracy is considered key. Though strict in its moral expectations, Congregationalism is based upon a founding principle that religious leaders should not act dictatorially. Instead, each individual chapel minister should answer to an elected group of lay officers and, ultimately, be guided by the wishes of the congregation that he or she is ordained to serve. One such congregation gathered at a soot-blackened chapel a couple of hundred yards up the Halifax Road.

* * *

Like the Crown Flatt ground that once upon a time would have been visible from here on its plateau across the valley, Springfield Congregational Chapel is nowadays but a half-forgotten memory. Stop off at the site today and in its place sits a modern doctors' surgery, before which spreads a gloomy patch of overgrown grass surrounded by a forbidding circuit of black iron railings. To the town planners of the 1970s, the neglected Springfield Chapel was merely one more eyesore best demolished for slum clearance. Ironically, given your average Congregationalist's stern disapproval of alcohol, the Bath Hotel, a public house once next door but one, stands as steadfastly by the roadside as it ever did. The painting and decorating firm that at one time sat in between is now an Indian restaurant.

Like several other such places of worship in the town, Springfield Chapel was built and paid for by the prominent local businessman and MP Sir Mark Oldroyd. Born in 1843, the public-spirited Oldroyd grew to become one of the richest and most powerful men in Yorkshire, if not the entire country. As owner of the largest textile-manufacturing empire in England, before his death, aged 84, in 1927 Oldroyd at one time employed some 2,500 workers. After helping to expand the mill founded by his father in 1818, Oldroyd would go on to own three more Dewsbury mills and one in Hunslet. In time, he would also bag a carpet mill in Germany, a textile mill in a part of Poland then known as Silesia and a couple of collieries. As the archetypal Victorian philanthropist, rather than just sit on his wealth Mark Oldroyd preferred to use it in the promotion of useful social causes, such as strengthening the relationship between workers and employers, and providing donations towards the building of schools, the first local hospital, Dewsbury Town Hall and Congregational churches. His interest in the latter was a direct result of his own religious background: after leaving Batley Grammar School, he had trained to be a Congregationalist minister at New College, London, before opting for a career in business instead.[3]

One prominent member of the Springfield congregation in the early 1900s was an insurance agent named Arthur Waring, destined, at various stages, to take on the roles of deacon, lay preacher and chapel choirmaster. In keeping with such respectable public positions, Arthur was a deeply religious and serious-minded man who, nevertheless, possessed a keen sense of humour and had a flamboyant approach when it came to conducting his choir. By 1910, he and his wife, Florence Harriet Waring, née Marsden and known to all as Florrie, had already produced one son, Henry Arthur, henceforth known as Harry. On 21 February that year, Arthur and Florrie presented Harry with a baby brother. Into the Heavy Woollen world of sermons, psalms and stirring brass bands came one Edward Marsden Waring. Though named after his father's best friend, Edward Washington, and further honoured with his mother's maiden name, he would one day be immortalised as just Eddie.

For all that its civic propaganda likes to boast otherwise, Dewsbury has produced but a sprinkling of truly famous people over the past few hundred years. Among the best known are a couple of respected Labour politicians in Baroness Betty Lockwood, whose many achievements include becoming the first chair of the Equal Opportunities Commission in 1975, and Betty Boothroyd, who, in April 1992, became the first woman Speaker of the House of Commons. At one time or another, the town has been crucible to a whole raft of less glamorous technical whizz-kids, too, including the pioneering computer engineer Professor Tom Kilburn, eighteenth-century astrologer and scientist John Michell – to whom we owe the theory of black holes – and Sir Clifford Allbutt, inventor of the clinical thermometer. In the literary world, the Reverend Patrick Brontë spent two years as rector of Dewsbury Parish Church, from 1809–11, while his daughter Charlotte was a governess at Miss Margaret Wooler's school for ladies at Dewsbury Moor, an establishment at which another of the three sisters, Anne, was briefly a pupil.[4]

In Eddie Waring, however, Dewsbury would have an entirely different breed of celebrity on its hands. From the chrysalis of this choirmaster's son would emerge a quick-witted butterfly, wafted high by the sheer exuberance of his own personality. The name 'Eddie Waring' would become known not only locally but across the length and breadth of the British Isles and as far away as Australia, New Zealand and the USA. A true child of his times, he would learn, in the words of Rudyard Kipling's much-loved poem 'If', to 'talk with crowds' and keep his virtue, to 'walk with kings – nor lose the common touch'. He would grow to number many of the biggest stars in sport, politics and show business among his friends and yet think of himself, first and foremost, as a jobbing journalist, rewriting the rules of that trade as he went along. He would be among the first newspaper writers to travel down under with a touring British sports team. He would all but invent character-driven live television sports commentary as we know it in Britain today and use the high-profile status that brought to raise funds for countless good causes. He would take the hitherto parochial sport of rugby league into the living rooms of a nation and, in so doing, become a household name loved by millions, while being unfairly – if, perhaps, understandably – viewed with suspicion by those closer to home, from whom he might have expected a little more empathy.

The young Eddie Waring would flower as a showman, a talented athlete, a coach, performer and frustrated impresario. He would hold audiences in the palm of his hand. In many ways a deeply private man, despite the extrovert public persona which established his reputation, the older Eddie Waring would guard his biographical details jealously, behind a protective shield that few of his fellow journalists were ever able to penetrate. 'He is a mysterious figure, shifting like a shadow in private life; slightly larger than life when presented with a microphone,' as the *Daily Express* writer Geoffrey Mather once observed.[5] At the height of his fame, Waring would enjoy the status of a true Northern star whilst simultaneously being slammed as an offensive regional caricature. In the process, he became the perfect symbol of the English North's ongoing struggle with its own identity, both in terms of how it likes to see itself (worthy and underappreciated) and how others often see it (chippy beyond belief). Yet to the Great British public at large, nurtured on a diet of Mike Yarwood, *It's a Knockout* and Challenge Cup finals on *Grandstand*, he was just good old Uncle Eddie, the voice of rugby league.

* * *

All that, however, was for the future. Harry and Eddie Waring had a childhood to get through first and a happy one at that. Though she is far too young to have experienced those twilight Edwardian years at first hand, Margaret Watson, the former deputy editor of the weekly *Dewsbury Reporter* and long ago adopted as the town's leading local historian, remembers a time when Springfield's mark on the community was still profound.

'Springfield Congregational Chapel was at the top of the road where I lived, near to Mark Oldroyd's mill,' she recalls, at the *Reporter*'s flat-iron headquarters, just across the road from Dewsbury railway station. 'Although I was a Catholic, I used to go to that church quite a lot. Eddie's parents weren't Methodists and they weren't Anglicans, they were "chapel-ers". Just as the name implies, it was the congregation who decided just how things were run; they didn't have a parochial church council or anything. They would all make decisions on chapel events after the service. They held harvest festivals, went on regular charabanc trips to the coast or local countryside and were very anti-drink: strictly temperance.'[6]

Eddie's only nephew, named Harry after his father and born in 1935, recalls Springfield's chapel services as joyous occasions. 'Congregationalism is a Nonconformist religion, similar to Wesleyanism,' he explains. 'They had their own type of service and a lot of it was nice hymn singing. I could best describe it as a hearty brass-band type of music rather than anything overtly evangelical. When he was old enough, Eddie would introduce hymns.'[7] He sang them too, as soon as he was able. The young Eddie became an enthusiastic member of the Springfield choir and, by all accounts, was blessed with a half-decent baritone voice, although he would one day declare: 'I did take lessons. Not good enough, of course.'[8]

'When I came along, I was the only child in this small family, so I got a lot of attention from Eddie, he was like a second father to me,' Harry junior continues. 'Apart from the games and quizzes he used to organise at the family Christmas parties, one of my first recollections of my uncle comes from going to chapel with my grandma, his mother, during the war years and hearing him singing. Even in those days, Uncle Eddie was a bit of a showman, and you could hear him over everyone else. He had his voice trained at one time, and I believe that this stood him in good stead in later years, when it came to standing in front of people and speaking. In the 1940s and '50s, I used to go to other chapels with him and he would introduce hymns there, too. He knew all the names: "Rimmington", "Pentecost" and so on.'

Back in 1910, meanwhile, although the majority of Springfield housing consisted of back-to-backs, each with two bedrooms, a single room downstairs and a chilly outside toilet, at the tail end of an age marked by optimism and innovation the area was considered a decent environment in which to live. Nevertheless, by the time Eddie arrived, though still maintaining close contact with their beloved chapel, Arthur and Florrie Waring were residents of nearby Soothill Nether. Their home, a two-storey house in Hollinroyd Road known as 'South View', sat in a busy little neighbourhood of around two hundred people, blessed with a panoramic outlook across the valley and situated on the very same slope upon which Crown Flatt stadium was also perched, a few hundred feet higher up. This would be home to Eddie for the first 36 years of his life.

That Arthur and Florrie were able to raise their family in such relatively salubrious surroundings owed much to the fact that the property's owners were Eddie's maternal grandparents. Like many in the area, Mr and Mrs William Henry Marsden had made a respectable amount of money in the textile industry, and a portion of the couple's savings had bought a cluster of terraced houses on leasehold land from a local builder, of which South View was one. Along with these properties, the Marsdens owned a corner shop, not far from their own chapel in Batley Carr, in which Florrie had worked as a girl. In her days as a young adult, Florrie also found work as a milliner (the genesis, perhaps, of her future son's eclectic taste in hats). In this way and more then, Florrie's father, William, would provide another major influence on both of his grandsons' formative years. Although he died in 1924, in the young Harry and Eddie's eyes their grandfather and landlord was living proof that sound business acumen, when combined with those long-established Victorian ethics of hard work and self-determination, could indeed be a route to material and personal advancement. In fact, in a straightforward business sense, it was Harry who most obviously put those lessons into practice. At the culmination of the Second World War, the elder of the two brothers launched a successful firm of electrical contractors still remembered by those of a certain vintage in the town today.

In future years, Harry would also inherit the responsibility for looking after the Waring family's Hollinroyd Road properties. His son, Harry junior, recalls that 'the houses were by then not very attractive, so they didn't earn much rent. In fact, they cost more than their income to maintain. There were two rows of terrace houses at ninety degrees to one another, one row of four overlooking the valley and one of five going up the hill.' Today, whilst Hollinroyd Road itself still exists as an unmade and seemingly forgotten-about back lane nestled in the crooked elbow of the Leeds and Wakefield roads, which themselves buzz along busier than ever just out of sight, South View and the majority of its neighbouring properties are long since gone. Indeed, all the houses which stood on the street's left-hand side were demolished in the late 1960s, victims of a scheme to widen the fast-moving Leeds Road, which runs parallel on the easterly route out of town.

The remainder of the land on which those houses once rested is nowadays overgrown scrubland, its history betrayed only by the odd inscrutable lump of time-stained rubble. There are clues to the style and positioning of South View, however. A single row of stone-built terrace houses – numbered evenly, 18 to 30 – still peers out on the right-hand side of the incline, much as the Waring residences would have done on the left. Otherwise, the years have taken their toll. The faux and long-faded grandeur of a small stone staircase leads up to what are now unkempt yards rather than gardens, offset by rubbish skips and unsightly half-finished breeze-block extensions. Despite the spirit-raising efforts of one or two carefully tended bungalows, the best days of this particular stretch of Hollinroyd Road are long since behind it. A little further up the hill, on either side of the dirt road, sit the remains of an old stone gateway, formerly a toll bar for horse-drawn traffic, and a small patch of woodland. To a twenty-first-century visitor, this forlorn little enclave feels almost eerie: a stagnant, if peaceful, backwater in an otherwise hectic world. Yet it is easy to imagine how, once upon a time, it might have seemed if not posh exactly then tentatively upwardly mobile. While the people who owned these homes would have been all too aware that life's mountain remained to be climbed, they could, at least, rest content in the knowledge that a camp had been set up in its foothills.

By no means poverty stricken, then, the Waring family could hardly be said to be a long way up the social ladder either: lower middle class at best, with a lifestyle inextricably tied to the economic fortunes of those who paid the rent. 'Eddie always felt he was working class,' says his nephew. 'He had a strong sense of social conscience, and I think his chapel upbringing influenced this. Because they broke away from formal churches, the Congregationalists operated in a democratic way. Although he came over as light-hearted and easy-going, there was a serious side to Eddie and once he focused on an objective he would make it happen. He was quite firm.' As, when she needed to be, was his dear mother, who, though widely remembered as a quiet and caring woman, worked with the same tireless determination as her husband for her family and chapel, and was equally blessed with a tremendous sense of fun. At least one Dewsbury signing from Wigan, Charlie Seeling junior, would later confirm that it was only thanks to Florrie's 'angelic' support that he had been able to settle into the town at all.

As his public persona developed, Eddie would all too infrequently let his defences slip a little and reveal snippets of these happy days from a distant past, in which he would walk the family's pet Scottie dog, Dusky, play his outdoor games and dream, no doubt, of great deeds to come – most probably on the stage or football field. One such occasion came with an appearance on the long-running BBC Radio 4 programme *Desert Island Discs* in February 1974, during which he admitted to the show's creator and presenter Roy Plomley that he had indeed once nursed an idea of making his living in music. 'I remember asking my father in later life what he wanted me to be – I was then a newspaperman,' Eddie revealed. 'He said, well, he would have liked me to have either been a minister or a pianist or a singer. Well, I was none of the three, although I think I would have liked to have been a singer.'[9]

It was also while cast away on this fictional desert island that Eddie Waring first publicly revealed his love for a particular piece of music written by a family friend, the composer Handel Parker. Of the many trips and excursions that the Springfield Congregationalists habitually took, one of the most regular was to Shipley Glen, a boulder-strewn beauty spot some three miles north of Bradford. It was in Shipley that Handel Parker, a one-time child prodigy who, aged seven, had played flute in an Oxenhope drum and fife band and made his debut with the Haworth Baptist Harmonium as an eight year old, spent much of his later life until his death, aged 74, in 1928. The parallels with Waring's own father were obvious. Parker, too, was at varying times a choirmaster, conductor, organist and composer, but, aside from the family friendship, it was the mournful, melancholic nature of perhaps his best-known work, 'Deep Harmony', that meant most to the bright-eyed young man on the Shipley Glen tramway. Indeed, so affected were the Waring family by the piece that Parker presented the original manuscript to Arthur, who, in time, passed it down to Eddie. Today, a copy sits proudly in the personal collection of nephew Harry. With its echoes of the famous Cup-final tune 'Abide with Me', the hymn would evoke fond memories throughout Eddie's life. He chose it, as played by the Black Dyke Mills band, as one of his tunes on *Desert Island Discs* and asked to hear it again, courtesy of a ten-piece brass-band arrangement, on a similar BBC Radio 2 programme, *Be My Guest*, just before his retirement in March 1980. 'I can still sing the bass part of it, too, if you want it,' he teased his listeners, 'but you're not going to get it.'[10]

Nor were Eddie's musical tastes exclusively highbrow. As Waring grew older, he would describe himself as 'a great radio man' and was as partial to a catchy pop tune as anyone, even if, in the case of another of his *Be My Guest* selections, 'Delilah' by Tom Jones, the biblical connection remained. On the same show, he also spoke of a lifelong passion for the light operatic works of those quietly subversive social satirists Gilbert and Sullivan, choosing 'We Sail the Ocean Blue' from Act One of *HMS Pinafore* and recounting a once embarrassing tale of long ago. 'I am a great fan of Gilbert and Sullivan,' he confirmed. 'In fact, I was the president of a Gilbert and Sullivan society for quite a while. I used to take part in anything [Springfield Chapel] had going. One year, they put on Gilbert and Sullivan and they had *Pinafore*. Now, I like *Pinafore* very well, and they had a chorus of sailors. One of my youthful memories is the horror of discovering that I was the only sailor in the chorus of *Pinafore* who had a bare chest. In the haste of dressing, and I have it at times nowadays, the hat and the collar and what have you, I had omitted the vital vest. So something from *HMS Pinafore* please, with blushing from me in consequence.'[11]

* * *

Although chapel life would play a crucial role in shaping the personality of the young Eddie Waring, the establishment at which he received his earliest scholastic education would prove equally influential. Along with just about every other child in the local community, including his brother, Eddie was a pupil at Eastborough Council School – nowadays Eastborough Junior, Infant and Nursery School – tucked away neatly on the other side of Leeds Road, just downwind of his Hollinroyd Road home.

As well as Betty Boothroyd and Baroness Lockwood, another Eastborough pupil destined to follow Eddie Waring on the road to fame was long-time Conservative MP for Shipley, Sir Marcus Fox. And appropriately, given the school's reputation for sporting excellence, the well-known cross-channel swimmer of the 1950s Eileen Fenton taught there. Upon the author's visit to what remains a charming and happy little establishment, in which a number of its very youngest pupils, no doubt used to a preponderance of female teachers, insisted on calling this 43-year-old, balding male interloper 'Miss', several staff members were off to watch the older boys in an after-school cricket match. The highly respected headmaster of Eddie's era, John Edwin Tolson JP, must have been beaming down in pride.

The first headmaster under whose influence Eddie would have fallen at Eastborough went by the name of Mr Foster. And certainly it is through that gentleman's entries in the school logbook – an item which the then current Education Code insisted every school had, as 'a bare record of events which constitute the history of the school' kept 'under strict care of the head teacher' – that we can glean much of what Eastborough Council School was about prior to and during the earliest years of Eddie's attendance in the infant section (like everything else in these parts, the school is sited on a hill; its carved stone lintels reveal that the boys' door was once at the top, girls' in the middle and infants' at the bottom).

'This dreadful war is taking a heavy toll on our old boys,' wrote a rueful Mr Foster on 4 December 1916. 'Up to the present, 23 have made the Great Sacrifice.' Generally, though, despite a national mood of gloom, with the occasional influenza epidemic thrown in for bad measure, the school's staff seem determinedly committed to ensuring a lively education for the children in their care. Trips to local parks and museums abound and the only real problem that Foster deems worthy of mention, aside from the war itself, is a smaller than average intake: 'I never remember such a dearth of new boys,' he reflects on 8 February 1917. If that was indeed the year in which Eddie Waring took his first tentative steps into what was in those days known as standard one – and, despite the lack of surviving documentary evidence to either deny or confirm that fact, it very likely was – his new school was certainly ready for him and the war was not going to last forever.

For all that such logbooks provide a glorious resource for anyone of even the remotest historical bent, going by the infrequency of his entries, the world-weary Mr Foster at least appears to have considered their completion a duty he could do without. Though informative in their way, Foster's notes tend to be cursory and written in a scrawl that indicates they were rushed. Even so, there is much to discover. On 21 March 1919, for example, he writes that this has been the 'worst year for attendance since opening of school'. On 14 July, there is the briefest account of how the Peace Celebrations held to commemorate the end of the First World War were celebrated in Dewsbury 'by a pageant of all the schools in the County Borough. We represented Scotland.' On 3 October, he reveals that those same schools were closed on the 'express desire of the King to grant an extra holiday in honour of the victory of the Allied Forces', before adding: 'The railway strike will prevent anyone going to the seaside, which was my intention.'

The big change in the school's fortunes, however, and consequently those of Eddie Waring, came with the arrival of the aforementioned Mr J.E. Tolson JP as headmaster, on the morning of 12 April 1920. Four days after placing his feet under the table, Tolson, a short and friendly Toby-jug of a man, felt able to confide his first impressions. 'I have found the boys attentive,' he wrote, 'and the staff particularly keen to help me in my new duties.' His first task was to rearrange the school timetable more to his liking and then, with that inaugural feat achieved, the sometime town councillor could turn his attentions to exerting still greater influence on the direction his school would take. The young Edward Marsden Waring is mentioned nowhere in the logs by name, but thanks to the new man's more expansive attitude to putting ink to paper, the subsequent picture of an educational environment in which he would flourish is vivid.

As under Mr Foster, there are trips here, there and everywhere, whether to local parks and museums or further afield to Bolton Abbey and seaside resorts such as Bridlington, Filey and Hornsea. The sanctioning of a 'school seaside camp' is sought and obtained from the district council's education committee, to which '40 boys will be selected to make the journey'. In September 1921, some 60 boys were taken to Filey, leaving Tolson to note: 'Many of them had not previously seen the sea, and expressed their delight at the wonders of the shore and rocks.' An appreciation of culture, too, was a cause to be championed. Back when his tenure at the school was just a fortnight old, Tolson wrote that: '24 boys from standards VI and VII visited the local theatre yesterday evening to witness a performance of the "Merchant of Venice". They formed a particularly appreciative portion of the audience.'[12] And, on 18 October 1920, the headmaster reveals for the first time that: 'For the past fortnight, the members of staff have issued a sheet of sporting notes which, we hope, may develop into a school magazine.'

Most obviously, there is a devotion to the self-improving qualities of physical exercise. In premonition of Eileen Fenton's later cross-Channel glories, the school commenced weekly swimming lessons at the local baths and developed a successful three-man swimming team, of which Eddie Waring was emphatically not a member. Even when, on 25 May 1921, a coal shortage led to the suspension of those classes, it was not long before the team was back in the water and winning with its customary aplomb. The one area of school physical activity in which Eddie most definitely did star, however, was on the football field – football, in this instance, meaning round ball rather than oval.

As a boy, slight in stature but fleet of foot, though he played a little social rugby league and took as keen an interest in the fortunes of the Dewsbury team as anyone, Waring's earliest sporting achievements came as a distinguished member of the Eastborough School soccer team. According to family legend, in 200 matches he scored around 100 goals, playing mainly on the left wing. Certainly, from around 1920 onwards, he was a member of a talented side that included among its number the well-known future professional Trevor Rhodes, soon to sign forms with Port Vale.

Mr Tolson first writes of the team's success on 18 March 1921:

The football team (yesterday afternoon) won the Shield given by the Dewsbury, Batley and District Schools' Football Association. During the season we have played 20 league matches and have only once been beaten. Messrs Fisher, Gibson and Speight deserve great credit for the training they have given the boys not only on the football field but during the Physical Instruction lessons. The splendid physical condition of Eastboro' boys has been commented on during the matches.

According to one later local newspaper feature – quite probably penned by Waring himself – some of Eastborough's most eagerly anticipated games were the local derby clashes with Ravensthorpe. And, as Tolson's next entry on the subject of football reveals some seven weeks later, they didn't always get things their own way. 'Football team beaten by Ravensthorpe in final of "News" Cup,' he writes. 'Presented with Shield won as League Champions for season 1920–21. Play time was extended this morning to recognise the event.' Undeterred by this lack of absolute perfection, the boys would duly collect the cup as planned in 1922 and follow that success with a second successive victory a year later.

Representative honours, too, came Eddie Waring's way. He won a place in the inter-town Dewsbury team and was a member of the side that reached the final of the Yorkshire Schools Shield, where he and his teammates were narrowly beaten by Barnsley at Oakwell. Upon leaving school, Waring also captained the Springfield Sunday School team in the Local Boys Welfare League and played for a time with Dewsbury Moorend and Selby Town. The experience at Barnsley had clearly suited him as, after turning out on a number of occasions with the Yorkshire Amateurs, he had trials at both that South Yorkshire club and Nottingham Forest.[13] If it had been left to Eddie, he might very well have continued along that path, but, in those far-off days long before the astronomical wages and pampered rock-star lifestyles of today's Premiership stars, his father Arthur had other ideas and urged his younger son to pursue a 'proper' career.

Harry Waring recalls that some 25 years after Eddie's departure from Eastborough, his uncle's impact upon school pride could still be felt. 'When I went into the primary school as a seven year old,' he says, 'I was taken by one of the teachers to see the headmaster. I was introduced to him as "Eddie's nephew". Not "Harry's son" but "Eddie's nephew". In Eddie's day, he had built a reputation as a bit of a football star in the local environment – kids' stuff, obviously. When I was at school, there was only one football photograph on the wall and it was Eddie's team. He wasn't particularly well-known nationally yet, but the school still remembered him. I was always a little bit in his shadow, but, on the other hand, I enjoyed some reflected glory.'

Nor were Eddie's sporting exploits solely reserved for the soccer field. A living embodiment of Juvenal's *'orandum est ut sit mens sana in corpore sano'* ('pray to have a sound mind in a sound body'), the teenage Waring was very much an all-round athlete who might just as well be found cycling up and down one of those ubiquitous hills as kicking an inflated bag of leather about, playing cricket or having a game of table tennis. Along with the 17 medals he won for his exploits in Association football, he earned silverware for feats on the running track too. He took a keen interest in amateur wrestling and boxing and briefly ran a physical training and wrestling club in his own gymnasium. Away from sport, during the period in which his father was president of Springfield Sunday School, Eddie served there as teacher, steward and choir member. He also began to develop an interest in writing that had first taken flight at Eastborough School when, along with many of the other children, he had written for and helped edit the school paper, *Boro' Football Weekly*.

As we have seen, the seeds of that modest publication were first sown by Mr Tolson in October 1920, some six months after he took up office. Upon completion of his first year in charge, the headmaster logged the opinion that, of all his achievements during that time, he was particularly proud of the establishment of a weekly school magazine. 'An average of 300 copies per week has been sold,' he wrote in April 1921, 'and though most of the matters related to School Sport, the paper has given me the opportunity to cultivate a good feeling between the parents and the school.' By October, he noted that in future, he intended to rely more on the boys' own efforts.

Remarkably, at least one copy of *Boro' Football Weekly* still exists – Vol. IV No. 13, owned by Harry Waring. Upon its yellowing front page, dated 23 January 1924, are three advertisements for local businesses: one for Megson's Central Cafe and Restaurant, Market Place, Dewsbury; another for Bickers Ltd, who 'Give Points Start to All Customers'; and a third promoting the qualities of J&B Scotch whisky, with the slogan 'Always Play Fair'. The masthead, meanwhile, is set against a humbug-style black-and-white background and upon it are caricatures of a goalkeeper punching a ball, a jester and a stripy-blazered supporter, complete with knickerbockers, school cap and speech bubble declaring: 'Now Boro'!!!' The Eastborough motto, *'Semper Optimus'* ('Always the Best'), is in evidence too, along with, at the foot of the page, a list of contributing 'editorial staff', namely P. Armitage, L. Farmer, L. Winder, J. Brook, E. Wood and one E. Waring, all looked over benevolently by Mr J.E. Tolson. 'I wrote rugby league notes,' Waring later told his *Desert Island Discs* interrogator Roy Plomley, 'obviously edited very much by the master in charge of the paper, but it put into me the idea that it might be some sort of a liking, particularly if I could do sport.'

The magazine had a business manager, too, the Physical Instruction teacher Mr J.C.L. Speight, who, we are informed upon turning the page, was rushed off his feet selling the previous week's copy. There is news that a holiday fund has been started, so that: 'Boys who like to save a penny or twopence may now bring their contributions weekly to school, where they will be collected and saved till the time arrives for the Chara trip.' It is revealed that an outing much further afield is also under consideration: 'Most of our readers will be aware that the British Empire Exhibition will be opened at Wembley this year, and some of us have thought what a fine education it would be to our boys were it possible to make arrangements for a visit by a small party. The venture, of course, would be rather expensive, and, moreover, would entail two long journeys and a little loss of sleep. The result would be worth it, we think.'[14] And elsewhere, in the editor's 'Random Remarks' column, we discover that: 'With a much depleted team, Boro' continued their League programme on Saturday morning, Carlton being the visitors to Sands Lane. Lionel Winder deputised for Tinker in goal, whilst Brain, Horsfall and Armitage were all absent on account of illness. Boro' wishes them a speedy recovery.' Those cry-offs clearly meant a reshuffling of the pack, for we are then told: 'Waring made a very convincing debut at inside right, and besides scoring two goals himself, had a hand in most of the others.' The superstar thus described would later confess that, as a 13 year old with tongue planted firmly in cheek, this may very well have been one of the reports he'd had a hand in composing himself.

Two

THEATRE OF DREAMS

'I don't know whether that's his head or the ball; we'll
soon see when he gets up.'

As the days of school trips receded and the prospect of finding
paid employment loomed large, for Dewsbury's most academically
gifted and subsequently high-profile individuals, their next stop
would be Wheelwright Grammar School, a little further up from
Springfield Chapel just off the Halifax Road. It is for that reason,
presumably, that so many accounts of his life have described Eddie
Waring as a former Wheelwright pupil. In fact, he never went
there at all.[1]

There was nothing wrong with Eddie's intelligence. On the
contrary, he had a mind as keen as anyone's, more so in many ways.
Yet with sport and music his twin chief interests, and possessed of
an impulse to cram as much into his days as was humanly possible,
his was an imagination always likely to be fired more by hands-on
practical experience than by sitting around in some dry and dour
school library sifting doggedly through piles of dusty old books.
The outgoing, enthusiastic and ambitious Eddie Waring was not cut
out for hours of serious study alone in his room. He needed to be
out there engaging with the real world, meeting people, pushing
back his personal boundaries and making a name for himself. The
sooner he could embark upon that course of action the better.

As it happened, the opportunity for Eddie to sever his ties

with the classroom came at the grand old age of 14. The exact circumstances of his departure from Eastborough are now lost to the mists of time, although Harry Waring recalls being told that his uncle went to work pretty much immediately for Hirst and Hellawell, a Dewsbury firm of office suppliers. One thing is for sure, for a boy to leave school at such an age was in those austere days of grinding recession far from uncommon, and usually as a result of financial necessity. And, as Mr Tolson's log entry of 25 April 1921 makes clear, the world into which they were thrust could be a tough one indeed. 'There is much distress in the neighbourhood in consequence of unemployment,' Tolson wrote, some three or so years before Eddie Waring's turn came to take his chances. 'A dozen of our boys are having meals provided at the Cookery Centre.' On 23 June, the headmaster noted that the 'distress' had increased, with '40 boys now provided with dinners and teas in school'. A lack of work and 'a bad state of trade' in the town was the prevailing state of affairs, whilst large numbers of those children still in school were periodically absent with 'impetigo and other sores', scabies and those seemingly constant outbreaks of influenza.

For all that the Waring family must have viewed their offspring's first footsteps into adulthood with trepidation, Eddie at least went on his way with steadier foundations than most. Notwithstanding his chapel and family background, Eastborough was, after all, a school where a collective emphasis on social duty and a high regard for cultural and sporting endeavour were as integral as the mortar binding its stone. Though a cursory glance through the school's punishment book of 1926 onwards reveals a strictness of regime hardly unusual for the times – 'four strokes for dirty writing and passing of letters, two strokes for trespassing in Girls school, and so on'[2] – on the whole, the unifying qualities of shared experience and team spirit were never in doubt. On 25 October 1922, for example, chronicling the sudden death of his predecessor, Mr Foster, four days before, J.E. Tolson records that lessons were suspended at 10.45 a.m. in tribute. 'All the boys lined the route between our school and Leeds Road, and standards V and VII went into [St Philip's] church to assist in the singing.' As well as providing Eddie with lifelong memories, Eastborough Council School had certainly been character building. He would stay in contact with his inspirational headmaster long after the last school bell had rung for them both.

Though we cannot be certain if he was one of the pupils involved, perhaps a clue to Eddie's departure from the school can be found, once again, in the school logbook. On 17 September 1923, term examinations began, which, according to Mr Tolson, were unsatisfactorily attended due to a nearby cattle fair and 'boys being kept at home on certain afternoons to accompany mothers on char-a-banc excursions'. Nevertheless, when the government inspector visited shortly afterwards, he filed a highly positive report of the school's activities, offering the opinion that: 'Judging from the manner and bearing of the older boys, the school exerts a good influence.' Before the end of the following school year, on the morning of 5 December 1924, 12 of those older boys to whom he had referred attended an examination at the Municipal Technical College – later plain old Dewsbury Tech – 'in order to qualify for entrance to the Junior Technical and Commercial School'. On 9 January 1925, Tolson reported that ten of the prospective entrants had been successful, adding that: 'This, together with our usual crop of "leavers" at this period has seriously depleted standards VII and VIII. Most of the outstanding boys have gone, and the remainder are below our usual average.'

Whether or not Eddie Waring was indeed one of those 'outstanding boys' – and one much later newspaper interview does refer in passing to Eddie as having attended 'secretarial college' upon leaving school[3] – it is safe to say that his qualities of outward popularity and inner self-motivation would have proved useful to an employee of Hirst and Hellawell even if, as seems clear, he by no means intended to spend the rest of his life at the firm. To start with, Eddie would most probably have worked in the offices, but in time he took on the more suitable role of typewriter salesman. Though he would not actually buy a car of his own until

1954 – a stately grey Triumph Mayflower – in those days before official driving tests,[4] there would have been nothing to stop him obtaining a licence and going about his business in a company car, should that have been necessary. His nephew Harry, however, suspects that his uncle completed most of his journeys either on foot – no mean feat given the up hill and down dale nature of his Dewsbury stomping ground – or by public transport, a subject in which, over the years to come, Eddie Waring would develop an almost fanatical interest.

The first sign that Eddie preferred to thump away on typewriters rather than sell them came very early on, when he began sending short unsolicited articles to the town's two weekly newspapers, the *Dewsbury Reporter* and *Dewsbury District News*. At first, these were mainly cinema reviews and stories about local sporting events, but in time his contributions grew to the extent that he would now and again report marriages, funerals and the activities of his beloved Dewsbury RLFC.

Despite his promise with a soccer ball, rugby league had always played a major part in Eddie Waring's upbringing; given his love of sport and Hollinroyd Road's proximity to Crown Flatt, it would have been strange if it had not. His first hardback book, *The Eddie Waring Book of Rugby League*, published in 1966, began with a piece of doggerel verse, apparently taught to Eddie as a nursery rhyme by his father. It was a poem, Waring wrote, about the legendary Richard 'Dicky' Lockwood, whom Arthur considered 'the greatest player ever to put on a pair of boots': 'He's scarcely five foot high and only just nineteen, he can run and kick, and collar, you can bet your bottom dollar there never was a one like him before . . .'

Dicky Lockwood, a diminutive labourer from Crigglestone, near Wakefield, stood just 5 ft 4 in. tall and, in his earliest playing days, went under the nickname 'The World's Little Wonder'. As the first manual worker ever to captain England's rugby side, he made history at a time when the powerful Northern clubs dominated a single code. Then came the revolutionary spilt of 1895, when a group of 21 club representatives gathered at Huddersfield's George

Hotel and concluded that if the powers that be down south would not listen to reason over the principle of broken-time pay for working-class players, they had no choice but to go it alone.[5] With the subsequent birth of the Northern Union, Lockwood – by now capped 14 times – left his then club Heckmondwike to join Wakefield Trinity. Once the fledgling competition was truly up and running, he would return to the Heavy Woollen District to play for Dewsbury, before retiring in 1903. Eddie Waring's links with the game that, from 1922, would become known as rugby league, went back to its very roots.

Though born 15 years too late to recollect the momentous events of 29 August 1895 himself, he knew plenty of people, including his own father, who most certainly could. They could explain how, in 1897, rugby union-style lineouts were abolished to make the game more exciting. They could recall the year, 1906, when rucks and mauls were replaced by the now familiar play-the-ball and teams were reduced from 15 to 13-a-side. They could tell stirring first-hand tales of thrilling domestic escapades such as Hunslet's 'All Four Cups' in 1908 and the first-ever tour by an international team, Albert Henry Baskerville's New Zealand All Golds, in 1907, followed a year later by an inaugural visit from the Australian Kangaroos. As a toddler, Eddie may even have been taken along to see Harold Wagstaff's legendary Huddersfield 'Team of All Talents', which, in 1915, repeated Hunslet's grand slam of seven years before. As he later put it: 'When I went to school in Dewsbury they played soccer, but the town was a Rugby League town. I was always mad on Rugby League.'[6] The game was in his blood.

Even so, until one momentous event in May 1929, the fortunes of the Waring family's home-town club could, thus far, hardly be described as groundbreaking. For one thing, although the Dewsbury club chairman, a local mill owner named Mark Newsome, had actually seconded the original broken-time motion at an earlier RFU meeting at London's Westminster Palace Hotel, his delegate at the George Hotel, a Mr Holdsworth, was the only man present not to vote directly for a breakaway after all. He felt sure, he said, that his club committee would ultimately ratify a 'yes' vote but, somewhat bizarrely, claimed not to have had time to consult them on the issue. The upshot was that when the first weekend's fixtures were unveiled, the name of Dewsbury was not among them; the club had fled back to the safe embrace of the Yorkshire Rugby Football Union. No doubt entirely coincidentally, Mark Newsome would in time be made chairman of the RFU. Otherwise, the change of heart proved disastrous. Dewsbury's best players weren't daft: they simply sought recompense for their loss of earnings elsewhere, and the team's fortunes slumped. It wasn't long before a cash-strapped committee turned its attentions to soccer, leaving the way clear for a new, revitalised rugby set-up to rise from the original club's ashes. At last, in 1901–02, and with Dicky Lockwood now in tow, a rugby-playing team from Dewsbury belatedly joined 't' best in t' Northern Union', a phrase which is still occasionally used to sing someone's praises today.

Nor, over the years to come, would the contents of the Crown Flatt trophy cabinet require much in the way of dusting. True, the early signs looked promising when Dewsbury were crowned Division Two champions in season 1904–05. It would be another seven years, though, before a further such triumph, when the club beat Oldham 8–5 to collect the 1911–12 Challenge Cup before a crowd of 15,271 at Headingley. A notable, if solitary, achievement. Other than that and a couple of runners-up appearances in the finals of the 1918–19 and 1921–22 Yorkshire Cup competitions – sandwiching a record home crowd of 26,584 against Halifax in 1920 – Dewsbury's seasons were, as your average cheerful Yorkshireman might put it, fair to middling. But then, towards the end of the rugby league club's first quarter century, the prevailing mood of underachievement began to shift perceptibly.

The 1925–26 season was the one that really got the town's enthusiasm for the winter game bubbling. Although a 16th-placed finish in a league table of 31 was again nothing much to be proud of, a 2–0 Yorkshire Cup win over Huddersfield gave Dewsbury their first piece of silverware in years. That success was followed by another victorious campaign in 1927–28, with Hull this time beaten 8–2, and it is easy to imagine how a teenage Eddie Waring, peddling typewriters by the score, might just have been sparked off in a completely new career direction. And then, at the end of season 1928–29, came a predominantly Northern sport's first exciting expedition to London's Empire Stadium – Wembley, the soon-to-be iconic venue of legends and the nation's true theatre of dreams.

No one knows for sure whether Eddie Waring actually went to that first Wembley Challenge Cup final, but given that whenever he subsequently wrote or was interviewed about the occasion – and that was many, many times – he was uncharacteristically vague about any personal experience of the day itself, it seems almost certain that he did not. Indeed, when asked directly, in 1979, about his first Cup final visit, he simply replied that he couldn't remember. All he could recall, he said, was that it had been a 15/6d day return, probably in the late 1930s, and that he had later fallen asleep at the London Palladium.[7] He most definitely did attend the game that sent Dewsbury on their way, however: the semi-final clash with Castleford at Huddersfield's old Fartown ground. In future years, Eddie would grow fond of boasting how the honour of being the first to qualify for Wembley had fallen to his home-town team, on account of how fellow finalists Wigan's seven-all draw with St Helens Recs at Swinton in the other semi-final had meant a replay, eventually won 13–12 by Wigan at Leigh.

When Eddie's book of 1966 was updated, re-edited and reprinted as *Eddie Waring on Rugby League* to coincide with his retirement in 1981, a brief new chapter was inserted towards the end. It was entitled 'A Few Memories – Rugby League Challenge Cup Final 1929, 50 Years On'. In it, Waring says nothing about the big game itself but does recall how: 'As a teenager one of my big moments in Rugby League was the occasion when Dewsbury qualified for the first ever Wembley.' He goes on to describe how, after an unexpected victory over Warrington in the third round, Dewsbury faced a Castleford side who, coached by former Dewsbury player

Billy Rhodes, had only been in top-level rugby league for three years. Despite the huge prize at stake, confidence was high. 'Both teams relied on home products,' he wrote:

> Unless you call Featherstone, three miles away, foreign, for that was the village where Joe Lyman, the Dewsbury captain and star player, came from. There was an exception in the Dewsbury side in full back, J. Davies, from Ammanford. 'Where on earth was Ammanford,' asked Castleford fans and Dewsbury ones for that matter. Otherwise it was an all Yorkshire 'do' and 'Ilkla Moor B'aht 'At' figured amongst tunes which supporters on the main stand side sang with gusto. The singing dealt with, it was three o'clock and down to the real thing . . .

Thanks, in the main, to an outstanding display by Dewsbury forward Joe Malkin, who had moved to Crown Flatt from Castleford for a fee of 'virtually nowt' (in Eddie's words), at the end of the afternoon's business the men in red, amber and black had indeed won through, although not without a struggle. A scoreline of 9–3, in front of a 25,000 crowd, flattered Dewsbury, but neither Eddie nor the rest of his favourite club's fans worried about that. History was about to be made and their team would take a starring role.

The Challenge Cup competition had been running since 1897, when 13,490 spectators watched Batley beat St Helens 10–3 in the inaugural final, at a brand-new Headingley stadium. Based on soccer's FA Cup, it would grow, as intended, into a vital money-spinner for the new Northern Union, helping to keep its ruling body financially afloat for the best part of the following century. Attendances were relatively healthy from the start, although only once, for a game between Wigan and Oldham at Rochdale in 1924, did the crowd figure for the final break the 40,000 mark. The traditional Northern venues, it was felt in official circles at least, simply weren't big or glamorous enough and, in 1928, a courageous and, to some at the time, quite possibly foolhardy decision was taken to move the game 200 miles south.

Initially, the favoured stadium for what was (despite the recent name change to 'rugby league') still referred to as 'the Northern Union's most prestigious event' was not necessarily the venue with which it would soon become synonymous. For when the full-time secretary of the Rugby Football League, John Wilson, set off on a recce mission to London, it seems that the place to which he was first headed was Crystal Palace, while White City had also been an early contender. Waring later wrote:

> Mr Wilson told me the story that 33 per cent of the gate was asked and even included 100 per cent of all money taken before midday on the Cup Final date. Mr Wilson well knew that most of the spectators would be travelling from the North on a Friday midnight train at a cost of 15/6d rail fare and that many would go straight to the ground rather than hotels. Just as the whole business of taking the Cup Final to London appeared to be falling down, the late Sir (then Mr) Arthur Elvin offered Wembley for a seven and a half per cent share of the gate and the deal was done . . .[8]

The modern-day Rugby Football League's official archivist, Professor Tony Collins, however, has pointed out in his social and cultural history of the sport, *Rugby League in Twentieth Century Britain*, that things weren't quite so straightforward. There were, Collins insists, broader reasons behind the RFL's choice of a venue originally built to host the 1924 British Empire Exhibition, under the drive of the future Edward VIII. 'The success of the FA Cup final since it moved to Wembley in 1923 was quite obviously something the RFL sought for itself,' he writes, 'but it was also attracted by the national symbolism of Wembley. As Bolton Wanderers, Newcastle United, Sheffield United and Blackburn Rovers had demonstrated in winning the FA Cup at its new home, Wembley was an arena in which Northern towns and cities could gain national prominence and significance beyond their immediate regions.'

In any case, with Wembley finally decided upon, the larger battle to persuade the sceptics of the viability of the project continued. Many in the North were aggrieved that the sport's showpiece event was being snatched from the grasp of the very people who supported it, physically and financially, week in and week out. Given the economic realities of the time, on the cusp of what would become the devastating Great Depression, it was a valid point of view, one which a 'satisfactory' debut crowd of 41,500 – some 300 down on that Rochdale turnout – helped only partly assuage. Nor must it have helped when, one month after the big game, Arthur Elvin announced that, in future, Wembley's cut of rugby league takings would increase to 25 per cent. This particular debate, in one form or another, was destined to rumble on for a good few years yet.

Those who did scrape together enough time and money to make the journey, however, seemed to have a whale of a time. For many, it provided the chance of a first-ever trip to England's capital city – an experience which would be repeated for generations to come. And what they saw there was a 13–2 victory to a star-studded Wigan side, who, led by the magisterial Jim Sullivan at full-back, proved more than a match for a home-grown Dewsbury team seemingly high on having got there at all. At least that's how it looked from the stands. In future years, the story would go around – propagated by Eddie – that the men from the Heavy Woollen District were visited by officials just before the kick-off and told to play open football in order to impress the Southern crowd. 'They did so, but it wasn't the natural play of a team whose forté was defence,' Waring wrote in his 1966 tome. Whatever the truth, a Wigan side comprising five Welshmen, three Lancastrians, two Kiwis, one Scot (centre Roy Kinnear, father of the late film and television comedian of the same name), one Yorkshireman and a Cumbrian proved way too strong, and plucky little Dewsbury's day out ended in disappointment.

Not that it did the club any immediate harm. Although the Dewsbury players had only losers' medals to show for their efforts, the confidence gained from a Wembley appearance helped them end the 1929–30 league season fifth, the highest-placed finish at Crown Flatt in a combined league table since a fourth-placed finish in 1912–13. And, though no one knew it at the time, their exploits may very well have planted an idea in the mind of one ambitious young typewriter salesman that the rugby game he had followed all his life didn't have to be quite so parochial as he might once have imagined. Though Eddie Waring and rugby league were Northern to the core, that didn't mean both couldn't one day take flight if they wanted it badly enough.

* * *

Filed away in the British Broadcasting Corporation's Written Archives Centre, in a leafy suburb of Reading, is a letter dated 10 December 1931. It was sent to the BBC's outside-broadcast director by a young man from Hollinroyd Road, Dewsbury. He signed himself E.M. Waring. It begins:

> Dear Sir
>
> I notice that there is the possibility in the near future of you broadcasting a running commentary on selected Rugby League games in the North of England. In consequence of this, I am taking the liberty of writing you wondering if you are interested in my qualifications to assist you in the broadcasting on these occasions. At present I am a Rugby League football writer for a newspaper in Dewsbury and from an early age I have been interested in this code. I have a good knowledge of the game and am familiar with the majority of players in both Yorkshire and Lancashire. Should this letter interest you, I should be very pleased to furnish you with any particulars you may desire.[9]

Initially at least, this attempt to launch a radio career met with a curt and businesslike response. Its recipient simply returned a polite note thanking the writer for his letter and promising to forward it to the BBC's north regional director, the man who would ultimately be responsible for filling any such position.[10] Sadly, the regional director's response is no longer to be found, although, given future events and a note on the memo stating that the outside-broadcast department was 'anxious to know if you have found a good commentator for these broadcasts', it seems reasonable to assume that the notion of Eddie Waring being involved in some way would not have been dismissed out of hand. Certainly, by 1937, his name pops up on the regional director's 'Reply Sheet', a signed undertaking given to the BBC's Manchester Piccadilly headquarters. On 4 February of that year, Eddie formally agreed to provide running radio commentary on one half of a Dewsbury versus St Helens match scheduled for 6 March at Crown Flatt, for which he would receive the princely sum of four guineas (four pounds, four shillings).

Most likely, Eddie would have been alerted to the chance of a start in radio by a report in the *Manchester Guardian*, which had revealed how the Rugby League Council had given BBC North permission to broadcast rugby league commentaries 'at the rate of about one per month'. However, he could also have gained notice that changes were in the air through his increasing access to the inside track. For, by 1932, the precocious Eddie had already begun to make a name for himself in Dewsbury rugby league circles as the co-founder and trainer of the town's high-profile Under-14 youth team, Dewsbury Boys. He was aided and abetted in that task by a couple of fellow Springfield Chapel-goers, Arthur Brook and Frank Bould, who, being older than Eddie, acted as its joint-managers. Brook, a haulage contractor from Thornhill Lees, and Bould, a railway canvasser, were typical examples of rugby league officials of the time: lower middle class in background and profession but very much part of a wider working-class community. Both men were also well known behind the scenes at Dewsbury RLFC. In 1936, for example, Brook was appointed to the role of vice president, while Bould also served as a member of the Crown Flatt committee. Owing to his budding entrepreneurial talents and Springfield connections, Waring, too, soon began to take a part in his home-town professional club's administration.

The high point of the Dewsbury Boys team's success, meanwhile, came in season 1934–35, when this team of now Under-16-year-olds – who boasted among their number a lanky centre prodigy named Ernest Ward – swept all before them in winning a record 20 successive games, along with the Yorkshire Boys Montague Burton Cup at Batley. In 1936, when his team was too old to play established youth rugby any more, Waring re-formed the side, this time under the moniker Dewsbury Black Knights. As members of the Yorkshire Federation of Supporters Clubs League, the Black Knights were an acknowledgement of the extent to which Waring felt a struggling club like Dewsbury needed to nurture, promote and protect its home-grown playing talent. In essence, he had foreseen the value of something akin to the academy production-line system that many rugby league and other professional sports teams have in place today.[11] Beyond that, with the application of such an eye-catching nickname, this snappily dressed one-time seller of office supplies was engaging in what marketeers today would see as brand management. That the innovation worked is not in doubt. Despite playing just two games under that tag before the close of the 1935–36 season, the name Black Knights captured public imagination to the extent that it was retrospectively applied to the Dewsbury Boys RL team that had gone before. Clearly, aged 26, Eddie Waring was a young man who already, and instinctively, understood the promotional value of image and publicity.

But what of the origins of the Black Knights name itself? In these days of Bulls, Rhinos, Wolves and Wildcats, when rugby league divisions can sound more like menageries than sporting competitions, it is easy to scoff at these appendages as newfangled Americanised abominations, little to do with the towns or clubs which they are intended to promote. Yet when the application of a nickname is carried out with enthusiastic and diligent professionalism, as in the case of Bradford, Warrington or Leeds, say, there is no doubting its effectiveness as a rallying point. The long-accepted story of how the Black Knights name came to pass is that Eddie simply noticed Thomas Brock's 1903 statue of Edward of Woodstock, aka the Black Prince, when coming out of the Queens Hotel – an establishment with which he and we are destined to grow more familiar – in Leeds City Square. Almost certainly, however, this account can be traced back to Eddie's days as a national newspaper reporter when, in search of a nom de plume with which he could moonlight on tours to New Zealand and Australia for the *Yorkshire Evening News*, he adopted the title 'Black Knight'. A more likely and certainly intriguing explanation is that the roots of the Dewsbury Black Knights are planted in Arthurian legend. For, according to Dark Age mythology, Sir Brunor le Noir, aka the Northern Black Knight and a one-time sworn enemy of Sir Lancelot, had his castle in Dewsbury. Eddie's nephew Harry specifically remembers how, during his childhood, his grandfather, Arthur, read Harry exciting stories of Camelot when ill in his sickbed with heart trouble. In fact, these tales of King Arthur's Round Table are some of Harry's earliest memories, and, given the closeness of Eddie to his father, it is surely inconceivable that similarly colourful tales of romance and adventure would not have left a mark upon the lively imagination of Arthur's young son.[12]

* * *

An awareness of the power of mythology is one thing; the practical opportunity to put that knowledge and imagination to good use is quite another. So, that Eddie Waring was by now well and truly embarked upon a career in newspaper journalism did neither his own reputation nor that of his Black Knights team any harm at all.

His approximate date of entry into the trade that would first extend his sphere of influence has been placed by former editor-in-chief of the *Dewsbury Reporter* Bernard G. Kaye as 'the late 1930s'.[13] Clearly, though, this cannot be the case. As we have seen, Eddie's first recorded reference to himself as 'a Rugby League football writer' comes in that letter to the BBC in 1931. And even if there was a bit of exaggeration going on – a perhaps not unreasonable assumption to make about an eager young job applicant – by 1936, a year in which his career was to take another major leap forward, Eddie most definitely was a fully fledged writer on the *Dewsbury District News*, earning around £3 per week and operating, as was the norm back then, under a pseudonym: 'Centre'.

A more accurate estimate would be the late 1920s or early 1930s, but, in any case, aside from that trick of memory or simple misprint, Bernard Kaye's recollections remain well worth repeating. Then a reporter at the *District News*, Kaye recalled that:

> The member of staff who was covering Dewsbury RL at that time was unavailable to get to Crown Flatt on Saturday afternoon. Eddie was there – he never missed a home game. He had been amongst the paying spectators as usual. He called in the office on the Monday morning and learning of our reporter's problem promptly sat down and produced a passable account of the match he had watched. Without going into unnecessary detail, the reporter, who was courting a girl over in Lancashire, fixed it (quite unofficially!) for Eddie to 'cover' Crown Flatt matches for the rest of the season, paying his entrance money (he wasn't allowed in the Press box, of course) and giving him a bob or two for his trouble. That was how E.M. Waring got started in journalism. At that time he was a salesman for Hirst and Hellawell, the typewriter firm, who were then in Nelson Street.

By 1936, each weekly edition of the *District News* carried at least one page of sport, and on 4 April of that year, in the regular diary column contributed to by 'Centre', 'Sport Spotlight', it was reported that:

> Dewsbury football supporters will again have an opportunity of seeing last year's successful Dewsbury Boys team in action. A match has been arranged between the team, now Dewsbury Black Knights, and Liverpool Stanley Old Boys team at Crown Flatt next Saturday.

It went on to say that the boys would be recalled from the clubs they had subsequently joined, and stated that they would be

> having special training under Mr E.M. Waring, who was coach last season. The Black Knights will have a complete new rig-out – black jerseys with a white crest of a helmet, black pants and striped stockings. Mr F. Bould and Mr A.T. Brook, members of the Dewsbury committee who took a part in organising the boys last season, are again taking over the management.

Nor was the good news confined to the sports pages. A week later, at the foot of page three, sat a photograph under the headline 'Dewsbury Black Knights Ready for Action'. In it, at one end of a team that, it was reported, had taken 'a powerful hold on public fancy', stood a characteristically dapper Eddie Waring.

Where Dewsbury Boys had earlier conquered all before them east of the Pennines, their Liverpudlian rivals had done likewise in the west. At the time the article was written, the Old Boys had reached two cup finals and headed their league table. Not surprisingly, the *District News* journalist wrote, 'I understand that at least one representative of a first class club is to be present with a view to spotting talent.' The outcome of his visit went unreported. But the 18 April edition of the paper did carry an extensive report of a game won by the Dewsbury side 12–6. 'There was a good crowd to see this revived champion Dewsbury Boys team and the spectators were thrilled by the clever football,' it revealed of this first Under-18 appearance. 'Dewsbury were rather slow to settle down and they did not show their best until after the interval. Their football in the latter period however was delightful to watch and the two "picture" tries they scored aroused much enthusiasm.' After a description of the tries and action, the report concluded: 'Negotiations opened on Good Friday for a match between Dewsbury "Black Knights" and a star Manchester side are still proceeding. It is likely that definite arrangements will be made very shortly.'

Just a week later, in the 25 April edition of the *District News*, readers were informed that 'Dewsbury "Black Knights" next week meet a team from Salford at Crown Flatt. The Salford Boys are selected from the best in the league and should provide the "Knights" with the stiffest task they have yet had to face.'The stiffest task they have yet had to face – and how many games had the Black Knights played since their re-formation again? Once more, the twin powers of promotion and publicity were up front, centre stage, and the hype continued unabated right up to the day of the match. 'At first this game was to be between the Knights and an individual team,' wrote an anonymous *District News* reporter:

> But in view of the Dewsbury Boys' record it was suggested that a champion side be selected. A Lancashire correspondent informs me that the team is particularly strong and should prove a great attraction. The Knights have taken special training and are keen to maintain their unbeaten sequence.

With the regular professional rugby league season now over, the game had no competition at the turnstiles. In consequence, another good crowd turned out to watch the Black Knights pick up a second victory on the trot, 11–6. After quoting an unnamed 'football fan' as saying that 'the future of the Dewsbury Rugby League club cannot be bad', the 9 April edition of the *District News* declared:

> This opinion was shared by many Dewsbury supporters who saw a brilliant exhibition. The Salford team contained some of the finest boy footballers in Lancashire, though on Saturday they met their superiors in the 'Black Knights'. Physically Salford had the advantage but this was countered by the teamwork and the more skillful football of the Dewsbury boys. There were many spectacular moves by the Dewsbury boys. Three tries were scored by the 'Knights' – each the result of open, fast football. The first try scored by Walker began on the Dewsbury '25' line and several members of the side handled.

For all the on-field success, though, that was to be that until, on 6 June, a *News* reporter – probably 'Centre' – wrote in a 'Spotlight on Local Sport' column:

> I have had many enquiries and heard many rumours about the Dewsbury Black Knights, who were the Dewsbury Boys team of 1934–35 and who became too old for 14–16 football. These boys played two games at the close of the current season and as a result handed £20 to the senior club. Although many rumours are being circulated with regard to the future of the Black Knights, I can say definitely that no decision has yet been made by those responsible for their introduction.

Then, on 8 August: 'The Dewsbury officials have decided not to run a Boys 14–16 team this year. It is expected, however, that the Black Knights will again be seen in action.' On 29 August, readers were told: 'The Dewsbury "Black Knights" Boys team which was formed last season will probably again be seen in action in the near future. The players have been called up for training and it is possible that matches may be arranged for them.' And finally, on 17 October, came news that: 'The Dewsbury "Black Knights" RL team which was formed at the end of last season by messrs A.T. Brook and F. Bould, play their first game of the season today when they meet a champion side from Hull.' Yet bizarrely, given what had gone before, the following week's *District News* carried not one sniff of the outcome. And there was no further reference to any future games for Dewsbury's 'famous' Black Knights over the rest of that year. Perhaps the game was postponed. Or maybe it was just the case that, one way or another, by now Eddie Waring had much more pressing matters on his mind.

Three

CENTRE OF ATTENTION

(Mock innocence) 'Hey! You can't do that!'

Eddie Waring was officially appointed secretary-manager of his home-town club on Saturday, 4 July 1936. Under the subhead 'Mr "Eddie" Waring Accepts the Position', the front-page story of that week's *District News* reported:

> Mr E.M. Waring, East View, Hollinroyd Road, Dewsbury, who takes up an appointment today as part-time secretary-manager to the Dewsbury Rugby League Football Club is well known to District News readers as our football representative 'Centre'. His new appointment, which arises through the removal of Mr Harry Fortescue to Bradford, will not interfere with his newspaper work.

Little did they know. Although, in the short term at least, Eddie did indeed continue to write for the *District News* and gather as much experience as he could on the wireless, the Dewsbury job would otherwise turn out to be pretty much all-consuming, watering further the seeds of his ambition. But what a job he made of it. By 1936, the Crown Flatt club was struggling badly, off the field and on. Of its two most influential committeemen, one, the highly respected Charles Preston, had recently died, while another, Ernest Ballance, though still around, was now contenting himself with a role as life member. With the departure of Harry Fortescue to Odsal, there existed a gaping hole at the centre of the club's affairs. Into the breach, just four weeks after one of the worst-attended AGMs in the club's thirty-eight years, stepped the precocious Eddie who, at twenty-six, was the youngest secretary-manager that any rugby league club had ever employed. Over the following eight seasons, Waring's flair for promotion and talent-spotting transformed Dewsbury's fortunes completely. He revitalised the club's finances and gave the town, and rugby league as a whole, its single most successful team of the Second World War era. They would win every available honour in the game.

Tellingly, however, later newspaper stories reveal that the circumstances of his appointment at Crown Flatt may not have been quite so straightforward as all that. At various times, as in an interview with the *Daily Express* in the 1970s, it has been reported that: 'At the tender age of 23, [Eddie] became secretary-manager of his hometown club.' This, as we have seen, is three years out. Yet, reading between the lines, it seems clear that whoever first recorded that detail had just misunderstood. In fact, 1933 was most probably the year in which Eddie first began to help out behind the scenes at Dewsbury RLFC. Certainly, in what is far and away the best-written and without doubt the most relaxed newspaper interview he ever gave, with the well-known television playwright and sportswriter Arthur Hopcraft, Eddie revealed how he had first been offered the role of Dewsbury's secretary-manager in 1935, some 12 months before his actual appointment. 'My father asked me not to take it,' he told Hopcraft, 'because it would mean that the man in the job at the time would have to be sacked. Well, I argued a bit, but I did as he asked.' And, as Hopcraft astutely reminds us, this was at a time when to be in or out of work had a vital significance. He goes on: 'Eddie stresses that story – the man left voluntarily a year later, and Eddie replaced him – because he likes to make the point that "I've never, all my life, taken anyone else's job; I've always created new work for myself."'[1]

One week after Harry Fortescue's departure from Crown Flatt, on the weekend of 25 April 1936, Eddie Waring's can-do influence upon a club he was already, in the background, in the process of revitalising was plain for all to see. On the very same day that the Black Knights were scheduled to face the best in the Salford and District League, a headline in the *District News* revealed: 'New Summer Venture – Baseball at Crown Flatt'. 'Dewsbury officials on Wednesday decided to allow Crown Flatt ground to be used for Baseball during summer,' the piece went on. 'The team will be named the Dewsbury Royals and will operate in the Yorkshire Baseball League.'

As it happened, along with Bradford City Sox, Leeds Oaks, Hull Baseball Club, Sheffield Dons, Greenfield Giants, Wakefield Cubs and Scarborough Seagulls, Dewsbury – clad in black shirts, trimmed with amber, and red caps – were among the competition's founder-members. Launched by National Baseball Association president John Moores, whose day job was running Littlewoods Pools, the Yorkshire Baseball League was intended to help launch the American version of rounders as a major English summer sport. As at Dewsbury, its three-and-a-half-hour games would be staged at either rugby league stadiums or the local dog track. A week after the Royals' first game, at home to Hull on 9 May, the *Dewsbury Reporter* (the higher circulation cross-town rival to the *District News*[2]) concluded that of the 1,500 people who turned up,

> Probably 80 per cent of those who visited Crown Flatt last Saturday . . . came out of curiosity. It was a pity, therefore, that conditions were so miserable, or by now there might be many more baseball fans in the Heavy Woollen District. Even as things turned out, a bitterly raw afternoon, with an icy wind with rain at times, most people would have their appetites whetted, for there was no doubt about it, the game had some appeal.

Back in the pages of the *District News*, meanwhile, it was revealed that 'football professionals can play baseball as amateurs'. This they duly did, with the likes of Ernest Ward and several more of his former Dewsbury Boys teammates chancing their arm at various stages. More pertinently, in a feature outlining the rules of this new sport, it was revealed that:'Mr E.M. Waring ("Centre"of the *District News*) will give a loudspeaker commentary and explanation.' He acted as live'sole commentator'for the following week's game with Bradford's Greenfield Giants, too, and would spend much of the rest of the summer in that role, including a game at Scarborough and a representative clash between North and South.

Alas, for the Royals themselves, things did not run quite so smoothly. By 13 June, Dewsbury had lost all five of their opening games, with the latest, a 24–10 defeat to Bradford City Sox, played out before a crowd of just 500, the lowest since baseball had been introduced to Crown Flatt. The root cause of the struggle seemed to be that where other teams had imported overseas professionals, Dewsbury relied upon local novices. Less Babe Ruth, more Bob Booth. Four more defeats followed until, with the Royals planted firmly at the foot of the eight-team table, a first league victory finally arrived on 11 July, just one week after Eddie had officially taken over at Crown Flatt. The victims were Scarborough Seagulls, put to the sword 54–6. The following week came another victory, against Bradford City Sox at Legrams Lane, 10–9. But with crowds dwindling alarmingly and no spare cash with which to attract the talent that might have saved them, the writing was on the wall. Although the Royals did claw their way off the bottom of the table with another victory, over Sheffield, to go with their 11 defeats, at the close of the season they departed from the league and York Maroons took their place.

As for the future of professional baseball itself, Dewsbury's demise notwithstanding it initially went from strength to strength. In 1938, the competition grew to include clubs west of the Pennines, and players from the newly formed Yorkshire-Lancashire Major League went so far as to beat the United States 1936 Olympic team, earning the right to call themselves world amateur champions. With the arrival of the Second World War, however, baseball in England slid to a halt and, owing to the relative shallowness of its roots, never recovered. With the cessation of hostilities, an attempt was made to relaunch the game in Hull, London and Liverpool but, for baseball, the moment had passed.[3]

* * *

Baseball was not the only entrepreneurial delight that the resourceful Eddie Waring would put before his home-town public. In his time at Crown Flatt, he would also introduce Dewsbury to the delights of professional wrestling, tractor pulling and even Russian Cossack dancing. For all that those innovative ventures were useful in helping to keep Crown Flatt in use all year round, however, upon his official appointment as secretary-manager in July, Waring's most pressing job was to find a reported £135 in order to pay off the previous season's wage bill. Harry Waring recalls that a loan from Eddie's father, Arthur, at least helped to take a chunk out of that deficit, and a 50,000 Shillings Fund set up by rejuvenated committeemen must have provided additional financial breathing space too. Whatever the actual figure of the debt, or the immediate method of coping, with a new, enthusiastic visionary in charge, it was not long before the club began to turn the corner and generate improved revenue streams of its own.

In fact, although the financial conditions at Dewsbury were indeed dire before Eddie Waring took over, contemporary press reports reveal that circumstances were nowhere near as disastrous as subsequent reports have described them. Even here, though, we ought to be wary of Eddie's influence at the newspaper in which the club's financial position was breezily reported. A week after the 1936 Challenge Cup final on 25 April, for example, under the subhead 'What About Money?' in that week's 'Sport Spotlight' column, came the following snippet of information:

The Dewsbury supporters are now wondering what the financial statement of the club will show when it is issued shortly. Naturally, I expect a loss on the season's working, but the Crown Flatt officials have watched their finances very carefully, in spite of limited income, and I do not expect the loss to be as large as generally expected.

The positive spin continued when, some six weeks later, a 'Football Surprise at Dewsbury' was announced. 'Pleasing Features of Balance Sheet,' the report ran, before going on to confirm that the club had made a loss of 'only' £41 5s 9d, after allowing for £73 4s 9d depreciation. There followed a list of receipts from sources such as shared cup gates, refreshments, programmes, car park fees and donations. The club's assets and outgoings were itemised, taking in costs like the players' wages and secretary's salary (which, according to the figures printed, was £200, a fall from the 1934–35 total of £212, accounted for by the fact that back then, like the players, coaches received cash incentives for winning, too). And then, in the best future traditions of burying what some less optimistic souls might have considered bad news, came the heartwarming story of a Thursday-night presentation to the recipient of that latter salary, Mr Harry Fortescue Esq., native of Hanging Heaton and one-time employee of Batley Corporation, latterly ensconced up the road at Odsal Stadium.

The presentation, we are told, was made by the club's oldest member, Mr Herbert Clegg, in recognition of Fortescue's 14 years of service. The man himself received a 'handsome secretaire, fountain pen and pencil' and was thanked by the club's latest president, Mr George Oldroyd, an Ossett woollen manufacturer, who wished his old friend every success in his new duties. In fact, just about every section of the club seems to have spoken and paid tribute, before launching a rousing rendition of 'For He's a Jolly Good Fellow'. Less riotously, there were solos by a Miss Phyllis Ward, and supper was served 'to about 50 persons'. For his part, a visibly affected Harry Fortescue said he now realised he had more friends than he thought. 'His heart would always be with the Dewsbury club and he felt sure there would soon be a change in the club's fortunes,' reported the *District News*. Ernest Ballance added:

Mr Fortescue had been a very conscientious and trustworthy secretary. He was so keen that, even when it rained for a home game, the secretary thought he was responsible for the conditions! (Laughter). Mr Fortescue had received splendid assistance from his wife, and would not have been able to devote so much time to the club without her valuable co-operation. Mrs Fortescue was ill and they extended their best wishes for a speedy and complete recovery.

If anyone understood the stresses and strains that such a high-profile position could inflict upon marital harmony, it would have been Dewsbury RLFC's new man at the helm. For, on 23 September 1933, around three years before his official induction at Crown Flatt, wedding bells had already rung for the twenty-three-year-old Eddie Waring. His bride in that ceremony – held at Springfield Chapel, naturally – was a local girl and near-neighbour of the chapel, Agnes Boddy, a hair machinist by profession and some three years his senior. The proximity of their homes and shared religious background suggests that the two were long-time acquaintances, if not long-term sweethearts. Like Eddie, Agnes was of stout local stock and lived just up the road from Springfield, in Tolson Street.

Though, at this distance, it would be unfair and, indeed, foolhardy to guess at the depth of affection underpinning the relationship, we can surmise that, for a 26-year-old woman whose time might well have been perceived, in those days, as having begun to pass her by, marriage to a bright, young and respectable thing like Edward Marsden Waring was most likely a welcome prospect indeed, whatever her own qualities. Equally, given Arthur's earlier instruction that his son should 'get a proper job' rather than pursue fortune and fame as a professional soccer player, it is a fair bet that there was a degree of 'isn't it about time you settled down' going on too. One thing, however, is for sure. The pair's marriage certificate records the groom's occupation in 1933 as 'commercial traveller'. In other words, for all his part-time journalistic ambitions, Eddie – full of ideas, one eye permanently cocked to the future – was also still out and about selling typewriters, busily going places amidst the bumps and troughs of those Heavy Woollen hills. In a landscape of humdrum struggle, toil and soot, what an optimistic, uplifting and – to some – unsettling figure he must have cut.

In contrast to Eddie's love of outdoor activity and energetic *joie de vivre*, Agnes seems very much to have been a 'traditional' 1930s homebird, happiest behind her own four walls. And the very first residence in which the newlyweds feathered their own marital nest was another of those Waring-owned properties along Hollinroyd Road – number 23, or 'East View' as it was at least initially known, in a perhaps humorous nod to the main family pile. Either way, 23 Hollinroyd Road was a rather more impressively furnished version of the South View home in which Eddie had grown up, just around the corner. According to his nephew, Harry: 'It was the only building in the row with rooms either side of a single entrance door, which had three or four steps leading up to it from a gate at the footpath some three or four feet away. It had an inside lavatory, too, and a bath under the kitchen window, which, when not in use, was covered with a board. The hot water was provided from a large Yorkist (i.e. black-leaded) range.' For Dewsbury's working folk, an arrangement like this would have been most satisfactory. For an ambitious young man like Eddie Waring, however, it might just have generated the spark of a quite understandable urge for better things.

Looked at today, the warning signs in a marriage that was, sadly, not destined to go the distance are there for all to see. As one of Eddie's Dewsbury contemporaries, Harry Peel, confirms: 'Eddie was a good secretary-manager. He was full of ideas. I would say that he had a one-track mind and it was on Crown Flatt.' If, for Agnes, this period was a time for settling down in preparation for middle age, one of her energetic husband's first jobs was to have a telephone installed, a far from commonplace domestic appliance at that time. Somewhat presciently in those days of four-digit telephone numbers, the Warings were listed in the phone book under 1471, nowadays the number for last-caller ID. In the years to come, the telephone would more than cover the expense of its purchase, as its owner took and received calls from a growing list of media and sporting contacts the world over. For Eddie, the world was an opening book. Along with his increasing workload and profile on the sports desk of the *District News*, he would soon become a regular, well-known voice on the wireless too. Yet it was at Crown Flatt where the seeds of an exciting future were most noticeably and immediately sown.

* * *

If Eddie Waring's tenure as secretary-manager of Dewsbury RLFC hardly began with a financial bang, fireworks were equally noticeable by their absence on the field of play. Despite his coming in with the express intention of introducing the brand of open, expansive and entertaining rugby league football previously associated with his Dewsbury Boys, over the first few months of Eddie's stewardship, the club continued to limp along alarmingly.

After the team finished second to last in the 1935–36 league table, with Eddie's appointment hopes were high of a change in fortune. Partly, this was fuelled by his own upbeat influence on the *District News*. 'At Dewsbury there is a feeling of quiet confidence and optimism,' claimed one anonymous writer in 'Sport Spotlight' on 29 August.

> Players have shown in their preliminary training promise of better football than that displayed last season. With the acquisition of four new players supporters are showing a greater interest and while the defeat at Wakefield last Saturday in the Lazenby Cup match was disappointing, it is generally agreed that such matches are no criterion of what can be expected in league encounters.

Giving a hint of the sort of expansive philosophy the Crown Flatt fans could now expect, the first of those 'four new players' had been Brendon MacNamara, an Irish full-back from Liverpool

Stanley who, thanks to his new manager's uncanny powers of persuasion, was offered lodgings with Eddie's brother and sister-in-law, somewhat reluctantly in the latter case. MacNamara, readers were told, 'formerly assisted the Bohemians rugby union club and gained honours with the Munster provincial team'. A willingness to plunder such untapped pools of playing talent would be a defining feature of Waring's career both at Dewsbury and beyond.

Most immediately, however, Eddie's 1936 charges faced an opening game of the season against Harry Fortescue's Bradford Northern at Crown Flatt. Dewsbury lost 7–4, leaving 'Centre' of the *District News* to reflect that a draw would have been a more fitting result. Still, a 'satisfactory' crowd of some 5,000 had turned up, generating receipts of £140 – 'in addition, quite a number of members cards were bought just before the game'. In their next match, the Heavy Woollen men went down 17–3 to Castleford, with 'Centre' this time noting that he had seen 'signs of improvement' whilst also bemoaning 'inconsistent finishing and slow scrummage service'. Interestingly, no one seems to have picked up on the blatant potential for a conflict of interest here. Presumably, the readers and journalists of the *District News* were just pleased to have an inside line to the heartbeat of the club, whilst their competitors across town at the *Dewsbury Reporter* could simply trumpet that theirs was a truly independent voice. Whatever the scenario, after the Castleford defeat, the 'Sport Spotlight' writer informed his readers that: 'Dewsbury officials have definitely decided that players must play open football. To maintain a place in the Crown Flatt side, players will have to maintain such a standard.'

In fact, over the course of a disappointing 1936–37 season in which Dewsbury would ultimately finish fifth from bottom, with only Bramley, Leigh, Newcastle and Featherstone Rovers below them, the optimism of 'Centre' continued unabated. At times, the level of spin bordered on the comical. A third defeat on the bounce, 19–5 to Hull, was described as 'a closer game than the score suggests', and when Dewsbury again lost to Bradford, 14–8, in the reverse fixture at Odsal, the *District News* report stated: 'It is surprising how easily the weather can alter the course of a match.' According to 'Centre', the heavy ground had not allowed Dewsbury to play. Best of all, though, has to be the headline placed on Eddie's report of a 16–8 defeat to Bramley, in the edition dated 7 November: 'Dewsbury Nearly Won', it roared.

Amidst all the optimism and upbeat flag waving, there were also signs of Eddie Waring's inherent determination and hunger for real success. On 3 October, with things clearly not going as planned, the *District News* ran a story headlined 'Dewsbury Clear the Decks'. It reported that:

> Dewsbury's wholesale offer of players for transfer has been one of the football sensations of the week. Whitehead and Jayne, three-quarters, are offered at £100 each. The fee for Ernest Oakland, loose forward, who has played in three matches this season, has been reduced from £120 to £75 and other reductions include: Daniel, three-quarter, £75 to £25; Ivor Davies, half-back, £100 to £75; A.B. Davies, centre, £150 to £100; W.H. Hall, scrummage half, £100 to £50; W.A. Rees, half-back, £75 to £25. Free transfers: Connolly, hooker; Watson, D.M. Jenkins and Bailey, forwards; Green, scrummage half; Hogan and Brydon, centres, and England, wing.

Clearly, desperate times called for desperate measures. The following week, Dewsbury lost again, 19–11, to Hull Kingston Rovers.

Given that, by the time of a draw with Leigh, the crowd had dwindled to just 1,500 people, members included, it is clear that the Crown Flatt supporters were hardly won over yet, either. Certainly, after a 29–13 defeat to Huddersfield in October, at least three 'regular first class members' were moved to write to the *District News* demanding 'sweeping changes'. Nor would the 1937–38 season have done much to lift their spirits. This time, Dewsbury only managed to finish 20th in a table of 29, and when they again dropped to second-bottom at the end of season 1938–39, with only Rochdale Hornets propping them up, the bad times, it seemed, were here to stay. Then, on 3 September 1939, the skies went darker still.

* * *

Though, thus far, they had not delivered much in the way of tangible success, Eddie Waring's first three years in charge of Dewsbury had revealed him to be an individual full of ideas and not averse to hard work. Quite simply, he took to his new responsibilities with an absolute sense of purpose. If the job required long hours, he would devote those hours and burn the midnight oil. If the job required travel, then travel he would. As Harry Waring recalls: 'There was a taxi rank outside Ernest Ballance's florist shop in Dewsbury Market Place, opposite the Town Hall. Ballance's was used as a rugby league focal point and team sheets were posted there. Uncle Eddie was always using their phone and would jump into a taxi to go up the hill to Crown Flatt.' Everything else came second.

An indication of Eddie's approach came with the demise of rugby league's two pre-Second World War London clubs, Acton and Willesden (who closed at the end of the 1935–36 season) and Streatham and Mitcham (who disbanded after playing one season and twenty-six matches in season 1936–37). Though on the whole well-disposed to the idea of expanding the game south – indeed, much later, Eddie would become president of the Southern Amateur League – he had no qualms whatsoever about picking over the carcasses of these failed projects if players to help the Dewsbury cause could be found.

As such, he was a regular visitor to the capital, and, on 4 April 1936, three months before his official inauguration at Crown Flatt, as 'Centre' he wrote: 'Old friendships were renewed and new ones made on Saturday when natives of the Heavy Woollen District resident in London visited Park Royal to watch Dewsbury team [sic] play Acton and Willesden.' Eddie described how, upon his arrival at the stadium, he was met by one Ivor Halstead, a former member of the *District News* staff now acting as publicity agent for the two London clubs. 'When interval time comes on this magnificent ground,' he wrote:

Mr Halstead usually gives a talk on the game and about the visitors, through the medium of microphone and loudspeakers. On Saturday, I had the privilege of speaking to the London public on behalf of the Dewsbury club and the rugby league game in the north. Although this experience was not new to me, it was one I enjoyed.

Clearly, Ivor Halstead can be seen as one more influential figure in the young Eddie Waring's life. As 'Centre' himself puts it:

Clubs in the south are having a hard fight to get the public really interested in the game, which is new to them, but Mr Halstead is convinced that progress is being made and, personally, I feel sure that a few more workers of his type would ensure its prosperity.

Nor is Eddie's interest in the event confined to the actual match itself, in which, incidentally, Dewsbury were beaten 12–2. His interest in showmanship and theatricality comes to light also when he tells of having met the actor and film star Mr Beckett (Billie) Bould, brother of Dewsbury committeeman Frank and now resident in London, 'who a year or two ago was a member of the Terence Byron Repertory Company at the Dewsbury Empire'. Eddie is clearly impressed at the way in which this Dewsbury native is carving a name for himself in the big city. We also get a taste for his burgeoning talent for networking when he states that:

Mr Beckett Bould has recently finished work on a film at Elstree. It was curious that he met for the first time Mr Ivor Halstead and Mr Charlie Roberts, formerly of Batley, who, in pre-War days was 'Raven Junior' of the *News*. Mr Roberts told me after the match that although Dewsbury had been defeated, he considered their performance equalled that of many teams who had visited the south. I noticed that 'Raven Junior' had a long chat with 'Cosh' Richardson, a member of the Dewsbury club committee, who played some 25 years ago, and James Arthur Pickard, who joined the Dewsbury team the year after 'Dicky' Lockwood retired. Harry Smith, the all-in wrestler, was also present . . .

On this particular trip, most of the members of the Dewsbury party arrived at around midday on Saturday and left at midnight 'after a splendid outing'. Eddie had made the journey to London and back by road for the first time, though whether he drove himself must be open to doubt, given that his usual preference was for taxis and public transport. Certainly, his open-minded attitude to the staging of rugby league in London contrasted sharply with the majority view back home. Indeed, the very newspaper for which he worked could not conceal its scorn at the notion. In this area, at least, Eddie Waring's influence was not sufficient to sway editorial policy.

Take the Challenge Cup final, which, by the time Leeds faced Warrington there on 18 April 1936, was in its eighth year of residency beneath Wembley's old twin towers. In the 14 March edition of the *District News*, under the headline 'Why Take Final to London?', that week's 'Sport Spotlight' made the paper's feelings perfectly clear. Taking 'the match of the calendar nearly 200 miles away from Lancashire and Yorkshire, where rugby league is at least on equal terms with "soccer", to a district where football still means "soccer", is not good policy, nor is it good for the game', its writer declared.

By this time, I am rather tired of hearing the old story that the Cup Final is as much a day out as a sporting event for we who live in the north. It might be, but I am convinced that the cost of the trip – it can't be done under 30 shillings at its cheapest – prevents thousands of really enthusiastic rugby league followers from seeing what should be the game of the year.

The writer went on:

> I hope this Wembley business will not be continued. The huge stadium is never more than half full for the match, and now that Odsal Stadium could be placed at the disposal of the League, it is high time to consider the return to the North of what is, after all, a 100 per cent northern sporting event. Odsal, when completely laid out, will hold 100,000 people. I am sure it would be crowded if the rugby league cup final were played there. Moreover, the journey to Bradford costs a few shillings only from the furthest parts of Lancashire and Yorkshire. After the Wembley experience of the past few seasons, surely it is time to assert that the cup should stay in the North.

Nor, upon the arrival of the big day itself, did widespread national radio coverage provide much of a sop. Although the second half alone would be given running commentary across the rest of the country (followed at 4.45 p.m. by Gramophone Records and then, once the BBC Dance Orchestra and a five-minute Interlude were dispensed with, Whippet Racing), in the North the game could be heard in its entirety. That, though, did not satisfy the sports editor of the *District News*. 'All rugby league club games are suspended today to avoid any internal clash with the Leeds–Warrington Cup Final at Wembley,' he sulked:

> And of all the contentious decisions made by the Rugby League in recent years, this has caused as much contention as any. There is confident talk of a 50,000 gate at Wembley this afternoon but at what a price! Not even half the keenest followers of rugby league football can afford a trip to London, yet not only is the titbit of the season transferred a good 150 miles from the most southerly outpost of the game's true home, but a complete standstill of league football is ordered until the final is played! Thus thousands of earnest rugby followers, who for a variety of reasons cannot go to London, will be compelled, if they wish

to watch a game, to fall back on junior fixtures, rugby union or soccer, or sit by their firesides listening to the fortunes of Leeds and Warrington! Even the best broadcast is a cold substitute for a good club game, but our football legislators have spoken and now we must do as we are told.

That downbeat view was reiterated the following week, albeit with a less hysterical haul of exclamation marks, when the subhead 'Warrington Humbled in Very Ordinary Final' was appended by the *District News* subeditors to a determinedly upbeat Eddie's report, in which he wrote that:

> The biggest crowd ever seen at a rugby league game in England poured into Wembley Stadium on Saturday to see Leeds beat Warrington for the trophy at a canter, with a final score of 18 points to 2. The attendance was officially returned at 51,250 and the receipts were £7,200.

Eddie further emphasised Wembley's positive benefits by pointing out that 'employees of the Calder Mills, Dewsbury, of messrs M. Oldroyd and Sons, make an annual trip of the final and a coachload left for London at five o'clock on Saturday morning and returned next day', before adding, '14,000 travelled from Leeds alone'. He had another chat with Ivor Halstead who, Eddie said, had done a great deal of publicity work for the final, 'while his propaganda for the new southern clubs has undoubtedly assisted in interesting the London public'.

Meanwhile, in adopting a more oppositional attitude, the *District News* could at least point out that it was merely echoing the opinions of a fair percentage of its own readership. On 25 April 1936, for example, the weekly 'Sport Spotlight' column carried the following article, published under the heading 'Why Build Southern Teams?' It began:

I am very glad to publish the letter of an old reader, who evidently shares my view that the rugby league authorities would be performing a greater service to the game by concentrating their activity in the north, instead of devoting so much time and money to propaganda in the South. Signing himself 'Disgusted', he writes: 'I think it is time the Rugby League cast their eyes on clubs in the north; never mind building clubs in the south. I think they are in a position to help some of the poor clubs. If they would help them to buy players at home in the north, I mean footballers, then those outside would have some encouragement to form other clubs. Honestly, it hurts to see the type of football we see played at Crown Flatt. This so-called football will never pay.'

* * *

For the nation at large, the Second World War, when it arrived, was a time of horror, hardship and tragedy. In Dewsbury too, it meant all those things. Yet for the town's struggling rugby league club, the war would also provide the impetus for a quite remarkable change for the better. Again, things did not exactly pick up immediately. But only days after Prime Minister Neville Chamberlain had uttered the immortal words 'this country is at war with Germany' came a sign that, in Eddie Waring, the club had indeed found someone who could sew a fine silk purse from a sow's rear end.

Worried that packed grounds would prove an irresistible target to the expected German bombers, upon the outbreak of hostilities the British Government initially called a halt to all professional sport. Unlike during the First World War, however, when, initially at least, the playing and watching of sport was considered by some in authority to be 'bad form', Britain's latest powers that be recognised the positive effects on morale that mass sporting entertainment could bring. Consequently, the ban was lifted almost immediately, albeit with conditions attached. Normally, attendances would be restricted to no more than 8,000 people, although, for larger stadia such as Bradford's Odsal Stadium, a crowd of 15,000 could be allowed. Furthermore, some grounds were to be requisitioned for the billeting of troops or housing of anti-aircraft guns, a blackout was imposed after dark and non-essential travel was restricted to 50 miles.[4] Amidst all the confusion, one man, at least, sensed a wonderful opportunity.

Though only 29 years of age, Eddie Waring escaped being called to the front line on account of a long-standing mastoid ear problem with which he would battle all his life – an ailment that, by 1960, required an operation to save his hearing. One poignant little tale of those war years, subsequently related to nephew Harry by the subject's sister, tells of how Eddie walked her brother, a soldier and one of Eddie's former schoolmates, to the town's railway station as he prepared to return from embarkation leave. 'Mr Waring carried his kit bag,' the lady recalled. 'He said it was the least he could do as he wasn't able to join him.' Tragically, in common with so many other such servicemen leaving the familiarity of their home town behind forever, the young soldier never came back.

Eddie, meanwhile, did see wartime service of a sort. He became a local auxiliary policeman, whereupon, true to character, he soon began organising charity rugby and soccer matches involving the police, the fire service and other organisations. When it came to participation, at only 10 st. 7 lb and 5 ft 7 in., the round-ball game was more his thing, although Harry, born in 1935, does have vague memories of seeing Uncle Eddie giving the oval-ball game a go at least once. 'He was quite slim in those days,' recalls Harry, 'not very big. I always remember how Dewsbury's Charlie Seeling, playing for the fire service that day, chased him to the corner flag but wasn't able to catch him, and he scored a try.' By then, Eddie had proved to be just as quick off the mark away from the field too.

Of rugby league's earliest casualties of the Second World War, perhaps the most high-profile were that year's New Zealand tourists. For, having arrived on these shores only on 29 August and faced just one team, St Helens, the day before war was declared, the Kiwis suddenly found themselves cast adrift. Not only was there now a ban on sport in Britain, but, upset by such a dramatic turn of events, the 26 players involved would far rather have been at home. Despite the enormous distance just travelled and the expenses incurred, they and the Rugby Football League were left with little choice but to cancel the tour, a decision that would leave the NZRL in particular struggling financially for years to come. It might, however, have been worse had a certain secretary-manager not been tuned to his police radio at 9 p.m. on 8 September. Over it came the announcement that the Government's ban on professional sport was lifted 'in safe and neutral areas'. Eddie Waring leapt into action. He would bring the unfortunate New Zealanders to Crown Flatt.

At least, that's how the legend goes. In common with many such yarns, the story of how Eddie Waring single-handedly set up a game with the Kiwis in less than 24 hours has assumed mythical proportions down the years, especially in Dewsbury. Eddie, it is said, went to work like a dervish, drumming up support for the venture in a local community which, quite frankly, must at that point have had more important things than sport on its mind. He dragged a local printer out of bed in the middle of the night to produce some 'match certain' stickers and then attached them to advertising posters all over town. There were even tales of how Eddie went out and found himself a bugler to ensure adequate half-time entertainment. Many years later, showing his usual flair for the propagation of a good legend and ignoring that earlier game at Knowsley Road,[5] he told the *Daily Express* how the Kiwis' Dewsbury game 'was the only match played in the country. I had many offers by players from other clubs to turn out for me, but I felt it was only fair to play the Dewsbury lads.'

What is certain is that thanks in no small part to Waring's efforts (and having the ear of the chief of police, the man responsible for deciding when and where crowds could safely congregate, must have helped), a game against New Zealand was indeed staged on Saturday, 9 September 1939, the only such rugby game to be played that day. As expected, the Kiwis came out on top, 22–10, but, as the cliché goes, the real winner was rugby league. A good-natured crowd of 6,200 – well above Dewsbury's normal turnout – packed up its troubles, brought along its gas masks and ensured gate receipts of some £459, from which the tourists picked up a handy bonus of £276, along with the usual collection of jerseys, ties and commemorative pins. Some five days later, and just seventeen days after their arrival, the Kiwis set sail for Auckland on the SS *Rangitiki*, some five to six thousand pounds lighter in pocket but with the contact details of Eddie Waring scribbled in many a notebook.

Meanwhile, for Dewsbury and the rest of English rugby league, there was still a regular domestic league competition to consider, and on 11 September 1939, three days before the tourists' departure, a crisis meeting of the Rugby League management committee was held. Aware of the need for the sport to continue in one form or another but mindful of wartime travel restrictions, it suspended the regular competitions scheduled to start on 30 September and set up instead two 'Emergency Leagues', based in Yorkshire and Lancashire. Once again, despite better times ahead, Dewsbury's on-field fortunes were hardly transformed overnight. In the first year of competition, they finished 11th in a Yorkshire Section table of 15. The following year, with the temporary closure of Hull KR, they finished 10th in a Yorkshire League table of 14. Then came season 1941–42, without question the most successful season in Dewsbury's history so far.

Although his club was undoubtedly assisted by unfortunate circumstances – the fact that the amalgamated War Emergency League table which Dewsbury topped at the end of the season had dwindled to just 17 clubs, for example, together with a further reduction to 14 in season 1942–43 – Eddie Waring's imaginative and quick-witted response to a challenge that laid other clubs low is a thing to be admired nonetheless. In essence, he put together a 'superteam', built largely on the back of new Rugby League regulations that, mindful of the way in which men now found themselves stationed away from home in the armed forces, or having to cut back on longer-distance civilian travel, allowed players to 'guest' with other nearby clubs, so long as the outfit to which they were originally attached agreed to the move. Clearly, teams located near to military bases such as Leeds, Bradford and Halifax now held a colossal advantage. Even so, few, if any, were swifter on the uptake than Eddie Waring.

As a wartime wheeler-dealer, he knew no equal. Paying particular attention to the local Caulms Wood army camp, he set about putting together a side that, over the next few years, would go on to win the Challenge Cup, the Yorkshire Cup and, in a manner of speaking, the Rugby League Championship two years running. By April 1943, some forty guest internationals had turned out for Dewsbury, with nine playing in that year's Challenge Cup final (which Dewsbury won on aggregate, over two games, 16–15 against Leeds), and the club had won every available honour. At various times, star names of the calibre of Vic Hey of Leeds, Barrow's Roy Francis and Salford's Gus Risman were just three to line up in the red, amber and black, before going on to be counted among Eddie's closest friends. Another 1941 team member went by the name of Shirley Crabtree, uncle of today's Huddersfield player Eorl, and later to be better known as wrestling's 'Big Daddy'. Whilst, in the words of the chant forever associated with that king of ITV Saturday lunchtime grapple, the club's wartime progress could never be described as 'easy, easy', by the end of 1941–42, Waring could boast in his club's annual 'Report and Balance Sheet' that: 'In this third wartime report a review of the season's workings at Crown Flatts is one that contains many satisfactory and pleasing features.'[6]

Waring continued: 'For the first time in the history of the club, Dewsbury won the R.L. Championship when 18,000 people saw us defeat Bradford at Headingley by 13 points to nil. It was generally agreed that we were worthy of that honour.' They were indeed. Although that season's Cup campaign was nothing to write home about, the club had nevertheless scored over 100 tries, with 99 in league games alone. 'We have scored many more points than any other team and the football throughout the season was of the highest standing.' Nor did the financial figures look anything other than encouraging. According to Waring, a profit of approximately £550 had been made on the season, after 'allowing £230 for depreciation'. One notable figure, he said, was

> the fact that we have paid out to other clubs during this season £1,706 against £580 received from other clubs. A difference of over £500 which in three war seasons brings the total to over £900 paid out more than received. Both in the playing sense, where we have lent players over whom we had control to other clubs and in a financial sense, we have played a big part in the continuance of Rugby League football throughout the country.[7]

Indeed they had, although not without a certain amount of controversy and even jealousy in many quarters. For if dapper suits, polished shoes and fine trilbies covering immaculately groomed hair indicated enterprise and professionalism in a born salesman, the flip side, and especially during times of war, was that you could equally come across as a bit of a spiv. Eddie Waring, already known to play it fast and loose with the RFL's prohibitive restrictions on player payments – expenses only and 30 shillings for the win – annoyed even more people when, during the 1940–41 season, he snapped up Wigan's veteran full-back Jim Sullivan, who had single-handedly destroyed Dewsbury in that inaugural 1929 Wembley Challenge Cup final.

Sullivan, still resident in Wigan and a member of the town's Police War Reserve, had moved to Crown Flatt against the express wishes of the Central Park board. In his book *Rugby League in Twentieth Century Britain*, official RFL historian Tony Collins takes up the tale:

> In October 1941 the RFL Emergency committee held a special meeting to investigate [Sullivan's] case . . . at which Wigan claimed he had demanded more than the twenty-five shillings payment allowed. They had refused to pay him more than the limit, implying that Dewsbury had not been so observant of the rules.

Although the RFL could not find any evidence to back up that charge, they did severely censure Sullivan for having made the request. Wigan's disapproval notwithstanding, the full-back continued to turn out for Dewsbury anyway. As Collins says: 'Controversy over Waring's recruitment practices continued throughout the war, the irritation of many being encapsulated by Batley's George Smith, who asked provocatively in 1943, "who is running the Rugby League, the [RFL] Council or Dewsbury?"'[8]

Indeed, 1943 was the very year in which disquiet at the brashness of Dewsbury's activities came to a most unpleasant head. After their team was beaten by Bradford in the Championship play-off semi-finals, Eddie Waring and his committee put in an official complaint that the Odsal side had fielded an ineligible player, Sandy Orford, who had signed as a guest for Northern just four games before. After considering the case, the Rugby Football League found in Dewsbury's favour, allowing the men from Crown Flatt to advance to the final in Bradford's place, whereupon they beat Halifax, 33–16 over two legs, and were duly awarded the Championship. At a reception for the victorious team held at Dewsbury Town Hall, captain Barney Hudson, on loan from Salford, said: 'The team spirit has been fine and the man who has made that spirit is Eddie Waring. All the players felt they could not let him down.'[9] That, though, was not to be the end of the matter. One month later, an incredulous Bradford also put in a complaint, alleging that Dewsbury too had fielded an ineligible player in that very same semi-final. This time it was Castleford's Frank Smith in the spotlight. Although Smith had played several knockout Cup games for Dewsbury, like Orford, he had not amassed the necessary amount of league games to qualify for selection in the play-offs. In the most bizarre ending to a league campaign before or since, Dewsbury were fined £100 and stripped of the title, with the 1942–43 Championship race rendered null and void.

Whether as a result of envy at a level of success his critics didn't have the nous to achieve for themselves or of genuine grievance at the damage his activities might be causing the game as a whole, such polarisation of opinion along those lines would dog Eddie Waring's career from that point onward. In this particular instance, however, what cannot be denied is the extent to which Waring's team of all-stars – a major draw card wherever they played – kept interest in rugby league high, as the sport and the country at large made their slow, grinding way through some of humanity's darkest days.[10]

It has been argued, quite reasonably, that for all their perceived misdemeanours, 'Dewsbury's success did much to keep interest in rugby league alive during the war.'[11] The chief problem seems to have been that, in Eddie Waring, the club was being run by a man very much ahead of his time. Yet, Dewsbury apart, one other club, at least, recognised potential when they saw it. After Eddie again led Dewsbury to another two-legged Championship final at the end of the 1943–44 season – where Wigan gained revenge 25–14 – the English game's perennial underachievers, Leeds, came knocking at 23 Hollinroyd Road.

* * *

Where Eddie Waring's tenure as Dewsbury secretary-manager delivered great success, the same could not be said for his subsequent year or so spent in the pressure-cooker atmosphere of Headingley. In his first season there, the Loiners finished an unspectacular tenth in a final War Emergency League table of seventeen. Dewsbury, the team Eddie left behind, came seventh. After peace was declared in the summer of 1945, the number of clubs competing in the 1945–46 season rose to 27, but, if anything, that simply reiterated how far Leeds were off the pace. This time, they finished 23rd, with only Rochdale Hornets, Bramley, Liverpool Stanley and York between them and bottom place. Dewsbury, meanwhile, came sixth. By then, though, Eddie had already moved on, owing, it was said, to 'difficulties arising through Mr Waring's inability to devote the whole of his time to the position, as he has still to carry on his duties as a War Reserve policeman'. Ironically, by the end of the 1946–47 season, Leeds had rebuilt to the extent that they finished fourth, before losing out in the Championship play-off semi-finals, 21–11, to Wigan. How much influence Eddie had on that rebuilding job is now impossible to quantify, but the Loiners did also make the final of the 1947 Challenge Cup, where they were beaten by deadly local rivals Bradford 8–4.

In hindsight, there were a number of reasons for Eddie Waring's failure to set Headingley alight in quite the way he had managed at Crown Flatt. Most obviously, there was the simple matter of time. He just wasn't there long enough to impose himself fully on his new surroundings. More pertinently, there was also the nature of the Leeds club itself. At Dewsbury, the emphasis was very much on community. Eddie's home-town club was a tight-knit family set-up. Everyone knew everyone else's business and the camaraderie essential for team spirit was more easily forged. It was a club where folk rallied to the cause. 'Would any club or individual care to make a present of jerseys to a troop of New Zealand troops in this country?' ran one wartime story in the *Dewsbury Reporter*. 'If so, Mr E.M. Waring, secretary-manager Dewsbury club, Crown Flatts, Dewsbury, will see they are despatched to the proper quarters. Included in the team are three players who are assisting Dewsbury when military duties permit.' It was a club that still took pride in the former members of its best-known youth team. 'Dewsbury Black Knights serving in Iceland have been sent a football and football boots from Crown Flatt,' went another such report. 'John Kane and Frank Thurman . . . are interested in Dewsbury's progress and in the welfare of other local footballers in the forces.'[12] Players, supporters and officials were all in it together. Expectations were relatively low.

At Headingley, meanwhile, the exact opposite was true. The Leeds club's hopes for the new man are evident in a contemporary newspaper report written by the *Daily Express* journalist Henry Rose. In telling how Leeds poached this 'go-ahead young manager', making him the highest-paid official in the game, Rose wrote:

I am not surprised that big money inducements have been made to Mr Waring to leave Dewsbury; surprised only that they have not been made before this. Since he went to Dewsbury his story has been one of unbroken success and well deserved success too. His enterprise and enthusiasm and high-powered management would carry a top job in Soccer. He is the youngest and the game's most 'live' manager.

Rose further pointed out: 'With the offer go various bonuses, and, allowing for a reasonably successful playing season, it would bring Mr Waring practically a four-figure yearly salary.'[13]

A more recent incumbent of a Headingley management hot seat, the former RFL public-relations officer David Howes, confirms the situation that Eddie would have walked into. 'Leeds is a strange club,' Howes admits. 'It does have the effect of burning people up. It obviously wasn't Eddie's forte and I don't think that was his happiest time. Just by virtue of what it is, with the cricket going on too, Leeds is more of an institution than a club. I did five years there and you have to work very hard to create a club atmosphere because it's really a business. It typified it when we renamed it Leeds Rugby Ltd in 1998, because that's what it is – a business. Normally in rugby league, what you do is get the football right and the rest will follow. At Leeds, it's all balance-sheets and so on. Eddie was used to being a one-man band at Dewsbury and you can't do that at Headingley. You have to answer to a board of directors. The culture is different.'

Plus, of course, there was a busy media career bubbling away alongside Eddie's management work. Having built up over a decade's experience in local newspaper journalism, Eddie was keen to parade his talents on a bigger, national stage. And, as we have seen, by 1937 he was honing his vocal talents on radio broadcasts, too. Certainly, during the Second World War, Eddie's commentaries were assured enough for the BBC to transmit them to troops serving abroad on the Corporation's short-wave World Service. The current Leeds president, Harry Jepson, recalls how, having first met Eddie Waring briefly before the war, he was called up and stationed in Italy, where, one day, a familiar voice came crackling over the airwaves.

'In late 1944, I was stationed at a place called Maddaloni, about 30-odd miles inland from Naples,' Jepson recalls. 'I was in the sergeants' mess one Saturday afternoon and someone put the radio on. It was the BBC North regional programme and they were broadcasting the Yorkshire Cup final, first leg: Hunslet versus Halifax. I don't recall much about the game but what I do remember is that it was the first time I had heard Eddie Waring's voice since I met him as Dewsbury secretary-manager with one of my best friends at the time, the Pontypridd stand-off Oliver Morris, who had then signed for Hunslet. I was listening to the game and Eddie said: "For those lads from Hunslet who are serving abroad, I want to tell them that I am sitting in the old pavilion, there's 9,000 people here, and I am going to open the window so you can hear the Parkside roar." And he did! One of my mates said, "What the heck's up with you?" There were tears in my eyes, there really were.'

Once again, however, even on the wireless, the human dynamo that was Eddie Waring was not to everyone's taste. And nowhere is the clash between Eddie's brashly modern go-get-'em mentality and the complacent attitudes of society's old guard more obvious than in one internal BBC memo, marked for the attention of a Mr Standing at the head office of outside broadcasts, dated 13 October 1939. Written by V. Smythe, head of the OB department's North Region, it takes as its subject matter: 'Rugby league football – suggested broadcast, November 18th, 1939 (E.M. Waring)'. 'This gentleman has been a long-standing nuisance and as a commentator he is by no means good,' it begins, revealing Smythe to be a chap who would clearly prefer not to have his cosy existence rattled by anything so vulgar as enthusiasm and individual initiative. 'I had to use him to get a balance vote in favour of broadcasting at a critical meeting, but it is no longer necessary to consider his claims either as a commentator or as a responsible representative.'[14]

Goodness! In terms of sports broadcasting, that must be somewhere on a par with the bloke at Decca who turned down the Beatles. For not only was Eddie Waring's involvement in the internal machinations of rugby league already central to the code's political health and welfare, his loyalty and ties to the BBC would, in due course, be set in stone. Here was a man destined to be not only a great BBC commentator but a national institution and broadcasting icon. First, however, there was a national newspaper career to get up and running, and for that he would travel 12,000 miles, to Australia.

Part II

HOPE

Four

EXPANDING HORIZONS

'How would you like to be getting into the bath with those great big hefty lads?'

Whatever his obligations to the wartime police service, clearly the idea of a trip down under and the career possibilities it might bring had been fermenting in Eddie Waring's mind for a while. 'I'd always wanted to go to Australia,' he once told the *Daily Express*, 'and in 1946 when I was still manager at Leeds, I got the chance.'[1]

In fact, so keen was Eddie to be involved with the tour – the first such sporting expedition undertaken since the end of the Second World War – he paid his own passage, a fare of £11 11s 3d. By now, he had bigger journalistic fish to fry, too. Through his contacts in the game, he arranged to report home for the local Leeds paper, the *Yorkshire Evening News*. Simultaneously, and more prestigiously, he was also commissioned to cover the tour by the national *Sunday Pictorial*, later to evolve into the *Sunday Mirror*. Whilst in Australia and New Zealand, Eddie would write and broadcast for the Australasian media, including Sydney's *Sunday* and *Daily Telegraph* newspapers, ABC (Australian Broadcasting Corporation) radio and Christchurch station 3YA, forging yet more contacts with international organisations that would serve him well in years to come. However, for him and for the players and officials with whom he was to travel, the first problem was getting there at all.

By 1946, tours to the southern hemisphere were a crucial part of the British rugby league tapestry.[2] The very first England–Australia game to be played on Australian soil took place in Sydney in 1910, in which the tourists triumphed 27–20 before going on to complete a series win, 22–17, in Brisbane. Since then, six more such tours (with a six-year hiatus for the First World War) had followed on a four-yearly basis until, by the time the Allied troops' washing had been nicely unclipped from the Siegfried Line, an eighth party of Poms – or 'Chooms' as they would become known in Australia on account of their funny Northern accents – were ready to make the 27-day voyage south. In terms of providing the finance necessary to allow the game not only to survive but to flourish, international tours were vital. Furthermore, their existence lent exoticism to a sport that, on both sides of the world, was engaged in constant combat with real and imagined parochialism.

Despite the fact that domestic rugby league activity in the UK had been pretty much back to normal in the 1945–46 season, to embark upon such a lengthy journey overseas at what remained a volatile time internationally was a venture not to be undertaken lightly. And indeed it was only upon the personal intervention of one Dr H.V. Evatt, the Australian Minister for External Affairs, who stressed the importance of such a tour from an ambassadorial point of view, along with an assurance from the British Government that it would provide organisational assistance, that Rugby League Council members, meeting in Manchester, felt confident enough to overturn their earlier refusal and accept the Australian Board of Control's initial invitation. The upshot being that, on 3 April 1946, 32 members of a touring party destined to become known as 'The Indomitables' were given naval permission to join the crew of the *Illustrious*-class aircraft carrier of that name in Plymouth. There, together with a host of returning overseas servicemen and, according to Waring, 'half a dozen priests from Eire', they set sail on what, for most, would be the adventure of a lifetime.

* * *

Upon his return some six months later, Waring produced his own pioneering handbook of the tour, *England to Australia and New Zealand*, nowadays a very valuable collector's item. In it, we are given not only a detailed chronicle of events as they unfolded but an equally remarkable insight into the workings of Eddie's own mind and introduced, at first hand, to just what a gifted writer he really was.

Eddie Waring's motives for publishing his book – the first of its kind – are stated openly in its introductory pages. 'Through the years,' he writes:

> international sport of all phases has been recorded so that the worthy deeds of athletic pioneers may be made known to future generations. But one great sport – Rugby League football – has been out in the wilderness. For what reason I cannot say, because this game, known in its infancy as Northern Union, has been, in recent years, the only British sport to maintain world superiority.

His dander well and truly up, he continues:

> Rugby League football has received little attention from the pens of authors. Why? Please don't ask me. There have been good writers and even better legislators who could have compiled a most interesting collection of anecdotes and reminiscences. But all, so far, have fought shy of the task. Now I propose to take Rugby League football out of the wilderness.[3]

Over the years, Eddie Waring has often been described as the first British journalist to accompany a touring rugby league side down under, an accolade the man himself was always happy to accept. In fact, it would be more accurate to say that he was among the first to do so, for in that 1946 party were another three such travelling wordsmiths: Walter Crockford (*Manchester Guardian*); Ernest Cawthorne (*Manchester Evening News*); and Alfred Drewry

(*Yorkshire Post*). Reading between the lines, Eddie would doubtless have justified that claim on the back of being the first journalist actually to purchase his ticket! Certainly, as the tour progressed, he became an increasingly influential figure with regard to its organisation. And he could, at one later stage, fairly claim to be the only reporter to have seen every post-war Test between Great Britain and Australia.

The pivotal nature of Eddie Waring's involvement in helping to coordinate this first post-war Australasian outing can be seen in a business report prepared for the Rugby League Council by tour co-manager Wilf Gabbatt. After bemoaning the activities of Australia's written media, Gabbatt writes that he feels it

> only fitting that I should refer to one member of the British press, whom the Council gave permission to accompany the touring party. It will be remembered, no doubt, my attitude with regard to Mr Eddie Waring of the *Sunday Pictorial*, and my observations regarding him at the final meeting of the Tour sub-committee. I therefore took the earliest possible opportunity of making my acquaintance with Mr Waring and discussed with him various policies that I was determined to pursue throughout the Tour, and it gives me the greatest possible pleasure to be in a position to report that I received from him every possible assistance and co-operation, at all times, for which I am most grateful.[4]

Indeed, so enamoured was the Rugby League with Eddie's contribution that its long-serving secretary, John Wilson, agreed to pen a foreword for his book. 'The author is a keen observer and records his observations with a frank, breezy enthusiasm which is as refreshing as it is entertaining,' was Wilson's verdict.

> You will sight-see with him in the Mediterranean, the Canal, Aden and Colombo, play deck games East of Suez, Cross the Line, and suffer the discomforts of that awful train journey across the Nullabor Plain. All these, however, interesting as they are,

are merely the hors d'oeuvres, the real feast is the Rugby League football games played in Australia and New Zealand. The thrill of watching your team on the packed Sydney Cricket Ground in a Test Match (and tell it not at Old Trafford or Headingley, they play Rugby League football across the cricket Test Match wicket!), the joy when they win, and the depths of sorrow and despondency when they lose, can all be experienced by Mr Waring's graphic writings.[5]

In commencing his tale, Eddie makes great play of the way in which the captain and commander of HMS *Indomitable* took the intrusion of this party of civilians in good heart, although you suspect that for the crew having a group of high-spirited international sportsmen aboard must have come as a welcome diversion. Originally laid down in 1937, at the Vickers-Armstrong shipyard on the northern banks of Morecambe Bay, a stone's throw from Barrow's Craven Park, HMS *Indomitable* was some 230 metres in length and weighed 23,000 tons, with a top speed of 30.5 knots. At various stages in its existence, the carrier had taken a 1,100 pound bomb through her flight deck, been bombed twice more by planes off the coast of Malta, got herself torpedoed by a Ju-88 bomber while covering the Sicily landings in 1943 and been hit by a kamikaze less than a year later, before returning to the UK in November 1945. After that little lot, putting up with 26 rugby league players and Eddie Waring must have been a doddle.

Indomitable by name, then, indomitable by nature. And the same might also be said of the Great British Lions under her care, in their Test matches with Australia anyway. Seldom was a nickname so well deserved. This eighth squad of British rugby league tourists, captained by the great Gus Risman, not only successfully increased their nation's series victory record to 7–1, they won 19 of their 24 other games on tour too, emphasising the dominance of British rugby league football during that era. One tale from the tour, possibly apocryphal, told of how, when the team's biggest players disembarked first at their Sydney hotel, one startled onlooker yelled: 'Right, then, that's it! No more bloody food parcels to England!'[6]

* * *

Eddie Waring's account of the Indomitables tour is a riveting and entertaining read throughout, describing event after event that must surely have played a key part in shaping the mindset of the young journalist. After leaving Plymouth and making brief stops at Gibraltar and Malta, Eddie writes, it was full steam ahead through the Mediterranean heat and on towards the Suez Canal.

Sailing on past Port Said, at which HMS *Indomitable* did not land, and along the hundred-mile, eight-hour 'slow march' up the canal itself, the ever-curious Eddie Waring informed his readers that he

> was fortunate in having the use of very good binoculars. The modern age of steam seems to run into the olden age of transport. With jeeps running on the road further in the sanded desert I could see lone riders with their camels.

Once through and out into the Red Sea, the mercury climbed several notches higher, leading to Waring's amazement that

> an itinerary is never issued to a touring team. Most of the party were unprepared for the extreme hot weather, and shorts and an outfit suited for this climate was just not part of the equipment we had taken. Take note you future tourists when going through the Red Sea, take a Red Sea outfit!

Approaching Aden, discomfort at the humidity continued to rankle:

> for the cabins – yes, I had a single cabin – were intolerably hot. I had a fan which occasionally worked, but was advised not to put it directly on to a sweating body, and as this was the only way one could keep the heat away, it was an almost hopeless position.

Among the available distractions were on-deck cinema shows, leading to an observation that, 'even with such good films as *Brief Encounter* and *Scarlet Street*, the hard stiff seats were too much until one got the idea of taking a pillow or, better still, a cabin chair, if you had one'. The thought of big tough props like Wigan's Ken Gee (15 st. 3 lb) or Bradford's Frank Whitcombe (17 st. 8 lb) shifting uncomfortably as Trevor Howard and Celia Johnson struggled to stiffen their upper lips is a charming one indeed.

From Aden it was on to Colombo, Ceylon, a location that, mostly, met with great favour all round. Waring relates how, while the party was drinking in Colombo's Palace Hotel, a group of British sailors noticed them and came over for a chat. After a while, observing that one lurking local was taking more interest in the conversation than might be considered polite, one sailor abruptly turned round and instructed him to push off. 'It's alreight, lad, I come fra' Bradford,' was his reply. The fez on his head, it seemed, was but the latest souvenir obtained by Bradford Northern winger Eric Batten who, according to Waring, 'was always much browner than anyone else, and was known as Abdul to his pals'.

Though essentially an observer of the tour rather than an active participant, Eddie Waring was clearly, by now, one of the boys. As another of the players on board, Bradford Northern's Welsh forward Trevor Foster, would later write:

> Uniquely, this tour had reporters travelling with the party and one journalist, the popular Eddie Waring, became organiser-in-chief. For instance, with 11 Welshmen in the party he assembled a Welsh choir to entertain people on board and at various theatres in Australia. In his journalist capacity he had a room set up with a telephone and express mail facilities so he could get his reports back to England quicker than ever before. The party felt indebted to Eddie, a real player's man and well-liked.[7]

* * *

After their longest spell at sea without sight of dry land – nine days – the passengers and crew of HMS *Indomitable* finally reached Australia twenty-seven days after the ship's departure from Plymouth, albeit on the western edge of that vast land, at Fremantle. To get to their ultimate destination in the east, it was originally intended that they would travel for some six days more, sailing around the Great Australian Bight.

Accompanying them on this final stage of the outward journey would be representatives of the Sydney press, most of whom had travelled at least 2,600 miles in the opposite direction for the privilege. Though Eddie Waring would be covering the tour for the *Sydney Telegraph*, that newspaper still dispatched a photographer, while its rivals, the *Sydney Morning Herald* and *Sydney Sun*, both sent well-known reporters. There was even a cartoonist from the *Brisbane Courier*. Yet that reception was as nothing compared to the one which awaited the Lions in New South Wales.

Throughout his journalistic career Eddie Waring would embark upon seven southern-hemisphere tours in all, but none were as eye-opening as his inaugural trip. As the first Lions team to visit Australasia in ten years, Gus Risman and his boys were feted wherever they went. Furthermore, owing to circumstances beyond their control, they would go where no rugby league tourist had travelled before. Most immediately, an initial two-day stay in Fremantle was extended to seven when HMS *Indomitable*'s fellow aircraft carrier HMS *Victorious* ran into trouble and was damaged whilst making the return voyage through the aforementioned Bight. Eventually, the Admiralty in London sent orders that HMS *Indomitable* should disembark its own passengers and pick up those of HMS *Victorious* instead, before heading straight back to England. Those bound for Sydney, meanwhile, would travel under naval escort on a troop train from Perth to Melbourne and onward.

There was, however, still time for Eddie to flex his deft literary muscles in praise of Perth. 'No better introduction to Australia could be given a first-time visitor than to spend a few days in this beautiful city of Western Australia,' he writes. 'It was autumn and the colouring of some of the famous plants was not so profuse as in other seasons. Kangaroo paws in their reds and greens, and the golden wattles were passing their best.'

In return for the hospitality shown by the HMS *Indomitable* crew, a match in aid of the ship's charity was also organised, between a Lions team clad in red and another in blue. Played at Fremantle and refereed by Eddie himself, it also allowed the ship-rusty Brits a first semi-serious run-out on Australian soil, while giving the Aussie press an early glimpse of what their fellow countrymen on the east coast would be up against.

That done, after a barrage of telegrams between Sydney and tour co-manager Gabbatt, the party finally embarked upon the last leg of an already lengthy expedition, by rail, across the great Nullabor Plain. For a group of individuals more used to the grey, rainy wintry afternoons of northern England and south Wales, the vast, fly-infested and deadly orange monotony of the Australian desert provided a fascinating if uncomfortable experience. Meals had to be queued for and eaten by the side of the track on wayside halts. Sleeping accommodation was severely limited, with the corridors and floors, according to Waring, 'a mass of humanity during the night'.

Displaying an interest in trains that is already fully formed, with a disarming attention to factual detail, Waring goes on to share with his readers the nuts and bolts of the Australian railway network, which, he declares, thanks to historical interstate jealousies, is a law unto itself. The line's first length, to the great gold mining centre of Kalgoorlie, for example, operated upon a 3-ft-6-in. gauge. Its second leg, meanwhile, from Kalgoorlie to Port Pirie, near Adelaide, employed a gauge of 4 ft 8 in. This from a man who would regularly hold quizzes at family Christmas parties on the best routes to such and such a place and who, when asked which book he would like to take to his fictional desert island some 28 years later, along with the usual Bible and collected works of Shakespeare, replied: 'I would like the old Bradshaw timetable, about five inches thick, where I could run so many journeys up and down the lost railway lines of Great Britain – that I would enjoy. And as a bonus, if I could have one overseas too, I'd think you were very nice to me.'[8]

Given the length of the overland journey, Eddie and his fellow travellers had plenty of time for contemplation. The first part of the trek alone traversed some 365 miles, mainly in a dead straight line through an unchanging, scorched landscape. 'In England,' he mused poetically, 'the longest such line is eighteen miles between Selby and Hull.' Occasionally, upon its food stops, the train would be visited by a local Aboriginal community, keen to sell its wares. Not for the first time, Eddie Waring's instinctive compassion for life's underdog is right there on the page. 'Coming down to the train with their boomerangs and imitation Kookaburro [sic] staves,' he wrote, 'this fast-dying race looked far from being healthy.' He went on: 'The most depressing sight was to see the millions of flies round their scantily clad bodies. But the flies appeared to worry me more than they worried the Aborigines.'

Not surprisingly, then, the train's arrival in Adelaide came as a great relief, not least because it allowed the party to have 'a much needed wash and brush-up'. Once back on board, an even sweatier 500 miles later, the party disembarked with equal gratitude in Melbourne, after which the remaining 512 miles to Sydney were again to be made on a non-sleeper, with as many as six 'hefty footballers' sharing a single cabin. A luggage change at Albury saw half the suitcases go temporarily astray. In Waring's own words: 'no International touring team has ever travelled as frugally as [this] team did.'

Nevertheless, when the tour was done and dusted, ever the optimist, Eddie Waring would look back on this discomfort with philosophical affection. 'Although the grumbles had been many and the inconveniences terrific,' he recalled, 'we had had many good things to atone for the annoyances. We had been the first International RL team to travel across this continent. We had seen every big city and all the States (with the exception of Queensland, which we saw later) and we learned a lot about Australia which we would never have known had we gone on with our original plan and taken the Bight.'

* * *

In future, when Eddie Waring went on a Great Britain tour down under, although he was always a welcome member of the main travelling party – an unusual honour for a journalist – he would more often than not book his own hotel room elsewhere.

Some have viewed this perceived idiosyncrasy with suspicion. Yet, as we will see, Eddie's Greta Garbo-esque need to be alone not only reflected an understandable desire for privacy as the demands of fame grew, it was the direct result of hard experience. For all that they were welcome visitors, Great Britain's tourists were frequently squeezed into the most downbeat hotels imaginable – at least that was how the Chooms themselves usually saw it. Five-star accommodation it was not.

Having arrived in Sydney in 1946, for example, Eddie wrote:

> We were housed at Paddington, not a salubrious district by any means, and the accommodation was so cramped that at one time there was talk of moving, as the 1936 Tourists did. It was, however, very handy to the Sydney cricket ground. From the bedroom windows we could see the ground, and it was well served by trams and many taxis. The Olympic, our hotel, was accustomed to footballers, for the Queensland team and the New South Wales country players were frequent visitors. But 32 all at once was rather a lot. So thought Gus Risman who was sleeping on the balcony – particularly when it rained one night.

Perhaps one of the most pleasing aspects of *England to Australia and New Zealand* for the modern reader is the innocence with which it describes an age when travel to the other side of the world for recreation was a very rare thing indeed. Waring is clearly fascinated with local culture and, being a natural-born communicator at heart, the colourful Aussie vernacular particularly arouses his curiosity.

'"It's a fair cow" is a favourite expression,' he notes, 'while the use of the word "bastard" must be a means of affection, as it is used so often among good friends.' Given his equal fascination with public transport, it is no surprise that one of the first aspects of Sydney life Waring describes is the city's tram culture: 'To see a Sydney mob crowding on to their "Toast Rack" trams on race day at Randwick or football day at the Sydney cricket ground is amazing.'

In these days before the building of the Sydney Opera House and despite the presence of the famous harbour bridge, Sydney, to Eddie Waring, was

> just Sydney, and you either like it or you don't. I like it, and despite its indifference and its toughness it has a personality which you can feel happy in. Throw punches back at it and you are laughing. Cry and you will go under. My first article for the Sydney Telegraph was entitled 'Stop your kidding, Australia!' It brought in a lot of criticism, but it made me many friends, and we threw punches through the letter column like nobody's business. But that is how they like it in Sydney.

* * *

After a three-day trip to the Blue Mountains and Jenolan Caves, some 80 miles west of Sydney, the Indomitables' first match ended in a comfortable 36–4 victory over a Southern Division side in the country town of Junee, where a good turnout of locals set the tone for the welcome to come. From there, the party made an unscheduled visit to Canberra, where the Lions again won their game easily and were given a tour of parliament, meeting the then Australian Prime Minister Joseph Chifley and the Governor General, the Duke of Gloucester. After these two opening fixtures, the Sydney papers declared that, while they were impressed by their style of play, this modern team was not as good or as big as the class of 1936. In fact, the Indomitables would become the only British rugby league team ever to return from Australia without losing at least one Test match. (So far.)

The lead-up to the tour's third game, a clash with New South Wales – from which most of the Australian Test team was expected to be chosen – can't have failed to alert Waring to a new, thrusting style of newspaper journalism. Unlike in England, where tactical analysis was more the thing, here the main emphasis was on gossip, personalities and the opinions of players. Alarmed by this, the British management imposed a team curfew and banned its players from talking to the press, but the game continued to be hyped in a blaze of publicity.

In the event, those pre-match stories turned out to be more entertaining than the game itself, a rather poor affair which England just about edged, 14–10. Furthermore, at least two of the visitors' scores – a goal by Gus Risman and an Ike Owens try – came shrouded in controversy, a turn of events that allowed Eddie to reveal what his attitude towards today's use of video referees might have been. When the doubts over both scores were confirmed by newsreel, the *Sunday Pictorial* correspondent concluded: 'These newsreel shots – they must have taken thousands of feet of all the big games – became very useful in settling arguments.' Before the tour was out, Eddie would have used up a good number of film reels himself.

After two more games in NSW country towns and a second win against New South Wales, the Lions headed up the coast to a packed stadium in Newcastle, where the welcome was a good deal less cordial than it had thus far been elsewhere. The game, in which England lost 18–13 after being reduced to 11 men and having a last-minute 'try' by Salford's George Curran disallowed, was marred by crowd trouble and a police escort was needed to return the British team to its dressing-room. The press-box, too, was crammed, with no allowance made for the international press, a sorry state of affairs that did, at least, allow the resourceful Eddie to add one more pioneering claim to his list, that of being the first journalist ever to use a laptop: 'so I took my typewriter and sat on the touchline with it on my knees.'

Even more remarkably, that Newcastle match took place just

24 hours before the First Test back in Sydney, a clear case of gamesmanship on the part of the Australians that must have been a factor in the result, an 8–8 draw. 'Test football in Sydney is unlike any in any other part of the world,' wrote a clearly thrilled Waring. 'With the aid of a wonderful Press, the whole situation is one full of dynamite. Sydney papers had diagrams of almost every English moves [*sic*] and they produced every possible reason for every possible result.' Before the game, as an eventual 64,527 crowd built in number and, he confessed, made Eddie 'tingle with excitement', he took himself out onto the SCG turf and began taking movie shots.

* * *

While Eddie Waring's eyes were opened by Australian press coverage of the tour, his ears quickly became attuned to the buzz of its broadcasting media too. 'On a big match day the sideline is full of commentators,' he wrote admiringly.

> I was signed up with the 2UW station which, each Friday night, covered the Sunday Telegraph Sports Parade. This consisted of an hour with sports as its main topic. Rugby league had a prominent spot, and we had various personalities in it. On one occasion the Welsh choir sang a couple of songs, which were well received, and Frank Packer, the popular owner of the Telegraph, very generously gave the boys £50 for their 'kitty'. This Welsh Choir was formed because it was felt that all Welsh Choirs are popular, but as often as not, the Welsh Choir consisted of Yorkshiremen, Lancastrians, and a couple of Cumbrians. Still it sounded good to be called a Welsh Choir, and when they got down to business and sang 'Cym Rhondda', 'Sos Pan Fach' or 'Calan Lan' (Clean Heart) which were the main items from their repertoire, they were really good.

Commercial radio, decided Eddie, had a lot to be said for it, providing it was not overdone.

At least it was entertaining and provided sport presentation far in excess of what we hear in England. Rugby League, which is given such small consideration by the BBC, is one of the main sporting subjects in New South Wales and Queensland.

And speaking of the latter, with the First Test and a further country game against Northern Division in Tamworth behind Great Britain, a gruelling tour schedule continued with the party's first sighting of the Sunshine State.

The venue for this tour's one and only clash with Queensland was Brisbane, where some 25,000 people turned out, in the midst of a coal strike, to watch the Poms go down narrowly, 24–25. As for Queensland radio, Waring judged it 'bright', whilst noting the efforts of one broadcaster in particular. In Brisbane, he said:

> George Hardman is the shining light. A jovial commentator and announcer, he was quick to exploit the activities of the boys at his Fireman's Ball and other social interests. George was ever-ready to give the game a boost, and men like him are assets to the code.

After that game in Brisbane, the party set out for the tropical north and Bundaberg, home of Australia's famous rum and the site of what Waring described as the Lions' worst display of the entire tour. The opponents were Wide Bay and although the British eventually won 16–12, the game was ruined by the fatigue of the travelling players. If they thought the trip to Bundaberg was tough, however, worse was to come when the tourists went to play Central Queensland in Rockhampton. Again, the Brits came out on top, 35–12, but the journey had been a nightmare after the ongoing coal strike caused the cancellation of regular services, forcing the party to endure a 178-mile, 12-hour trip in the back of a goods train. Next up was Townsville, en route to which the party this time endured a 20-hour overnight haul, during which Bradford's Willie Davies, Leeds' Dai Jenkins, Barrow's Willie Horne and Waring himself were forced to sleep on the luggage rack.

Understandably sick of the sight of trains by now, from here the Lions employed a revolutionary form of transportation as far as a British touring team was concerned: namely, the aeroplane. Thus did Townsville become the first place from which a British rugby league team, albeit leaving in dribs and drabs, flew.

Along with ensuring greater comfort, this new twist to the timetable allowed Eddie Waring to further develop his transport fixation. Flying might have been a new experience for the Indomitables but, noted Waring: 'Air transport in Australia is now a very big affair. The distances are so vast that flying is essential and Australia holds the record for the cheapest flying in the world. You can fly for 3d. a mile.' Along with rugby players, Eddie noted, other types of living cargo could be transported too. Cattle, for example, was regularly moved this way, whilst 'A Shetland pony travelled 900 miles by air and was a very good passenger'. Nor were the people employed to look after the travellers overlooked. 'The air hostesses are amongst the most attractive girls I have seen,' he reflected, 'many of whom could make a name on the stage.'

* * *

The Second Test of the Indomitables tour was staged on 6 July at the Exhibition Ground, Brisbane. Quite simply, if England could win this one, that draw in the First meant they were guaranteed to retain the mythical Ashes. As a result, an official attendance of some 40,500 people turned up, although, as Eddie Waring put it: 'Nobody knows just how many were there, for the gates were rushed, but I should reckon 65,000.'

Whatever the true number, it was certainly a record for any game in Brisbane and the rushing of the gates to which Waring referred almost resulted in the match not being played at all. For in the ensuing confusion, the players, officials, press members and others in possession of a valid ticket could not gain admittance to the venue. By the time both teams arrived, under police escort, such was the size of the crowd that every gate – including the official entry – had been shut, for fear that the thousands of fans still left outside would also surge through. Eventually, those that mattered most were sneaked in through the back and the game went ahead as scheduled.

'Every vantage point inside and outside was used,' wrote Waring, 'and the more reckless climbed high up on to an electric standard, which looked very dangerous. Wireless commentators had their tables brushed aside and they finished up by standing on them, looking over the spectators' heads. I never thought the match would be started.'

Despite the melee, England produced a performance to savour, marred only by the late sending-off of Wigan hooker Joe Egan, who retaliated when Eddie's former Black Knight Ernest Ward was knocked out by an Australian punch. By then, though, a 14–5 victory, and therefore the fabled Ashes, was secured.

Even so, if the Lions were to succeed in becoming the only team ever to return from Australia without losing a single Test, they still needed to back up a further cluster of country games with a Third Test victory in Sydney. And on 20 July 1946, the players duly delivered that result, 20–7, leaving Eddie flushed with a combination of patriotic pride and genuine concern that Britain's dominance might be harmful to the international game. Writing in the *Sydney Telegraph*, he reflected:

Australia's Rugby League defeat – and it was a decisive defeat – is causing a lot of heartburning as well as a search for scapegoats. Many have picked on coach Johnson as the victim. But it seems to me that one thing stands out clearly – the players are not good enough. Therefore, the solution is in rebuilding the framework of good, sound Rugby. Surely by now it must be obvious that something is radically wrong with Australian Rugby League when, for 25 years, the same country has won the Ashes.

* * *

After attending a farewell dinner given by the Australian Board of Control at Sydney's Tattersals Club, where the small Ashes cup was presented in private – much to Eddie and the rest of the group's annoyance – and a speech was given by the entrepreneurial founder of Australian rugby league, James J. Giltinan, the Indomitables once again took to the skies.

This time, their destination was New Zealand, where they were scheduled to play one Test Match, in Auckland, along with six other games. After an eight-hour flight across the Tasman – a journey made in three batches, with the heavier luggage travelling on later by sea – the party arrived to a typically warm welcome on a sunny Sunday afternoon. Once on Kiwi soil, Eddie wasted little time in renewing his acquaintance with New Zealand Rugby League chairman Jack Redwood, former manager of the Kiwi team whose second and final match of that ill-fated 1939 tour had been hastily arranged at Crown Flatt. Along with other officials of the New Zealand RL and a few onlookers, 'including our first Maori acquaintances', the squad was taken to its Auckland hotel, about which Eddie remarked: 'Immediately we realised this was one part, at any rate, where this country scored over the Australian folk, for the accommodation was the best available and particularly comfortable.'

No sooner had the party settled in than it was off again. 'We soon obtained firsthand knowledge of the New Zealand rail system when we travelled the 400 miles from Auckland to Wellington,' wrote Waring, before adding in trademark style:

The main lines and branches of the State railways have a total length of 3,320 miles and serve both the North and South Islands. Most of the long-journey trains have sleeping cars, but owing to our late arrival we were unable to get these and had to make our first journey in a vestibule type saloon car with bucket lean-back seats and pillows obtainable at the stations.

Upon arrival in Wellington, the tourists hit atrocious weather, although this seems not to have perturbed Waring too greatly:

I had the pleasure of making contact with the New Zealand Broadcasting Company, for whom I was scheduled to undertake a number of broadcasts. Government-controlled, it was well organised and run with Professor Shelley, from the old country, in charge. He had a capable lot of folk round him, and, introducing various members of the staff, he told me one of them came from Ilkley, so for ten minutes we had a really hot bit of Yorkshire floating around. There are commercial radio stations in New Zealand, but they also come under the jurisdiction of the Government.

In pointing out the differences between the New Zealand media's treatment of rugby league and that of their Australian cousins, Waring wrote:

The Auckland papers gave the team a good show but in its right place, and it did not monopolise even the sporting pages. Auckland is a Rugby League stronghold, against Rugby Union competition, and this is the only city in New Zealand where it can claim such superiority. The Rugby League people are keen to make progress, but they had to endure severe opposition in their rivalry with the amateur handling code.

The first direct evidence of this 'cutting-in business', as Eddie put it, came with the opening game in Christchurch.

In a nutshell, when it was announced that Britain's touring rugby league side would play the South Island, the NZ rugby union authorities immediately hatched a fixture of its own. 'Naturally,' wrote Eddie,

the RU folk got the larger gate, and the whole business did not reflect well. There was a lot of indignation [in Christchurch] over the treatment afforded the visiting English team. Many of the Kiwi boys had played with some of the League players in two Service games in England, and the Kiwis had had the benefit of the use of RL grounds. On the evening of the game I broadcast from Christchurch, and I put out a challenge to the Rugby Union folk for a match to be played between the English touring side and the Kiwis team – at Rugby Union. The object of the game to provide Food for Britain. Nothing was heard from the RU on the matter. What a pity, and what a chance to show that we were all sport brothers!

Though on the whole a diplomat when asked about the relationship between the rugby codes, Eddie was quietly shocked by such blatantly antagonistic attitudes on the part of union administrators on both sides of the Tasman. When contacted for a telephone interview by the British magazine *The Listener* before setting out for Christchurch, he outlined his concerns. 'I am troubled,' he said,

> at the opposition and lack of sympathy there seems to be between the Rugby League and the Rugby Union codes in Australia. And I have been told that here, in Wellington, boys who play League at school are not allowed to play the Union game. I feel strongly that boys should be allowed to play any code. There is room for both. League and Union players were good enough to fight in the war together; they should be good enough to play football together.

Intriguingly, *The Listener* then asked Waring if he had yet encountered the union commentator Winston McCarthy, a well-known and voluble champion of the 15-a-side code who, after beginning his radio career in 1937, had broadcast commentaries on games played in Europe by the Second New Zealand Expeditionary Force – aka 'The Kiwis' – during the Second World War, the first such live rugby broadcasts to New Zealand from the British Isles. 'No,' Eddie replied, 'but I would very much like to. Perhaps I'll strike him on the boat to Lyttelton tonight.' With his penchant for catchphrases and eccentric personality – 'Listen, listen, it's a goal!' he would shout – it is not inconceivable to think that Winston McCarthy could have been an influence on Waring's own later broadcasting style. Either way, Eddie was soon cheerfully telling *The Listener* how, only the other day, he had successfully telephoned his home in Dewsbury. 'It was as clear as a bell,' he said, 'and it made me feel all the more at home. Not many years ago when a football team went overseas it wasn't heard of for months.'[9]

* * *

From Christchurch, the team went by train to Greymouth, where the rain continued to lash down. 'The Greymouth ground was really a race track,' reported Eddie,

> and the only stand was too far away to be of any use. The ground was wet and had many pools of water. I managed to get one of the few seats and sat with my feet on an upturned bucket with my typewriter on my knee – and some kind reserve player holding an umbrella over me. That is how I saw the West Coast beat England. Their win was no fluke, for England had almost a Test team out but just could not settle. No player wanted to dive into the pools, and while they were waiting for the ball to float out the locals would dive in and chase away. The final score was 17 pts to 8 pts, and England had no excuses.

Upon arrival back in Wellington, the next fixture on a packed agenda allowed Eddie to reflect upon the status of the New Zealand Maoris. 'The Maori race is one which mystery and romance appears to surround,' he decided,

> yet not a great deal is known about its members outside New Zealand. Some have thought them a wild tribe, uneducated, and just coloured folk lacking in physical strength. Actually, that is the absolute opposite to the grand folk of the Maori race. They are coloured, agreed, but they are intelligent, charming, and well educated folk. There are differences, as always with whites and coloured folk, but the Maori race has played a big part in the development of New Zealand in a sporting and physical sense.

Years later, this fascination with Maori culture surfaced again in Eddie's music selection on Radio 2's *Be My Guest*. For his third choice, he picked the 'Maori Poi Song' – as performed by the Australian bass-baritone Peter Dawson – after revealing how he first heard the Maoris sing this jolly tune in 1946. 'It was a very thrilling moment to see them putting all their endeavour into this,' he told his listeners.[10]

As it happened, while the Maori team that faced the Lions that day in Wellington also put in plenty of effort, eventually they were outclassed 32–8. 'The Governor-General, Sir Bernard [Freyberg], attended the game and the players were introduced to him,' Eddie wrote.

> Before the party left Wellington they were guests at Parliament House, where the Prime Minister, Mr P. Fraser, and other members, made us very welcome. The long trip back to Auckland by train through the night was lightened somewhat by musical entertainment, mostly by the Maori boys. An impromptu concert was held in the train saloon and the highlight came when the Maoris taught Hughes, Foster, Batten, Ward, and a few others the Maori war dance, which they did to the accompaniment of actions and facial expressions. In return, we tried to teach the Maoris how to sing 'Ilkla Moor B'aht 'At'. Not very successfully, I am afraid, but still it passed the time.

In Auckland, a three-day trip to the volcanic thermal spa of Rotorua was followed by a game against the Auckland city side, narrowly won 9–7 by the visitors, and a one-sided 42–12 romp against South Auckland in Huntly. That first game was played at Carlaw Park, the scene also of the tourists' one and only Test match in New Zealand, which somehow they contrived to lose 13–8. Despite having by now picked up a severe chill, Waring was always one to see the bigger picture and reflected that: 'Winning the only Test gave the New Zealand team and officials an impetus, which did them more good than it did the English side harm.' After one final match against Auckland, won by England 22–9, it was time for the long voyage home.

'This party of Indomitables had done a great deal no other party had done,' Waring wrote proudly, after the group had finally disembarked at Tilbury Docks from this last lap of its journey, via the Panama Canal and Nova Scotia, aboard the ocean liner *Rangitiki*:

> And it had pioneered many ways by which future Tourists will benefit. Nearly 40,000 miles had been covered by ship, train, plane, and foot. Naturally, it was good to be home but the experiences, the contacts, and the friendships made and the sights seen were so fine that were I never to have another Australasian tour, I am glad I had this one with the Rugby League Indomitables.

Five

A MAN OF VISION

'Here are two bonny lads. You could buy them for £3,000.'

Upon returning from an exhausting trip around the world, your average Joe would spark up the kettle, put up his feet and reflect fondly on the adventure just gone. Eddie Waring was no average Joe. Along with consolidating his position at the *Sunday Pictorial*, he began pretty much immediately to stage a series of touring 'lectures', during which he presented the film footage he had gathered whilst away, held rugby league quizzes and chaired question-and-answer forums, involving many of the game's best-known players and coaches.

In so doing, Eddie was in many ways merely echoing an earlier rugby league tradition. From as early as 1910, it had grown quite common for officials such as Bob Anderton of Warrington, a tour manager in the 1920s and '30s, to travel around the north of England with slideshows, relating stories of those overseas events.[1] With the advent of film, however, Eddie was able to take things to another level. Over the course of the next couple of decades, Eddie Waring's roadshows, as they were colloquially known, would become unmissable events, frequently selling out well in advance of the big day. One reason for their success was their lively, interactive style, influenced no doubt by Eddie's own experiences as part of the Australian radio series *Sunday Telegraph Sports Parade*, on which he had appeared in 1946. Of that show, he wrote:

The usual quiz programmes were held and a sporting quiz, at half-a-crown doubled, was presented. The studio accommodates about 400, and the tickets are always snapped up before the day; in fact, there is always a crowd waiting for any opportunity to get in to see this show. With cheer leaders, who indicate when to applaud and when to subside, and the band leader, who, incidentally, looked remarkably like Brian Aherne, the presentation is full of colour and interest for the whole hour.[2]

Owing to his lack of a motor vehicle, Eddie would often travel to these 'lectures' by taxi or sometimes in his brother Harry's van. Harry junior recalls: 'Eddie didn't have a car until he was 40. He used to go everywhere by train or taxi, and in fact while he was manager at Dewsbury he prided himself on knowing the quickest and cheapest routes to places like Whitehaven and Barrow. So when he did his roadshows, from 1946 onwards, I would go along with him. My father had a vehicle so we used to take Eddie, who had a case of programmes, jerseys and films, and there would always be a player or two in attendance. He would open with a talk, show his films on an old projector and ask for questions. Then he would have a quiz and give programmes away to the kids as prizes. He used to love doing those roadshows. I think it was his way of spreading the gospel and publicising rugby league. He didn't make any money out of them – the club [where the show was staged] took the receipts. He was just given his expenses.'

If anyone made money from an Eddie Waring roadshow, it was usually the player whom Waring was there to support, for the events quite often took the form of benefit nights. Despite his sharp dressing and flash image, financial gain, it seems, was never the chief motivating factor for Eddie. This, after all, is the same man who, aged 36, quit a highly paid regular job at one of the biggest clubs in rugby league to travel to the other side of the world at his own expense. That it turned out to be the best decision he ever made can only be seen with hindsight.

'Eddie's parents thought that you didn't get anything for nothing and had to go out and earn it,' confirms Harry Waring. 'But Eddie never did anything with money primarily in mind. He was a purist in that sense and did it for the love of the sport. The very idea of rugby league inspired him. It was a nonconformist game and, being a free spirit himself, that attracted him greatly. At heart, he was a players' man. Mick Sullivan, for example, says that whenever he was short of money on tour, Eddie was always there to bankroll him.'

Nor is the fiery former winger Sullivan, the most-capped British player of all time on his international retirement in 1963, alone in his admiration. Many other players who had the good fortune to accompany Eddie Waring on one of his seven tours have a similar story to tell. The free-scoring centre Eric Ashton MBE, for example, a tourist with Waring in 1958 and 1962, not to mention a supremely gifted World Cup-winning captain and future coach of Wigan and St Helens, recalls: 'One thing Eddie always did was look after players. He got them free cinema tickets and things like that. In the years we were there with him, he always found accommodation elsewhere, but, if you wanted him, he would be there. Because he had been going out to Australia so often, he had a lot of connections and never ever forgot the players. I became a good friend of his over the years. When I came into the game, Eddie was already number one. Everybody knew Eddie Waring. If you became a friend of his, you thought you were a little bit of a someone, you know? There was a bit of stardust on him.'[3]

Another former Wigan great with a try or two to his name, the barnstorming Welsh winger Billy Boston MBE, Eric Ashton's partner in the three-quarters at Central Park and a fellow tourist in probably the greatest British side ever to visit Australasia in 1962, also remembers Eddie Waring with fondness. 'I found him fabulous,' says Boston, who, as a 19 year old, scored a record 36 tries on his first trip down under. 'I first met him on the 1954 tour. I'd only played about five or six matches for Wigan when I got picked to go, and Eddie introduced me to Australia. He was a great fellow. When we went on tour, he used to fix everything for us. He used to get us into free films, and it was free this and free that. That was Eddie.'[4]

Not that life with Eddie Waring was one big party. As Eric Ashton points out: 'He was an outgoing character but Eddie had a serious side to him too. He wasn't one for jokes all the time. He expected players to be serious on tour. He liked them to have a good time but, overall, it was a case of "Come on, we've not come all this way to mess around." Well, he couldn't say that to us in '58 and '62, because they were very successful tours, but that was his attitude. Touring players shouldn't take things for granted.'

Then there is the man who, in 1958, became the youngest player ever to tour Australasia with Great Britain, the inimitable Alex Murphy OBE, of whom it was once famously remarked: 'If you want to know just how good a scrum-half he really was, ask him yourself.' In a later age, when the advancing years had slowed down his legs, if not his mouth, with Eddie's assistance Murphy would launch a high-profile media career of his own, primarily in the pages of national newspapers and in particular the *Sunday Mirror* and *Daily Mirror*. As a co-commentator on the BBC, he would sit alongside Eddie Waring for some ten years. Looking back on his time as a raw eighteen year old, however, on the first of three tours down under, Murphy remembers that: 'In Australia, Eddie was the only journalist who was presented with the team wherever they went. He was a lovely man. I have never seen anyone help as many players away from home as he did. There was a fellow in Australia called Ted Harris, who was a big friend of Eddie's. He was chairman of Ampol Ltd, the petrol people – a massive company. Through him, Eddie organised cars to run everyone around in. Usually, when you went to Australia, you had journalists picking up tittle-tattle and writing stories for back home. Not him. He never stayed at the hotel, never stayed with the players, but got to know everything. That's how much he was trusted by the lads.'[5]

And although his direct influence on the specifics of organisation decreased as time progressed, Eddie nevertheless maintained the closest of contacts with the men pulling the strings. In 1962, he got much of his inside information from a tour manager named Stuart Hadfield. Four years earlier, that role had been taken by someone who was even more of a larger-than-life character than either Alex Murphy or Waring himself. His name was Tom Mitchell, chairman of Workington Town and fondly referred to by some as 'The Godfather of Rugby League'.

A former rugby union player of some 16 years' standing with an ongoing interest in athletics and physical fitness, the bearded Mitchell, usually clad in a wide-brimmed floppy hat and tinted school-ma'am spectacles, had much in common with Edward Marsden Waring. Though products of differing social backgrounds – Mitchell was of upper-middle-class Cumberland farming stock – both were justifiably proud of being thought players' men and both needed little convincing of rugby league's inherent capacity for promoting character in those who played it. Along with his spell as Great Britain tour manager, Mitchell, a future president of the Rugby League Chairmen's Association, was also one of the founding fathers and a proud patron of the British Amateur Rugby League Association, or BARLA as that organisation became known upon its launch in 1973.[6] The pair's friendship, forged on that 1958 Lions tour, would prove particularly useful in future, when the time came to negotiate BBC television contracts.

Still later, before his death in 1998, Mitchell would relate how:

> Eddie, several times on previous tours, stayed downtown in Sydney. How he got his news I don't know. He was very pro-British to the extent of causing aggravation with some of the Australian Press. He helped me where he could from his experience with past tours and warned of possible pitfalls.[7]

Indeed, the Australians themselves realised Eddie's importance to the touring set-up. In 1962, for example, Sydney journalist Allan Barnes observed:

When the Australian Rugby League team lines up in front of its British opponents at the Sydney Cricket Ground next Saturday, the boys in the green-and-gold may well claim they are playing 14 men. The crack would not be directed at referee Darcy Lawler, but at a Yorkshireman sitting hunched in the Press seats of the Members Stand. This is Eddie Waring, officially correspondent with the Englishmen for leading English and Australian newspapers and the BBC, but unofficially one of the most influential men in British Rugby League. The only man to see every post-war England–Australia Test match, Waring in the past has often been dubbed the REAL manager of various British touring sides, the power behind the league throne. It is certain that the Yorkshireman with the streaks of grey hair in his shock of black hair is a valued strategist, adviser and publicist for the Chooms.[8]

* * *

Meanwhile, back in the Britain of 1947, his staging of roadshows was far from Eddie Waring's only involvement in the welfare of players. His wartime activities with Dewsbury and Leeds had already rendered him au fait with the game's administrative realities and loopholes. Nor, on tour, did he miss an opportunity to nurture his international list of contacts, always with the best of intentions.

On meeting the parents of Lou Brown, for example, a New Zealand-born Wigan player who had played in that 1929 Challenge Cup-final victory over Dewsbury, Waring wrote:

I gave a promise to help to get Lou back from England to New Zealand. On my arrival back in England I found that Wigan Rugby League club directors had taken care of Lou following his illness and had arranged for his passage back to Auckland. His house was full of his medals, cups and trophies, which he had won as a young star Auckland athlete. Later he was to fall on rough ground, but he was able to get back to the scene of his early triumphs. Unfortunately, he was not to see a great deal of them, for six months after his return, word came through that he had passed away. It was better he was at home.[9]

Waring's status as an unofficial agent meant he became involved in all sorts of transfer deals, too, with both sides seeing him as a middleman they could trust. He related one such episode in his 1981 book *Eddie Waring on Rugby League*. 'In 1947,' Eddie wrote,

a five-year ban agreement was made between the English league and the Australian Board of Control which stopped any player going from one country to another. Just before the ban took effect, two Australians signed for English clubs – Test winger Lionel Cooper and full-back John Hunter. The Huddersfield club had asked me on my return from Australia if I would get them Cooper, who had scored a great try in the first Test on the Sydney cricket ground in 1946. I had spoken to Lionel and he voiced one stipulation: he wanted a travelling companion. I had been impressed in Sydney with the young, dashing . . . full-back Johnny Hunter and suggested he should come with Cooper. Eventually the deal was done, the pair costing Huddersfield only £1,500, a remarkable signing for the Fartown club, probably the best they ever made.[10]

Nor did Eddie's rise up the ladder of success preclude a continued interest in the local amateur scene to which he had once contributed so much with his Black Knights. Most obviously, that interest centred on the Shaw Cross Boys Club, situated just across the way from Crown Flatt and not far from Waring's Hollinroyd Road home, just up the Leeds Road. Although Eddie had no direct involvement in its affairs, his brother Harry was a club leader from the early 1950s, while nephew Harry junior actually played for the team, which, over the years, has earned a reputation for churning out international rugby league players of the very highest order. Such illustrious names as Mick Sullivan, Garry Schofield, David Ward, Roy Powell, the Redfearn brothers, Alan and David, and

Mike 'Stevo' Stephenson all cut their teeth there, while the club's current coach, Lee Gilmour, is a full-time professional with Great Britain and St Helens.

Despite being relegated to the first division of the amateur National Conference in 2007, Shaw Cross continue to thrive, running as many as 12 teams a week, from Under-8 to open age. Also in 2007, the club celebrated its 60th anniversary with a special function at Dewsbury Town Hall. Guest of honour was current secretary and all-round linchpin Douglas Hird, a former local journalist who has been there from the start. 'We used to see Eddie often,' Hird says. 'He was keen on amateur rugby league in the county because he was on the sports committee of the Yorkshire Association of Boys Clubs, which met every month. Eddie and myself were among the rugby league representatives.'[11]

Along with following his nephew's on-field exploits with interest, Eddie also went along to Shaw Cross to give talks on the 1950 and 1954 tours. For a fledgling club living a hand-to-mouth existence, the money raised must have been an incredible help. 'After the war, there was no money about,' Douglas Hird confirms. 'You were thankful for anything. We had no premises; we·had nothing really. We started by buying a second-hand set of green-and-black jerseys for half a crown each, and we played our first match away against Healey in Batley because we had no home ground. When we got a pitch, we raised £30 to buy a second-hand Nissen hut, which we erected ourselves. The local bus company gave us some used bus seats to put down each side and we had a combustion stove in the middle. We thought it was wonderful. This being just after the war, rationing was still on and we got six pounds of sugar a month, while margarine and tea were all rationed too. We had to be registered for coke for the stove. But they were very pioneering days. We had no real facilities, just a kettle in the corner to make a cup of tea. The parents used to come and make us some sandwiches.'

All of which is a far cry from the nicely furnished headquarters the club plays out of today. After gradually extending the old Nissen hut, Hird and his pals were eventually in a position to tag on some baths and extra changing-rooms. Then, in 1965, Shaw Cross were given a grant from the Ministry of Education, as it was then named, enabling the club to build a part-wood, part-stone building. That lasted until 1998 when, upon winning National Lottery funding, and in keeping with the craze for animal-inspired nicknames, the newly titled Sharks opened the two-storey clubhouse in which Douglas Hird works so diligently now.

During the author's visit to the Sharks' tidy little ground, reached by a pathway that cuts behind the primary school next door, the pitfalls of supplying so many players to the professional game were clear. Having lost around eight players that way before the season had even begun, Shaw Cross had struggled to compete in their division. Their opponents, on the other hand, Eastmoor Dragons of Wakefield, were hoping to make the play-offs. Though a far cry from the hype and glamour of the sport's modern-day television coverage – there is a puddle of vomit on the 30-metre line, whether through pre-match nerves, exertion or last night's ale only its perpetrator could say – the match itself provides cracking entertainment. As usual in rugby league, even at an amateur level, the basic skills of handling, running and tackling are taken almost entirely for granted. Passes are sprayed instinctively from hand to hand and lack of defensive commitment is just not an option. The hits are at times thunderous and all the old clichés apply. Bodies are put on the line. No quarter is asked, nor any given. Players quite literally spill blood for their teammates.

There is a fair-sized crowd on hand, too, mostly collected on the raised bank that runs parallel to the main road opposite. Elsewhere on this spare piece of parkland, watched over by semi-detached maisonettes and bungalows rather than terraced houses and belching mill chimneys, all set against an apparently unnoticed backdrop of spectacular green hills and valleys in which lies neighbouring Batley, the tower of Staincliffe church jutting through its watercolour haze, one young woman pushes a newborn baby in a pram. 'God, look at t' ears,' quips one wit, presumably referring to the child rather than the mother. On the field, a silver-haired second-row forward is sent to the dugout with what Australian commentators would call 'claret' pumping from a wound on his nose. When asked how he got the injury, he blames an opponent's elbow: 'But t'referee just said, get your head in t'right place then.' Hoity-toity this sport is not. And ten minutes later, the same player is back, smashed nose and all, scoring the 66th-minute try that ensures Shaw Cross a 22–16 victory.

In celebrating the club's 21st birthday in 1968, Eddie Waring shared his own thoughts on the value of rugby league as a focal point for the local community. In a special commemorative brochure, he wrote:

> The contribution of the Shaw Cross Boys Club in producing footballers for many senior rugby league clubs is well known and no doubt dealt with at length elsewhere. More important, I feel, is the contribution the club has made for good citizens to the county borough of Dewsbury and further afield. I have a warm spot for the town and its football. The famous Dewsbury Boys and Black Knights of which I was coach were possibly the forerunners and inspiration for clubs likes Shaw Cross. My own personal interest in the Shaw Cross Boys Club was always maintained because of the keenness and enthusiastic support my late brother Harry gave to the club. He served as club leader and had much affection for the club until his death. He was very proud to be associated with the club, proud of its achievements in sport and pleased with its contribution of turning boys into men for Dewsbury.[12]

* * *

Although Eddie Waring was already attuned to the possibility of enhancing his range of broadcasting opportunities upon his return from Australia – and not necessarily only on radio – he was equally busy in the world of print. Very quickly, he began to forge a reputation as an important campaigning journalist, most substantially in rugby league publications but also, increasingly, with the *Sunday Pictorial* and, later, *Sunday Mirror*. So ubiquitous a figure did he become that it wasn't long before the *Pictorial* could refer to its man as 'Mr Rugby League – the one and only Eddie Waring'.

However, those formative years writing for the *District News* notwithstanding, the earliest signs of Eddie's growing confidence in the power of the written word are to be found in the lively and provocative trade paper *Rugby League Review*, initially published on the first Saturday of every month. Its editor was a wilful and somewhat vainglorious young chap named Stanley Chadwick, a printer by trade with a knack for pressing the buttons of administrators and public alike.

In Eddie Waring, whose literary talents were now out in the open thanks to his book of the Indomitables tour, Chadwick knew a useful man to have on the team when he saw one. 'Since the days of the first European war, when the old *Northern Union News* went out of existence, Rugby League football has been a long time without a journal of its own,' Chadwick wrote in 1947, in a feature called, with his trademark lack of modesty, 'Rugby League Personalities No. 4 – Mr Editor'.

> Although the game has been full of personalities and incident, and has always had a large and loyal following, no effort was made to cater for rugby league enthusiasts between the two wars by giving them a paper devoted solely to their code. It was left to Stanley Chadwick, a Huddersfield journalist, to fulfil a long-felt want and to present *Rugby League Review* to the public.

This self-penned history lesson went on:

> The first number of the paper was published on August 31st 1946 and quickly gained a ready sale and an international reputation. Fearless and forthright in its editorial criticism, the *Review* has not yet found full favour with all in higher rugby league circles, but the many letters received from readers contain ample expressions

of appreciation to show that the venture is welcomed by the ordinary man and woman who form the backbone of the code.[13]

Chadwick had a point. By that stage in its existence, rugby league was crying out to be taken more seriously by the world at large, and, to the everyday spectator at least, it seemed as if the game's ruling body had neither the ability nor the inclination to put the matter right.

Following the retirement of John Wilson as secretary of the Rugby League in 1946, there was a new man at the helm, the former England rugby union international, Cambridge University student and RAF officer William Fallowfield, whose reign would last almost 30 years, until he too finally left office in 1974. Over the course of his three decades in charge, Bill Fallowfield would reveal himself to be a formidable operator indeed. This well-educated and canny master of political divide and rule, with an attitude that might most charitably be described as superior, is said to have fallen out with anyone and everyone as the mood took him. A control freak to the soles of his immaculately buffed shoes, according to the 1971 Caine Report on the game, the dictatorial Fallowfield would often be 'too busy' to talk to the press. He neglected to pass on information relating to sponsors and television deals to the clubs and instigated legal proceedings against anyone who so much as dared breathe a hint of public criticism in his direction. With an ego larger than one of Wembley's famous twin towers, he and the self-styled media mogul Stanley Chadwick were a head-on crash waiting to happen.

Positioned squarely in the middle of that simmering distrust, meanwhile, was Eddie Waring, blessed, when it mattered, with the more positive traits of both men. Where Fallowfield could see the coming benefits of television – often in the face of stubborn resistance – Eddie shared that vision. Where the Independent Labour Party member Chadwick would champion the little guy and give a voice to those whose bread-and-butter devotion to the code had sustained it through good times and bad, Eddie would time and again trumpet the game's grand democratic traditions. Never, though, whatever the pressure to conform one way or the other, was he anything other than his own man.

To give Stan Chadwick his due, although he was a dyed-in-the-wool Northern fundamentalist at heart, with an ingrained belief that 'rugby league was a cultural expression of the "true England" that was to be found in the working people of the industrial north', seldom if ever did he fail to provide Eddie with the space to expound his own more progressive views.[14] One such article, 'London or the North?', published in October 1947, illustrates this perfectly. 'Eddie Waring, Rugby League expert of the *Sunday Pictorial*, invites your views on this very important question,' runs the standfirst.

> Read his carefully prepared review, complete with hitherto unpublished facts and figures, and then answer the three questions put by Mr Waring. 1. Can Rugby League succeed in London? 2. Can the Rugby League Council stand the expense it is likely to cost? 3. Is it right to concentrate on London in preference to say, Doncaster, Blackpool, Sheffield, Barnsley, Bolton and many other Northern towns?

Beneath those questions, Eddie outlines what he sees as the salient points of the debate, pointing out that:

> The whole angle of London is so important that all sides should be considered before worry, time and money is expended. Only then if the Council are agreed it has a fair chance of success should the scheme go forward; if they are not satisfied then it should be scrapped.

Interestingly, given events to come, in writing about the claims of Doncaster in particular, Waring reveals:

> I visited this town along with the RL Secretary [i.e. Bill Fallowfield], who spoke well and wisely to this bunch of League minded folk.

Since then they have secured 1,000 members, almost obtained a ground, got a junior League on the move without one penny piece or help whatever from the Rugby League. What will happen if and when they get the League backing to go full out with their plans?

He goes on:

Unlike the Editor of *Rugby League Review*, I believe in the Wembley Cup final. However, even in these days of shortages we still have the right to free speech, and difference of opinion is rightly held by us both. The Wembley Cup final, to my view, was the winning move for National establishment of Rugby League. It could also be the key card of winning the London move.[15]

A few weeks later, in December 1947, we get the reader reaction to Waring's piece, as promised. 'Victory for the North!' screams the headline, above a rather more conciliatory subheading: 'But Expansion Is Favoured'. 'My article on the subject "London or the North?" with its three questions resulted in a good deal of discussion,' wrote Eddie. 'Naturally, the majority of letters favoured concentration in the North, but there was a general viewpoint which indicated the concern of the average follower who desired the game to extend itself.' Waring then reveals:

Many of the letters received showed what keen interest is taken in Rugby League football in areas outside those already playing the game. This has also been the case with my recent book, over a hundred applications being received from places like Ryde [Isle of Wight], Newlyn [Cornwall] and the London district. This again indicates the outside interest in Rugby League. The seed is obviously there.[16]

Although an internationalist and entrepreneur at heart, Eddie was seldom one for indulging in idle flights of fancy. To him, the practical application of facts, hard work and common sense would be as important as imagination and vision if rugby league was ever to reach the wider audience it deserved and needed. For many in the game's traditional heartlands, the idea of laying down bases for the code in places like America, France and even Wales was as grounded in reality as Tinkerbell's fairy dust. Yet to Eddie, it was those who insisted that the game could end its long history of hand-to-mouth economic struggle by retreating into one small corner of northern England who were the real dreamers. Did anyone seriously think that without the adoption of rugby league by Australia and New Zealand the fledgling Northern Union would ever have reached its 20th birthday? International sport brought glamour, recognition and money, three things that rugby union's poorer relation could simply not afford to be without. So when Eddie Waring stuck the proverbial boot in with a piece entitled 'Now or Never! Drop World Expansion for the Job at Home!' you really did know something was awry.

'I was present at Bordeaux when the International Board of Rugby League Football was formed,' Waring wrote, in the front-page story of the March 1948 edition of *Rugby League Review*:

> Previously representatives of England, France and New Zealand had met to discuss International matters, but this was the first time an official title was adopted. M. Paul Barriere (France) was the chairman of the meeting. Mr. Walter Crockford and Mr. Tom Brown (England), Mr. Jack Redwood (New Zealand) and M. Peilot (France) were other representatives. The secretary of the Rugby Football League was appointed to the position of secretary to the Board. Others present, in the capacity of interpreters, were M. Maurice Blein (the first secretary of the French Rugby League, who is now a journalist and broadcaster); M. G. Fraiche, a prominent sportsman in Bordeaux (and also representative of '*Rugby League Review*'); and Mr. George Hargreaves, Paris representative of Messrs. Thos. Cook and Son. Ltd. (travel agents). Only two English Press representatives were present:

Mr Harry Sunderland, who has done a great deal for French Rugby League in the early days, and myself.[17]

So far so good.

Waring's real gripe emerged upon his return to the UK, however, after a visit to the fledgling club Mansfield. 'The glamour and colour of the French trip faded into the common light of Rugby in the raw,' he wrote:

> Travelling from Mansfield to Warrington, I wondered if the same careful attention and expense which had been put into the French conference would be put into the development of the game in England. Needless to say the die-hard follower of the game at every lecture I give makes a point of that, and there is no doubt in my mind what view he takes.

Clearly troubled by this personal urge to see rugby league achieve its true potential, whilst simultaneously uncomfortable at how the game might be ignoring the needs of those who sustained it, Waring was once again stuck firmly in a conflict which continues to bother the minds of contemporary rugby league thinkers to this day. His answer, as usual, was to revert to cool-headed logic. 'To those who advocate London so much, I suggest they move gradually South by concentrating, first on Doncaster, then Mansfield, then Leicester, Coventry, and so get a trail of sound clubs,' he writes. 'In the light of many failures – Newcastle, London, Ebbw Vale, Pontypridd, and others – can this be done successfully? I believe it can, but the R.L. Council must get a blue printed plan with no holes in it.' Expansion, though, was necessary: 'Either they take Rugby League into a bigger circle or it remains static.'[18]

In the following month's issue, dated April 1948, Eddie Waring's relationship with *Rugby League Review* was formalised, and the paper's 'distinguished contributor' began to write a regular monthly article. 'Former Secretary-Manager of Dewsbury and Leeds Rugby League Football Clubs; R.L. columnist of the *Sunday*

Pictorial; author, lecturer and radio commentator – Eddie Waring knows the game and men as no other writer does,' went the grand introduction. 'Always scrupulously fair in what he writes, his forthright pronouncements have earned him a high reputation as a sports writer.'

In the issues ahead, Eddie continued to live up to that reputation, engaging in constructive criticism when it was needed and providing detailed and privileged blow-by-blow insights into the inner workings of Rugby League Council meetings – the average fan's only real means of learning what went on behind closed doors. In the best journalistic tradition, Waring was the sport's unofficial watchdog, attempting to keep its officials honest and open to scrutiny. Unfortunately, although Eddie tried to be even-handed in all his pronouncements, his editor, Stanley Chadwick, frequently indulged in personal attacks.

The end for *Rugby League Review* came after a bitter and long-running feud between Chadwick and Bill Fallowfield, which originated when the Rugby League secretary denied the *Review* permission to publish the 1947–48 fixture list, despite one RFL committee having earlier decreed that it could. Never one to take such an affront lying down, Chadwick responded by setting out to savage, in print, the reputation of the 'playboy' who had singled him out for a snubbing. One month, in an echo of Oliver Cromwell's famous dismissal of the Rump Parliament, it was 'In The Name of God, GO!' The next, Chadwick was holding the RFL boss personally responsible for wasting valuable resources on 'stunts'.[19] Underlying it all was Stanley Chadwick's firm conviction – with no apparent basis in fact – that, given the opportunity, he could manage the sport far better himself.

The fatal blow for a publication that despite its editor's faults was nevertheless a valuable presence on the rugby league landscape came in July 1952, when Fallowfield's antipathy towards the fourth estate and Chadwick in particular resulted in him bringing a successful libel case against Chadwick and his publishing company, the Venturers Press, at Leeds Assizes. As the author

Geoffrey Moorhouse has reflected, in his 1989 essay 'Small Worlds', Chadwick's preposterously inflated ego was again to the fore in the front-page story that appeared in *Rugby League Review* after the judge ordered the Venturers Press to pay Fallowfield £300 in damages. 'During the past week,' Chadwick pompously intoned,

> the Labour Party, and in a lesser degree the Rugby Football League, have dropped all pretence at being united organisations. Mr Attlee and Mr Richard Stokes have fired the first shots against the Bevanites, while Mr William Fallowfield, with the backing of the RL Council, has taken the gloves off against *Rugby League Review* and its associates. In both cases the spectacle has been less than edifying and must surely have a damaging effect on the respective bodies' prestige and public following.[20]

Stanley Chadwick and Aneurin Bevan: brothers in arms – in one man's head anyway.

* * *

Although the axe had fallen on *Rugby League Review*, Eddie Waring was hardly inconvenienced at all. For one thing, by now 'Mr Rugby League' was firmly established with the *Sunday Pictorial*. For another, his eyes were trained equally keenly on a broadcasting medium of the future.

The story has often been told of how Eddie Waring was first turned on to the potential of television by a visit to the USA, as he returned from that 1946 Indomitables tour via Fiji, Honolulu, San Francisco, Los Angeles, Dallas, Chicago and New York. In California, it is said, he met no less a figure than the comedian and film star Bob Hope, who told our man that television was the up-and-coming thing, and that he should get involved as soon as possible. Faced with this version of events in later life, true to form, Eddie would always play along, telling of how, during his visit, he had conducted tours of the Hollywood studios and later immersed himself in the way that televised sport was being delivered to the

American public. 'I suppose you might say I could see the potential of Rugby League on television in England,' he told the *Daily Express*. 'So I learned what I could.' In fact, although that version of events is broadly true, the trip described actually took place four years later, in 1950, and by then Eddie had already served notice that he was well aware of television's future possibilities.

On 21 April 1949, for example, he wrote to Peter Dimmock, the BBC's assistant head controller of television outside broadcasts. Still giving his address as 23 Hollinroyd Road, he began: 'May I introduce myself through Peter Wilson of the above paper. I am on the staff of the *Sunday Pictorial* covering Rugby League and cricket. I believe also my name was mentioned to you last year in connection with R.L. Television.'[21]

Here it might be assumed that Waring is referring to what is often claimed to be the BBC's first live rugby league broadcast, namely the Challenge Cup final of 1948 between post-war giants Wigan and Bradford Northern, which, given the absence of national coverage at that time, was transmitted to the London area only. In 1950, so the history books tell us, the rapidly expanding BBC then had another go when Warrington and Widnes met at the Empire Stadium. This time, the game was also broadcast via the BBC's new Sutton Coldfield headquarters to the Midlands, although, thanks to freak weather conditions, it could also be received by the lucky few who owned a set in south-west Lancashire. Legend has it that while Eddie made his debut as a television commentator on that first occasion, for the second he was on his way to Australia with the Lions and so missed the opportunity to further hone his skills.

In fact, correspondence held at the BBC's Written Archives Centre reveals that the matter was not quite so straightforward as that. In approaching Peter Dimmock, Eddie went on to state that his purpose in writing was not in connection with rugby league but to put forward an idea regarding a possible programme about Northern sports stars in general:

For instance there are many Yorkshire, Lancashire, Notts, Derby cricketers whom your public only know by name and would be interested to see, particularly if they demonstrate their capabilities. Other sporting stars from football (soccer and rugby), speedway riders, swimmers etc might be included in the programme. I think I could arrange a list of names which would have more than ordinary interest in so far as being Northern and Midland stars they are more often read about than seen.

Dimmock passed Waring's letter to his television outside broadcasts producer, Michael Henderson, who wrote back on 26 April to thank Eddie for writing, promising to forward his suggestion to the studio producer, S.E. Reynolds, who was apparently about to start a monthly sports magazine programme any time soon. Having read between the lines of the original note, however, Henderson then made what, in hindsight, turned out to be something of a historic suggestion. 'We have been using George Duckworth as our Rugby League commentator,' he wrote.

He is not, as yet, completely at home in the medium and in any case, we prefer when we are televising a whole game, such as football, to have two commentators. This helps to give the commentator a rest and a chance to see more of the tactics before the next session and also gives the viewer a change of voice. I would therefore be interested to meet you and give you a test if you feel like it.

Now, either one BBC department is unaware of another's recent history – a not unusual phenomenon perhaps – or, more likely, Eddie had not commentated on that 1948 final as previously supposed. Certainly, Henderson then goes on to suggest that Eddie should sit with Duckworth and himself at their commentary point for the 1949 event and 'perhaps have a go for a short period'. That would be a strange offer indeed if Eddie Waring had already been in on the occasion some 12 months before. More evidence to the contrary comes with a further letter from Eddie, this time to the BBC producer Keith Rogers, dated 14 May, just seven days after the 1949 final had been broadcast. In essence, this letter is a response to an earlier missive, sadly no longer to be found, in which Rogers gives an appraisal of the tyro TV commentator's Cup final performance. In it, Eddie outlines his own thoughts, and, it is clear, both the BBC and the man himself consider that at this stage he has plenty of room for improvement. 'I appreciate you writing to me and the criticism you make,' Waring writes.

> First, my personal reactions to the broadcast [were] of a better second half than a first. I am pleased to know my voice was clear, the sounding of being old must be associated with the hesitancy for I am still in my thirties and on ordinary broadcasts I have not had this mentioned. The reiteration was something I should not have done and [I] must put that down to inexperience in Television. I think the jerkiness was probably due to my idea of passing on what I saw. Instead of saying Ward passes to Davies, he passes to Kitching, I was inclined to simply say the player's name when it reached his hands. This, I think, would probably sound jerkiness [sic] and not cause a smooth running in the words.

Ward, Davies and Kitching: just three members of the 1949 Bradford team that took on and beat Halifax in front of a capacity Wembley crowd of 95,050. Overall, though, Eddie professed that he 'felt comfortable in Television'. He continued: 'I certainly don't mind the criticism, in fact I welcome it and appreciate the trouble you have gone to in passing on your views which will not be ignored.'

As the launch pad for what would develop into one of the great television careers, it was hardly a flying start, but Eddie was far from put off by that less-than-glowing initial appraisal. He told Keith Rogers that he was eager to act upon a suggestion made by the BBC man that he, Eddie, should take the first opportunity to come to London and see a rugby union match, or something similar, and 'learn by hearing Michael Henderson'. Henderson, in return, wrote to Eddie, informing him that the BBC's first outside broadcast of the new rugby union season would be on Saturday, 26 November at Twickenham, where Harlequins were due to face Blackheath. For all the apparent warmth of that invitation, at this early stage one nevertheless gets the distinct impression that the established BBC bods were unsure. Would this doggedly ambitious wannabe have his uses, or was he simply a nuisance whose enthusiasm would run dry if put through enough hoops? Certainly, after inviting Eddie along to sit in the van and pointing out that Peter Dimmock would also be in attendance as producer, Henderson almost casually adds: 'your commentary on the Rugby League Cup Final last [season] was not very favourably received by the Pundits at Alexandra Palace.'

Whatever his intentions, some three weeks later, at the end of October, Michael Henderson received another missive from Eddie. It thanked him for the invitation, confirmed that he did indeed hope to get down to London and requested any necessary passes for the commentary box. Or, he helpfully suggested:

> Maybe you may think it would be as well to view the game from a set in Town. I have been viewing whenever possible and feel I have learned much from it. I shall probably be in London during the next week or so to finalise my Australasian arrangements. I leave for Australia and New Zealand after the Cup final 1950. Probably I may be able to see you whilst I am in town. You seem to be making great strides with T/V. [sic], when will it be coming North? I have a friend who got some Birmingham tests the other evening.

That Eddie Waring travelled south as proposed seems likely, as, on 16 December, he received a letter from Henderson's secretary, Margaret S.B. Macklin. In it, she wrote that although Peter Dimmock was currently away at Sutton Coldfield, he had asked her to write and thank Eddie for 'the interesting Press cuttings' earlier forwarded. She outlined details of the BBC's next upcoming 'rugger' match, on 24 December, when Blackheath faced Bedford at the former's Rectory Field ground, and spoke of a final England trial at Twickenham on 7 January, which, said Mrs Macklin, would in all probability be the better game. 'I'm afraid we have no Twickenham passes to spare,' she wrote,

> but if you [would] like to come and make yourself known at our Control Van (which will be in the Car Park, usual position) we will be pleased to see you. Mr Dimmock cannot guarantee that he can let you 'have a go' but says it will be quite all right if you wish to come to either of these matches. P.S. We are keeping your Press cuttings unless, of course, you'd like them returned.

For his part, Eddie later revealed to the *Daily Express* that: 'I paid my money to get in and sat behind the commentator to see what it was all about. I don't recall much about the match. I was quietly looking and listening to what he was doing and saying.'

As it happened, the BBC's growing national television service finally did make its first appearance in northern England some two years later, on the weekend of 12 October 1951. Just over four weeks after that, on 10 November, the region in which rugby league had been spawned over half a century before was finally able to look on in wonder as a first televised live game crackled across the Pennines and beyond. It came in the form of an international clash between Great Britain and New Zealand, played at Station Road, Swinton, broadcast to the North via the transmitters at Holme Moss, high on the Pennine Hills above Holmfirth.

The choice of venue was no accident. Technical restrictions meant that any outside television event had to take place within a couple of miles of the BBC's Manchester studio. Nor was it altogether a snap decision. The BBC bosses had been tentatively discussing the possibility of screening rugby league games with the

RFL for a while. Eddie, increasingly active in radio, was by now all but guaranteed a place on any presentation team, especially as his 'Mr Fix-It' facilitating skills were increasingly being put to good use behind the scenes too – a contribution invaluable to the BBC, given the suspicion with which many club chairmen viewed the newfangled invention. As was his wont, with the heady whiff of opportunity in his nostrils, Edward Marsden Waring set about making friends and influencing people.

Primarily, he did that in the pages of *Rugby League Review*. 'Rugby League Must March with Progress – Television Is Our Opportunity', ran the headline above the Eddie Waring column on 25 October 1951. Rugby league, he said, must 'get in on the ground floor'. He backed up that theory by relating how, during his trip home from New Zealand the previous year, he had enjoyed 'plenty of opportunity of closely studying TV in commercial form'. In New York, for instance, he had stayed in a hotel that had, wait for it, 50 floors!

> I was on the 35th, and in every room there was a television set. With a selection of half-a-dozen or more channels to choose from, it was pretty certain any evening I could watch either baseball, American gridiron Rugby, boxing or wrestling. The long bars in the streets – public houses we should call them – were always full if some big sporting event was on. I made my Coca-Cola last for some time to get the attitude of the American 'fan' to this TV business. What I was most aware of in all this was the terrific possibilities of TV in sport presentation and the BBC will soon catch up to the Yanks providing one thing – THAT THE SPORTING FOLK OF ANY SPORT WILL CO-OPERATE.[22]

British readers had first been made aware of Waring's activities in the USA courtesy of his *Sunday Pictorial* column of 27 August 1950, when, via transatlantic cable, he wrote:

After doing a broadcast on the relative merits of Rugby and American football, I visited Bob Hope on the set of his new picture. I was surprised to find that he knew quite a lot about the Australian [Rugby League] set-up. I suggested he might do a picture 'On the road to Wembley' with Bing Crosby. Bob said he could make an easier living playing 'The Groaner' at golf. Anyway, it would have to be a silent picture. They sent two of the British team off for talking during the Australian tour![23]

Whatever Bob Hope's actual influence on Eddie Waring's career path, there is no doubt that Eddie did return to British shores recharged and excited at the direction in which he had seen television sport headed. As he himself later put it: 'I made up my mind about two things: when television came to the North it was going to cover Rugby League, and when it did I was going to provide the commentary.'[24] Now all he had to do was convince the people who ran the sport that they too should grasp the opportunity.

Some twelve months after his return, writing in *Rugby League Review*, Waring went on a PR offensive.

No doubt some clubs will feel it might affect their gates if a match is televised. I do not think so, for all 'fans' will still want to watch the match itself and those who would not go in any case are the ones who will watch. And this is the opportunity to win more customers for the code.

Warming to his theme, he went on:

There are many angles to help the clubs should the BBC televise a match. For instance it would be possible, say two hours before the kick-off, to give a fifteen minute preview of the game . . . there are many possibilities and no doubt the BBC will examine them all. If the Rugby Football League is really anxious to get down to business then I know the BBC will listen to all suggestions likely to interest and help viewers.

And therein, as ever, lay the rub. For though he was a fervent supporter of rugby league's democratic decision-making traditions, no one appreciated more than Eddie Waring the danger in allowing every club official – no matter how self-serving, unimaginative or obstreperous – a say. If it was not in their own short-term interests, there was every chance that clubs would simply refuse to cooperate. 'Rugby League must not be on the outer when the wheels and the screens begin to turn,' Eddie implored.

> We have some excellent publicity minded men on both the RL Council and the League Management Committee. Not all, of course, are so inclined, and whether the progressives can persuade the stick-in-the-mud element to bestir themselves to move fast for once I just do not know. For far too long many Rugby League clubs have been thinking so small that they have now become small in most things they do. They are satisfied to have the steady 5,000 spectators a week. How often have we heard the cry: 'We can live on 5,000 each home match if we could only get them.' If they would only think big they would get the big crowds. At last we have the opportunity to go Big in a Big way through the channels of the television set. I repeat what I said some short time ago: Rugby League football is ideally suited for television purposes. Sound radio will still have its place in the sun for Rugby League. TV might bring what has now become the parrot cry of the followers of the game: 'Why are we not recognised nationally?' TV might well supply the answer IF it is given a chance.[25]

* * *

Today, of course, it is almost impossible to imagine how a professional sport might get by at all without the huge amounts of money, prestige and exposure that large television contracts provide.

Back in a grey, beleaguered Britain still in the grip of food rationing and post-war austerity, however, until Eddie Waring got to work it was genuinely touch-and-go whether the 13-a-side code would ever take the plunge at all. And even after the not-so-small matter of a first-ever live nationwide transmission had finally been laid to rest at Station Road, the implications of television's impact upon the game would remain a hot topic of discussion, for one reason or another, throughout the rest of rugby league's modern-day history.

In fact, in the 1950s and early '60s, scarcely a week went by without one club or other – with Wigan and Hunslet usually in the forefront – leading calls to throw out the cameras entirely. The 1951 Festival of Britain may have briefly raised spirits in the capital, but elsewhere, and particularly in the North, the mood was as drearily introspective and downbeat as ever. This, after all, was a Britain with few cars and no motorways. Wherever one lived, other parts of the nation felt cut-off and distant, their inhabitants and customs alien. To your average Londoner, the north of England felt like a different country, and vice versa.

Even the arrival of dashing prime minister Sir Anthony Eden, whose radical Clean Air Act of 1956 went such a long way to removing the smog and belching smoke of factory chimneys that had for so long blanketed England's urban North under a filthy cloud of all-pervasive soot, failed to spark much optimism in the parochial rugby league boardrooms of Yorkshire and Lancashire. Yet outside of those walls, the Western world was in a state of far-reaching social change. Transport and travel were on the verge of becoming easier and more affordable. The old 78-rpm shellac gramophone records were on the way out, to be replaced by hip new 45 singles and stereo LPs. Across the Atlantic, some kid with a quiff called Elvis Aaron Presley was frightening American parents to death with his pelvis-thrusting antics on *The Ed Sullivan Show* – a phenomenon that was already introducing British families to the concept of the hormonally challenged teenager.

One man who remembers those turbulent TV times well is the former Hunslet secretary and current Leeds president Harry Jepson. 'Television wasn't popular,' he recalls. 'It's very difficult to realise now that some clubs – and Hunslet were one – couldn't stand television cameras. In 1965, Wigan were fined £500 for refusing to play in a live televised cup tie against Bradford because they maintained they would lose money. That's a long time after the first televised game.' Indeed it was, and there had been many other such contretemps in between, as the booming crowds of the immediate post-war years began to fall steadily away throughout the 1950s and early '60s. For many, television was an obvious culprit. After all, it was asked, why would anyone swap the comfort of a living room for the wintry stands and terraces of a football stadium?

A sign of just how unstable the 13-a-side code's relationship with BBC Television really was at this stage can be seen in the fact that, for a while, the RFL withheld permission for the Corporation to transmit the Challenge Cup final. Its recalcitrance was down to a simple question of mathematics. In the 1951–52 season, the BBC had televised four games to the nation, including that inaugural Test match at Swinton, followed by the first-ever televised domestic league clash (Wigan versus Wakefield on 12 January) and the Wembley Cup final, the latter fixture costing the BBC a fee of £150. A year earlier, in 1951, 94,262 people had turned up at Wembley to watch Wigan beat Barrow. In 1952, that figure had dropped by some 22,000 to 72,093. Quite obviously, the fact that the finalists, Workington and Featherstone, were two small-town clubs with a relatively tiny population between them must have had something to do with the shortfall. The RFL, however, was adamant that television was to blame and declared an outright Cup-final ban. In 1955, the year in which the RFL's management committee decreed that no league games at all could be shown on TV only to have that decision overturned at a general meeting of the clubs one month later, the crowd for the Cup final again fell, to 66,513, as Barrow faced Workington in the Challenge Cup final's one and so far only Cumbrian derby.

For champions of television's bright and glittering future, then, like Eddie Waring, these were tricky times in which to win the debate. In 1953, when a round of league fixtures was played on the same day as a televised England–France match, the usual domestic attendances fell by half. The following year, live coverage of the Rugby League World Cup final from Paris saw crowd figures in the north of England drop by a third, and when, in 1959, the BBC televised the Third Ashes Test between Great Britain and Australia, the results were equally disastrous. Not only was the attendance at the game itself some 20,000 lower than the capacity at Wigan's Central Park and, indeed, the lowest of the series, clubs such as Leeds, Bramley and York all attracted their lowest-ever post-war attendances. For its trouble, the RFL was paid the measly sum of £1,250, less than half the gate money supposedly 'lost' from the Test match on its own. Later, ahead of the 1960–61 season, Warrington got together a successful campaign to ban live coverage from all rugby league grounds only to discover, along with their colleagues, that in the absence of the cameras, attendances actually went down, regaining an upward trajectory with their reintroduction. Even so, in a triumph of hope over experience, four years later the Wilderspool club was in campaigning mode again and this time managed to rally approximately half the professional clubs to its cause.[26] In 1970, after another disappointing attendance at a televised Yorkshire Cup final, Bradford Northern chairman Harry Womersley implored: 'We have to stop this monster that is destroying us.'

With the benefit of hindsight, of course, this was an argument that neither Warrington nor any other club could win. In any case, although the initial amounts weren't great, there was money to consider. As the years went by, broadcasting fees began to generate increasing amounts of vital income in a game that, financially, had always fought above its own weight. Once televised rugby league was up and running, the clock would never be turned back.

Nevertheless, the Northern game continued to display a scarcely checked hostility towards the BBC and all that it, in a wider sense, was felt to represent. As far back as 1927, the year in which the then newly independent BBC first began to broadcast rugby league matches on radio, dissenting voices had hit the air. A gentleman named E.G. Blackwell was the first BBC commentator to feel the rough end of league supporters' tongues, after rugby league made its wireless debut with his commentary from the pre-Wembley Challenge Cup final between Oldham and Swinton at Wigan.

By far the greatest amount of opprobrium, however, was reserved for the BBC itself, an organisation deemed, on the whole, to be paternalistic, arrogant and completely out of touch with Northern working-class culture. Also in 1927, the RFL Council lodged its first official complaint to the Corporation that the day's results weren't being read out on the Saturday teatime news, along with the soccer and rugby union scores. The widespread perception of the BBC was that, stuck away in its London ivory towers, it pandered primarily to the prejudices of a Southern middle-class liberal elite. If the so-called lower orders had any role at all, it was simply to sit down, tune in and be educated into better standards of behaviour and intellectual rigour. Culture, to the BBC, meant opera, scientific talks and highbrow literature in cut-glass accents. It did not mean bingo, beer and rolling around in the mud (unless that mud was on the playing fields of Rugby or Eton, of course).

Though the British Broadcasting Corporation's founder and first director general, the fiercely moral Lord John Reith, had undeniably well-intentioned ideals for his organisation, not least among which was the belief that the BBC should seek to elevate rather than go for the lowest common denominator, the result was that ordinary folk often complained of being patronised. As a member of the public, you did as 'Auntie' told you and any note of criticism was batted away with an almost irritable note of haughty imperiousness.

In his 1972 book, *The Biggest Aspidistra in the World: A Personal Celebration of 50 Years of the BBC*, the *Daily Mail* television critic Peter Black wrote:

It [the BBC] was, for example, positively testy with listeners who did not build their week's listening by choosing from the programmes in *Radio Times*. 'To leave a set switched on in the hope that before the evening is out one will hear something that one wants to hear invites mental indigestion and a chaotic state of mind in which one hears a hundred programmes and understands none.'

Those same listeners, writes Black, were also beseeched to

enlarge their capacity to respond to the programmes by turning out the lights so that their birdlike powers of concentration would not be distracted by familiar objects in the room: 'If you only listen with half an ear you have not a quarter of a right to criticise.'[27]

Even when the Corporation did finally condescend to broadcast variety shows as a means of rallying wartime spirits, it did so with barely hidden reluctance.

Not that the broadsides fired at the BBC always came from the wounded bloody infantry. Shortly after the Second World War, for example, there was a decided frisson of disquiet among the metropolitan chattering classes when the BBC's long-held aversion to regional accents was relaxed just enough to allow the Halifax-born actor and entertainer Wilfred Pickles to read news bulletins, a move again explained by the widespread mood of wartime egalitarianism. Until then, Lord Reith's frankly barmy answer to the question of why every BBC announcer traditionally spoke as though they had just swallowed a barrel of plums was that he did not want his organisation to cause offence to anyone wherever they lived in the country; received pronunciation had simply been adopted as a neutral lingua franca. With the arrival of Pickles, however, building on similar radio appearances by the bluff, pipe-smoking Bradfordian playwright J.B. Priestley, the Northern genie was out of the bottle and nothing was going to put it back.

Though the appointment of Wilfred Pickles was a welcome and pivotal moment in acknowledging the North's influence on British cultural affairs, it did little to stem the dissatisfaction in rugby league circles. In 1946, the Huddersfield supporters club complained: 'Many of us in the North have a suspicion that someone with an

1895 complex rules in a high place at the BBC.' Some five years later, the weekly *Rugby Leaguer* newspaper organised a 25,000-name petition calling upon the BBC to do the game justice. As RFL historian Tony Collins has pointed out:

> While there may have been an element of exaggerated self-importance in these criticisms of the BBC, the Corporation clearly did have problems presenting the sport . . . Drawn entirely from the public and grammar schools, the BBC's sports broadcasters in the 1930s had little real knowledge of rugby league, and the reporting of the game was often left to rugby union reporters such as Frank Shaw . . . Nor did professional sport gel easily with the Reithian ethos, especially when it appeared to be in direct opposition to amateurism.[28]

Yet, as Eddie Waring could have told them, if they had cared to listen, the amateur, Corinthian spirit was an integral part of the so-called professional code too.

Another crucial feature of the BBC, to this day, is the way it has managed to engineer an overriding spirit of loyalty among its own rank and file, whatever their local grumbles, whilst promoting an internal mindset of its own, independent of the real world outside. If everyone's a critic, the theory goes, then you must be doing something right. And one thing is for sure: the resulting bunker mentality has ensured that its employees can invariably be counted upon to toe the party line.

With the arrival of television, of course, distrust of the BBC's motives and broadcasters reached still deeper levels of intensity, and no commentator was caught more regularly on the critics' barbs than Eddie Waring. Indeed, he had only been in the job for around a year when RFL boss Bill Fallowfield declared: 'There is no doubt that the public are not happy with the commentaries on rugby league which are made either on television or sound broadcasts.' In time, those initial acorns of disquiet, an accepted occupational hazard for any sports commentator, would grow into a ruddy great oak tree of antipathy, which tested not only the BBC's loyalty towards one of its most famous and popular faces but the friendly and open public nature of Waring himself.

For now, though, Eddie Waring continued to beat a path through what was, after all, a still-to-be conquered medium. At that first televised Test match at Swinton in 1951, he was joined in the BBC commentary box by three other men: Alan Clarke, Alan Dixon and Harry Sunderland. As the BBC's head of sport, the first of that trio, Clarke, had already run head-on into rugby league's particular brand of public militancy when, in 1948, some 21 years after those initial complaints regarding the failure to give out league scores on the Home Service, he is said to have told supporters that 'rugby league [got] far more space than the game warranted'.[29] The second, Dixon, was an already well-established radio announcer in the North, while the third, the idiosyncratic little Queenslander Harry Sunderland, was a different barrel of barramundi entirely.

Six

THE COURT OF
KING EDDIE

'It's a coat colder on the east coast.'

It has often been said that Eddie Waring and Harry Sunderland did not get on. Maybe they did, maybe they didn't. What should be pointed out, however, is that although the two have been portrayed as competitors, on just about every occasion that Waring mentions his fellow BBC commentator and journalist in print, it is in the most glowing of terms.

In the *Rugby League Review* of October 1947, for example, Waring wrote: 'I know of no better organiser than Harry Sunderland to crack at London. It is his pet ambition and his Utopia.' Elsewhere, there are similarly positive references to a man whose reputation as an entrepreneur and all-round visionary was first established in this country when he arrived as tour manager of the 1929 Australian Kangaroos.

Sunderland was destined to return twice more in that role, in 1933 and 1937, before eventually settling in the UK for good in 1939, after accepting an offer to become manager of Wigan. In time, however, he would become more closely associated with such expansionist projects as introducing rugby league to France and championing its expansion into America. Indeed, whilst it may be just coincidence, in 1950, the same year that Waring visited Bob Hope's film set, Sunderland's route home took him through Fiji, Honolulu, Los Angeles, Chicago and New York, though whether on the same voyage as Eddie we cannot be certain. Writing in *Rugby League Gazette*, the official journal of the Rugby Football League and therefore a deadly rival to *Rugby League Review*, Sunderland banged the drum loudly for a project that would also remain close to Eddie Waring's heart over the years to come. 'The type of American who might be coached and drilled into playing our game is big, fast, strong, can handle a ball equally as well as our Rugby League men – and they can tackle,' wrote Sunderland.

> Could they refrain from interference, from obstruction, which is a feature of their game? Could they take and give the bumps without the aid of big padding and helmets? Could they play 80 minutes as our men do? The men I saw in the Los Angeles Stadium when 90,000 watched the Washington Redskins play the Los Angeles Rams were big men, fast men, and they hurled the ball, or kicked it, 50 to 65 yards without effort.[1]

After outlining what he saw as the potential financial costs of such an enterprise, Sunderland concluded:

> At the present moment it is merely a dream – just as the plans of the late A.H. Baskerville, G.W. Smith, Lance B. Todd and others were dreams when they organised their pioneering tour of England in 1907. It was a 'dream' when we planned to show a sample of our game to the Frenchmen in the Stade Pershing in Paris in 1933, and it was a dream when the men who met in October, 1928, decided to take the Rugby League Challenge Cup final to Wembley.[2]

If it did exist, then, perhaps it is here where we find the source of any antipathy. At the time he wrote his American feature, Harry Sunderland was 60 years of age, whilst Eddie Waring was 20 years younger. Not unnaturally, the older man may well have viewed the younger as a threat.

For although Waring's open-minded outlook on the game marked him out as a distinctive presence, he was neither the first to promote change nor the last. By stirring up those of a more parochial disposition, he was in many ways following the trail already laid by Sunderland, albeit with considerably greater tact. In his twilight years, Eddie too would guard his top-dog status with great diligence and show a calculated degree of resistance to the idea of being usurped. Over the years, he seldom missed a single match, and as the decades advanced, his age became the most jealously guarded secret of all.

And where Eddie Waring walked in Harry Sunderland's footsteps, it could equally be argued that Sunderland was following the example of a still earlier BBC commentator, the original All Golds pioneer and future Wigan and Salford stalwart Lance Todd. 'Wherever or whenever people discuss rugby league,' wrote Gus Risman, in his 1958 autobiography *Rugby Renegade*,

> the name of Lance Todd must crop up. For here was the greatest character who ever graced the game of rugby, a personality comparable to such as Herbert Chapman in soccer. Toddy, as he was known throughout the game, was a New Zealander who played for the All Blacks. In 1928, he became manager of Salford and it was under his inspired leadership that Salford became the team of all talents.

Lance Todd, said Risman, 'was rugby league itself. When the BBC wanted someone to broadcast about the game they called upon Toddy, and hard as the BBC may have tried in recent years, they have never been able to replace him.'[3]

* * *

Another branch of the media in which Harry Sunderland and Eddie Waring moved in close proximity was the national newspaper scene.

Back then, along with its headquarters in London, just about every publication boasted a busy Manchester office, complete with its own Northern editor, reporters and regional sensibility. As a result, there existed a lively and committed rugby league press pack, a close-knit bunch of individuals who, somehow, were both supportive of one another's efforts and simultaneously ultra-competitive. Very much part of that circuit, both at its height and towards its demise, was the journalist Brian Batty, who replaced Don Mosey as *Daily Mail* rugby league correspondent in 1964, the year of Harry Sunderland's death.[4]

'That all the papers had Manchester offices was crucial,' says Batty, of an era when editors would pester rugby league reporters for column inches, rather than the other way around as is so often the case today. 'It was a great time. Travelling on all those tours, you got to know so many people. I made some good contacts, which was great for getting stories. That was a time when a reporter could slip his informants a few quid, and sometimes, I'm afraid, you had to be a bit sneaky in other ways too. I remember when Frank Myler quit as England coach. I left the story in the office and went to Hull that night with three of the other guys in the car. I couldn't say a word to them about it and I felt awful. I knew that next morning they wouldn't be very happy, but that was the job. In the end, I spent 29 years with the *Mail*.'[5]

In these days when not one single national newspaper has its own dedicated full-time rugby league hack, a list of Waring's earliest journalistic contemporaries reads like a small telephone directory. Among the best known were big jovial Allan Cave of the *Daily Herald* (catchphrase 'Under My Beret', or, as Harry Jepson insists they pronounced it in Hunslet, 'Under My Burrette'), Alfred Beecroft of *The People* and the great Joe Humphreys of the *Daily Mirror*. As time went on, those writers would be joined or succeeded by the likes of Jack Bentley (*Daily Express*) and Neville Haddock (*Daily Sketch*). All were building on a tradition going right back to the breakaway itself, established by such journalistic pioneers as Bradford's Tom Riley (aka 'Bong Tong' of *Yorkshire Sport*),

A.W. Pullin ('Old Ebor' of the *Yorkshire Post*), Arthur Beanland ('Flaneur' of the *Leeds Mercury*) and Joe Leech (*Wigan Examiner*).

By the time Eddie Waring hit his jaunty stride, a new style of rugby league reporting was afoot, and in 'Mr Rugby League' we find the man largely responsible for introducing it. Until the 1950s, British sports reporting was strictly rooted in accurate presentation of facts and tactical analysis. In rugby league, as in all sports, writers were expected to be able to read a game and break it down accordingly. In Dewsbury, at least, Eddie Waring had done that too, but, perhaps as a result of what he had seen at first hand in Australia, he began increasingly to concentrate on personalities and gossip about transfer deals rather than on straightforward match reports. That latter obligation was often sub-contracted out to what, in the trade, are known as 'stringers', i.e. often unqualified local correspondents. For Eddie, the 'story' or 'angle' was the thing, and, given his reputation as an unofficial players' agent with a contact book thicker than the bridge of your average prop forward's nose, such tales were not hard to come by. Exclusives were relentlessly pursued, and as a result it wasn't long before he was upsetting folk again.

'A lot of clubs didn't like Eddie because he used to get inside information and publish it in the *Sunday Pictorial*,' confirms Harry Jepson. 'But everybody used to get the *Sunday Pictorial* to read what Eddie Waring had to say. Sometimes you got information from Eddie Waring before it had actually come out at the club.' And although Waring isn't named personally, it is quite clear to whom the Wigan directors are referring in an extended rant published in one match-day programme during September 1950. 'We've had enough of this!' it began.

As if enough trouble had not already been stirred up by the varied writings of irresponsible persons regarding the probable future of the Tourists on their return, one scribe in his Sunday diatribe has to go so far as to air his knowledge of what is going to happen at Wigan when our eight boys return, and openly names three players as likely to be leaving! We feel sure the people of Wigan, at least, are heartily sick of having to tolerate, week by week, the stuff that some Editors deem fit to print as knowledgeable Rugby League journalism. Let us state emphatically that this particular writer's comments are the figments of his own vivid imagination, or perhaps his association with our old friend Bob Hope, duly pictured in the same columns, has made him consider forsaking the realms of journalism for the less exacting, but probably more appropriate, role of comedian.

Phew.

Eddie Waring, then, was very much in the vanguard of that more aggressive brand of tabloid sports journalism with which we are familiar today. Yet it was not just the clubs who found his relentless search for a headline-grabbing angle unsettling. Although, on one level, a popular member of the gang – 'He was a likeable guy, Eddie, a real character,' according to Brian Batty – so successful did he become that a certain level of enmity was guaranteed in some of his colleagues, especially when his burgeoning BBC presence began to earn Eddie a big audience in the South and elsewhere across the British Isles.

The bitterest rivalry by some distance was with the ex-Lancashire cricketer Phil King, who, since his playing retirement, had reinvented himself as the rugby league reporter of the *Sunday People*. Famously, after having travelled to Australia to cover a Great Britain tour in the 1950s, King was said to have been welcomed with the words: 'Would you be Mr Eddie Waring?'

'Not for a million dollars,' came his reply.

Primarily, of course, it was occupational jealousy. As a former professional sportsman used to being in the national limelight, although writing for the *Sunday People* was hardly working down a coal mine, it must have bothered King deeply to have this cheerful, exuberant flash bugger stealing his thunder. 'Phil King and Eddie were great rivals,' confirms Batty. 'They both used to do these columns with paragraph-long news snippets; quite good really. As a person, Phil King was all bluff and bluster. But let's be honest. It was a cut-throat profession, rugby league journalism. We were in there to get stories. If you had a butcher's shop and you could sell something the other bloke down the road couldn't sell, you'd sell it. It was tough going. You had to be on your toes. My boss would say, "Have you got that on your own?" and I'd say that I was pretty sure I had. I used to have sleepless nights because I was worried that if I hadn't got it on my own, I would look bloody stupid. You could understand Eddie and Phil not getting on. Their job was to get a scoop every Sunday and get it in the paper.'

A perfect example of the way nonconformist Eddie was at once part of the press pack and somehow apart from it can be seen in his contribution to the rugby league trade press that has been such a vibrant feature of the game since the 1940s. Certainly, he directly influenced a young Oxford University student named Harry Edgar, whose campaigning *Open Rugby*, launched as 270 photocopies of 4 handwritten pages in 1976, developed into a hugely influential monthly magazine that fired many a thinking league fan's imagination and indignation. 'I wanted to promote and spread rugby league,' says Edgar himself, nowadays editor and proprietor of nostalgic quarterly *Rugby League Journal*. 'I was a bit like an evangelist, really, and, to be honest, that's what Eddie was. His own background was that of a young enthusiast who wanted to expand the game. He was a very big influence on me. I first met Eddie when he came to Whitehaven doing one of his roadshows during the "Big Freeze" of 1963. I was one of the kids he got up on stage. The next time he visited Whitehaven, I had progressed to becoming involved with the club, writing the programme, running the supporters club and so on. So, as one of the club's main enthusiasts, I was actually put on the panel. Eddie remembered me from being a kid, which was really nice. I had total respect for him.'[6]

However, his influence on *Open Rugby* and those earlier *Rugby League Review* writings apart, Eddie Waring's most obvious contribution to rugby league literature came in the form of his very own annual – known not unreasonably as the *Eddie*

Waring Rugby League Annual. From their birth in 1959 until their demise in 1968, there were eight such titles in all.

'Everybody bought Eddie's annuals,' recalls Harry Jepson. 'They came out in summer ready for the winter season, with all the fixtures in. Each annual would summarise the previous season and look forward to the next. As soon as they came in the shops, if you had the two and six, you'd get one.' Quite aside from any financial profit, the chief benefit of the annuals to Eddie was the increase in personal publicity they generated. Clearly, having your name and beaming face positioned alongside a photograph of St Helens winger Tom Van Vollenhoven in the act of scoring a try – as was the case on the cover of issue one – wasn't going to do anyone's media reputation any harm. By 1959, Waring's television career was only just on the verge of true lift-off, rendering this latest publishing venture crucial in establishing him in the minds of both his employers and the public as a hugely significant figure – indeed, as 'Mr Rugby League'.

In that first issue, Waring's pen portrait describes him as a *Sunday Pictorial* columnist who has 'televised or broadcast in all post-war Cup Finals from Wembley except 1946 and 1950, when he was en route for Australia'. By the time of his eighth, the words 'Television Personality' are most prominent, a sure sign of just how far Eddie and that medium had travelled during the years of the annual's existence. Some things, though, did not change. The style throughout stayed punchy and bright – 'St Helens were the 1958–59 champions with the mostest!' he yelled in 1959 – while just about the only named contributor of any substance was Eddie himself. There were exceptions to that rule, including the regular presence in those pages of one W. Fallowfield, secretary of the Rugby Football League, a sure indication that despite his earlier links with Fallowfield's bête noire Stanley Chadwick, Waring's diplomatic skills were continuing to serve him well. 'Rugby League Dying?' Fallowfield asked in 1959 – 'Phooey!' Amidst adverts for 'The One and Only' Eddie Waring's column in the *Sunday Pictorial* and, from 1963, the *Sunday Mirror*, the news-gathering talents of Joe 'Rugby League Is My Business' Humphreys in the stablemate *Daily Mirror* were promoted too. Then there were the 'What The Papers Said' columns, in which a number of Waring's fellow journalists, including Phil King, were given space to share brief comments on the previous season's showcase matches.

Interesting, then, that when a rival publication to Eddie Waring's appeared in 1962, *Windsors Rugby League Annual*, no such courtesy was returned. Its publisher, Jim Windsor, was a well-known Yorkshire bookmaker who, along with being a former player at Leeds and Bramley, and one-time director of that latter club, liked to boast how he had created the first rugby league pools coupon in history. Although they were outlived by Waring's publication by some three seasons and developed an irritating reputation for falling apart in your hands, the three issues of *Windsors Rugby League Annual* that Windsor and his editor, the popular caricaturist Ken J. Adams, went on to produce felt more like a substantial pocket yearbook than the flimsier pamphlets that Eddie had given his name to. Most obviously, that was down to the fact that they had more pages, containing articles by just about every rugby league journalist around, with the notable exception of one E.M. Waring.

Phil King, however, was well to the fore. Up near the front, in fact, where the 'brilliant and exclusive on-the-spot story of Great Britain's victorious tour of Australia', as written by the man who 'will be remembered by thousands of fans as D.P. King, the former brilliant and hard-hitting Lancashire and Worcester batsman', sat directly opposite an ad for *The People*. 'Get right in the game with Phil King!' it roared, alongside a picture of the man himself, complete with fashionably slicked-back hair and neat pencil moustache, an image one part 1930s movie star, one part seedy Dr Alan Statham in *Green Wing*. 'Follow Phil King, Rugby League's TOP writer, TV and radio commentator in the *People* every Sunday,' it went on. 'King knows every aspect of the great game, its players and the men who manage them. Read King for the inside stuff.'

* * *

Geographically, the great Northern cities of Manchester and Leeds are not that far apart, especially when linked by a trans-Pennine motorway. Even so, one more major contributing factor towards Eddie Waring's overriding image of independence must surely be the way in which, right from the start, he chose to live and work in West Yorkshire.

Then as now, the majority of national rugby league journalists had their homes and offices west of the Pennines, where the Northern offices of their newspapers were universally located. In Leeds, although he was surrounded by such respected Yorkshire-based journalists as his fellow 1946 tourist Alfred Drewry (*Yorkshire Post*), John Bapty (*Yorkshire Evening Post*) and the latest in a line of father-figure Waring mentors, the long-serving *Yorkshire Evening News* journalist Arthur Haddock, for Waring to be so physically set apart sent out a message. When push came to shove, here was a man who would go his own way.

Most obviously, that meant centralising his activities at the city's well-appointed Queens Hotel, handily placed next door to Leeds train station. Over the decades to come, the name of the Queens would become synonymous with Eddie Waring – for a long period it was even rumoured that he lived there. Though that assumption turns out to be false, it is easy to see how it came about. Certainly, from the early 1950s, the hotel became the hub of an enterprise that might have been named Eddie Waring Ltd. Along with having a favourite suite of his own at his disposal should he need it, and the ongoing use of the taxi-rank out front, Eddie gathered news, held meetings, made and received telephone calls there and even had his post delivered to that address. Why did he spend so much time at the place, one might legitimately ask. Was he unhappy at home?

On the contrary. For although his long-standing marriage to Agnes had finally buckled under the strain of her husband's ambitious go-getting lifestyle upon his return from the 1946 Indomitables tour, by the turn of the decade Eddie had entered into a new relationship with a bright, breezy and beautiful Scottish-born nursing sister named Mary, who, he would later joke in his trademark mysterious style, he had met when 'she was coming down from the mountains with the water and I captured her'. Whatever the circumstances of the pair's actual meeting, at 37 years of age, in her, he had found his soulmate, the love of his life. In the years ahead, Mary Waring would not only be Eddie's best friend, she would be his confidante, business partner and, during his troubled final years, devoted nurse. In 1949, Mary gave birth to her and Eddie's only son, Tony, an arrival that left Eddie overjoyed. Henceforth, nothing would be too much trouble where the raising of young Tony was concerned. He would be given the best education that money could buy and, as he grew older, accompany his father on business excursions at home and abroad. In later years, he even tagged along as Eddie's unofficial 'minder'.

Today, Tony Waring is a successful, self-employed marketing director based near Southampton, far from the rugged green hills and these days dormant satanic mills of his West Yorkshire upbringing. On England's south coast, sailing dinghies and bigger boats are more the thing, but the memory of those times exerts a powerful influence on a man who is still very much his father's son, both in looks and in his outlook on life.

'My father was a genuinely decent bloke who went out of his way to help people wherever he could,' recalled Tony, when we met in the somewhat flatter location of south-west Hampshire. 'People used to ask me growing up, "What's it like to have a famous dad?" Well, he always was famous to me, I really didn't know any different. By the time I was seven or eight, he was on television very regularly, and people were mostly congratulatory because he was such a popular figure. For me, my father's fame was a mostly positive experience. But, yes, there was a more private side to him too. He took his responsibilities to my mother and I very seriously. As a family, day trips were always a big thing. When I was a boy, we would go over to the coast regularly. I remember taking my grandma, Florrie, to Flamborough Head, where the lighthouse is.

My grandfather died before I was born, but my grandmother and I got on extremely well. She was a vibrant, very busy little lady. She had a tremendous sense of fun, which, I'm sure, must have rubbed off on my father.'[7]

Though fatherhood had been a long time coming, when it did, in the light of his prior experience as 'a second father' to Harry Waring junior, Eddie was always likely to be a 'hands-on' kind of dad. So it turned out. With Harry, Eddie's penchant for turning everything into a game had resulted in such activities as an indoor rugby match, played on the rug before a blazing fire, in which, according to Tony's cousin: 'Uncle Eddie, on his knees and wearing a white shirt and red, amber and black tie, was Dewsbury and I, just turned nine years old, was a Black Knight. We all wore Brylcreem in those days and by the time we had finished his shirt was full of grease from my hair. He got a telling off from his mother, who was preparing Christmas dinner. So we went into the front room, where I had to play the part of a fan coming into his office with the autograph book he had just given me as a present.' As secretary-manager of Dewsbury at that time, Eddie signed his nephew's book, 'Championshiply Yours . . .'

With his own boy to mould, this emphasis on activity and sport continued. 'I went to Moorlands prep school in Leeds,' remembers Tony, 'which, in those days, was a red-brick building in Headingley where we played soccer in the winter. Then the school decided to play rugby – rugby union, of course – and they got my father to come along as coach. I must have been about 11 or 12. Anyway, my father used to come and stand on the touchline, advising the players and giving them a few hints. Having started the team from scratch, it was quite difficult, because rugby union is a complicated game, and we only played one match in that first season, against another prep school called Clifton House in Harrogate, which we won. My father pointed out that we could tell people that we had had an unbeaten season.'

As his time in charge of the Black Knights had proved, not to mention those roadshow evenings in which he was gazed upon in wide-eyed wonder by the likes of Harry Edgar, when it came to dealing with youngsters, Eddie Waring was a natural. Among his father's many tales, one in particular can be counted upon to bring a smile to Tony's face. 'They were doing a quiz at one of his roadshows,' Tony recalls, 'when one of the boys was given the chance to win a jersey if he could name the Australian player who was being described. Well, the lad stood there with his mouth open, clearly having no idea. So my father decided to give him a clue. Thinking of Harry Bath, he asked: "What do you have on a Friday night?" To which the lad replied: "Fish and chips."'

As for Tony himself, when he went away to Rossall School on England's north-west coast, midway between Cleveleys and Fleetwood, he continued to play rugby union, and indeed he carried on doing so at university in Edinburgh. 'I remember playing in an away game at Blackpool one Wednesday,' he says. 'My father, who of course couldn't normally come to see us play on a Saturday, was able to come along and watch. It was quite funny, because there was a real buzz around the home team's dressing-room. "Eddie Waring's here!" they were saying. "Who has he come to see?" They thought he was scouting. Our lot had a good laugh about that. My father was tremendous and encouraged me in everything I wanted to do. At one point, I even showed an interest in athletics and shot-putting so he came home with a shot and there was I, practising at home. He was very much in the forefront of the "well, here's something new, let's give it a try" way of thinking. Without being overbearing, he was very encouraging and enthusiastic. If you showed an interest in a thing, he really supported you.'[8]

From his humble origins in working-class Dewsbury, Eddie Waring's career had progressed to the extent that he could now afford to send his son to one of the best-respected scholastic establishments in the country, whose explicit intention, as its own early literature had it, was to offer an education 'similar to that of the great public schools, but without the great cost of Eton or Harrow'. This may have been one more reason for the chippier and more class-obsessed members of the rugby league community to view his motives with suspicion. For Tony, however, though he would doubtless have had his lonelier moments, like any child in that position, life in a boarding school seems to have suited him just fine. 'My parents regularly came to see me on a Sunday,' he says, 'and I always thought I was tremendously lucky because they always made sure that I had a really great day. We would go up to the Lake District, eat lunch and then have dinner at the Imperial Hotel, Blackpool, on the way back. I would hear about the more boring things that other people had done and realise just how devoted my parents were. Even so, it was only later that I realised that my father would have been busy working until late on the Saturday, driven over from Yorkshire and had a tiring day out, and then made the long drive back again. My parents were great. We got on tremendously well.'

And when Tony Waring says busy, busy is exactly what he means. 'My father was always balancing his journalism and broadcasting media work,' he says, revealing that, at one stage in the 1960s, Eddie was offered the position of Northern sports editor of the *Sunday Mirror*, a job he had to turn down because he was already so busy. 'I remember one newspaper series that he particularly enjoyed doing was his regular "I See Stars" column for the *Sunday Mirror*,' recalls Tony. 'From being a boy, he had always been interested in lots of different sports; that's something a lot of people don't realise. He had a tremendous breadth. As far back as 1946, in Australia, along with his rugby league work, he would also be interviewing people about cricketing prospects and so on. I myself heard him interviewing Denis Compton about football and cricket on a disc in the early '50s.'

For his 'I See Stars' feature, Eddie would travel all over the country, talking to people like controversial showjumper Harvey Smith; Queen's jockey Harry Card; gold-medal-winning long jumper Lynn 'The Leap' Davies; the Aussie golf legend Bruce Devlin; footballer Bobby Collins; and the first-ever female BBC Sports Personality of the Year, the swimmer Anita Lonsborough. Then there were his more regular duties.

LEFT: Eddie's maternal grandfather, William Henry Marsden, poses outside the family pile at 23 Hollinroyd Road. (Waring family collection)

RIGHT: Eddie's beloved mother, Florrie, pictured as a girl. (Waring family collection)

LEFT: Arthur and Florrie Waring provide baby Eddie with his first photocall, shortly after his birth in 1910. (Waring family collection)

RIGHT: The Waring family at home. Back row (l to r): Arthur Waring, Florrie Waring and two unknown friends from Manchester; front row (l to r): Eddie and brother Harry. (Waring family collection)

Eddie's first taste of sporting success – Eastborough School football team. Eddie is seated in the front row, second from right. (Waring family collection)

The young Eddie tried his hand at most sports. Here, he (on the ground) and his father, Arthur (far left), are pictured with the Springfield Chapel cricket team. (Waring family collection)

Mens sana in corpore sano – Eddie (front row, third from left) amid the weightlifters and wrestlers at his Dewsbury gym in 1934. (Waring family collection)

Eddie (far left) and the all-conquering Dewsbury Boys team of the mid-1930s, destined to become known as the Black Knights. (Waring family collection)

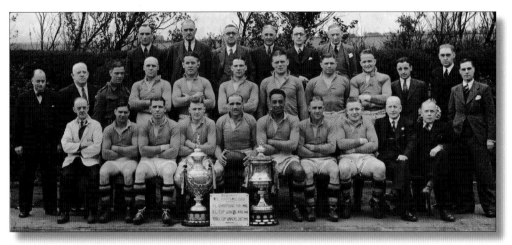

Eddie's wartime Dewsbury team celebrate having won all three trophies – the RL Championship, the RL Challenge Cup and the Yorkshire Cup – in April 1943. Eddie is on the far right. (Waring family collection)

Eddie Waring (centre) tosses a coin before refereeing Blues v. Reds at Fremantle, Western Australia, on the 1946 Indomitables tour. (Waring family collection)

LEFT: Eddie, Kiwi shirt in hand, embarks upon one of his many good deeds in a children's hospital in 1947, along with New Zealand captain Pat Smith. (Waring family collection)

RIGHT: The musical Eddie leads the Great Britain Lions 'Welsh' choir on the 1950 tour of Australasia. (Waring family collection)

LEFT: Eddie (fifth from left) and the 1954 Great Britain rugby league tourists prepare to take to the skies at Rockhampton, Australia. (Waring family collection)

LEFT: Eddie and actor James Garner on the Warner Brothers set for *Up Periscope* in Hollywood in 1958. On an earlier visit to Los Angeles, in 1950, star-struck Eddie is said to have been turned on to the potential of television by Bob Hope. (Waring family collection)

INSET: Eddie with the actor Karl Malden. (Waring family collection)

LEFT: Eddie's journalistic work with the *Sunday Pictorial* introduced him to many of the biggest sporting names of the day. Here he is pictured with gold-medal-winning long jumper Lynn Davies and friend at London's Piccadilly Circus. (Waring family collection)

LEFT: Family man. Proud father Eddie and son Tony (left) with nephew Harry and his son Andrew in the garden at Bramhope. (Waring family collection)

BELOW: 'Faint not, nor fear.' A nervous Eddie ascends the notorious spiral staircase in the South Stand at Headingley. (Waring family collection)

ABOVE: With the arrival of television, Eddie's face soon became well known in the living rooms of the nation, and of the North in particular. (Waring family collection)

LEFT: One of British sport's great iconic broadcasters pictured in the early years of a television commentary career that would earn him the title 'Mr Rugby League'. As one BBC executive put it: 'Eddie Waring is not just a commentator. He is The Commentator, and the five million viewers prove it.' (Waring family collection)

BELOW: Eddie's light-entertainment profile really hit the heights with the phenomenally popular *It's a Knockout*. In a special 1978 celebrity edition, he lines up with the likes of Frazer Hinds, Eric Morecambe, Stuart Hall, Shaw Taylor, Nicholas Parsons and Bob Grant, aka Jack in *On the Buses*. (© BBC)

LEFT: *The Goodies and the Beanstalk*. Bill Oddie, Graeme Garden, Tim Brooke-Taylor and Eddie Waring on the set of the anarchic trio's 1973 Christmas special. (© BBC)

BELOW: At the height of his fame, Eddie appeared in the star-studded 1977 *Morecambe and Wise Christmas Show*, watched by some 28 million people. Back row (l to r): Michael Aspel, Philip Jenkinson, Barry Norman, Frank Bough, Eddie Waring, Richard Baker and Richard Whitmore; front row: Eric Morecambe and Ernie Wise. (© BBC)

Game for a laugh. Eddie on the set of *It's a Knockout*, New Year's Day, 1980. (© BBC)

Eddie Waring after receiving his MBE from Her Majesty the Queen at Buckingham Palace on 23 March 1982, shortly after his retirement. (Waring family collection)

'On a Saturday night, after he had been doing a match, he would go back to the Manchester studios to do *Look North* and then go around to the newspaper offices to make sure his match report had gone in correctly,' continues his son. 'After that, he would finish off his weekly column, which ran in various editions of the paper, and it would be one o'clock in the morning before he could set off home to Yorkshire, "over the top" as he used to call it. Journalism was always a very strong element in what he did. He read all the papers – we used to get great wads of them delivered – to see if anyone had a story he'd missed. We also used to get newspapers sent over from Australia. My father read a lot of books too, mainly non-fiction, autobiographies and things like that. He took pride in knowing a lot of the prevalent newspaper people in London, like Hugh Cudlipp, the former editor of the *Sunday Pictorial* and later chairman of Mirror Group newspapers too. As far as my father was concerned, he always saw himself as a journalist first and foremost. Journalist and broadcaster, that way around.'

Meanwhile, the home to which Eddie Waring returned in his newly acquired Jaguar early every Sunday morning was not in Dewsbury but a detached house in leafy Bramhope, a well-to-do suburb to the north of Leeds. The couple's first house in that area had been a bungalow in 'The Rowans', just off Otley Road, but as Eddie's career took flight and his son began to grow with it, a larger residence was deemed necessary. The couple found it in nearby Old Lane, a quiet country road not far from Leeds Bradford airport. It was there, as her son recalls, that Mary ruled the roost, ever keen to ensure that her other half's feet stayed firmly on the ground. 'Some newspaper writer once referred to my father as "a phenomenon",' Tony smiles. 'So my mother would ask him, "What does the phenomenon want for breakfast?"' As Eddie's fame soared, guests – and often very well-known and important guests at that – would visit too, turning Langside, as the house was known, into a precious place of refuge.

This, then, is where the real appeal of the Queens Hotel lay. Of course, there were other potential reasons for Eddie Waring to be so coy about his private life. There was his failed marriage to Agnes for a start, a sad situation that, these days, few people would bat an eyelid over but which, back then, may well have been troubling to a man of such formative religious influences. Few who were close to Eddie Waring are comfortable discussing the issue even now, a sure sign of the loyalty he inspired in those around him. The one thing all are agreed on, however, is that with the marriage over, whatever their comparative circumstances, Eddie ensured that Agnes was cared for and supported financially until her death in the 1960s.

More generally, although Waring's own chapel visits decreased as the years went by, largely as a result of his weekend working patterns, he nevertheless held on to his faith. Correct in all that he said and did, he continued to raise funds for local chapels, present religious programmes and support his son, Tony, who attended the local Methodist chapel in Bramhope. Thanks, no doubt, to the influence of his mother's Congregationalist attitudes to temperance, Eddie seldom drank anything stronger than cider, didn't smoke and swore little. Early in the 1970s, he even got around to organising something called 'The Methodist Sevens', in which, he claimed, 150 teams took part and games were followed 'by a rally of 12,000 people in the Royal Albert Hall'.[9]

Another possible reason for his reticence in the area of personal disclosure, of course, is concern at the reaction of the BBC. Although the authoritarian John Reith had long since departed by the time Eddie shoved his foot in the television door, the BBC nevertheless retained strict codes of conduct, which its presenters had at all times to be seen to abide by. An irreproachable public image meant everything to the national broadcaster. It is certainly telling that, though an obvious subject for the Big Red Book, Eddie Waring was never given the *This Is Your Life* treatment, although by all accounts the show's producers, doomed to be rebuffed, did at one point give it a whirl. It seems ridiculous now, but in those less enlightened times, the slightest whiff of 'scandal' could end the career of any public figure – indeed it did so on more than one occasion. Then again, as a 'mere' rugby league commentator, perhaps Eddie was worrying about nothing. Either way, with a glittering future in television within his grasp, he was quite reasonably reluctant to take the chance. As a journalist himself, no one knew the sensation-seeking press better than he did. So why throw himself to the wolves? He didn't volunteer the information but nor did he lie about it. Eddie Waring's private life was no one else's business.

* * *

It wasn't that Eddie didn't enjoy being the centre of attention, because, as we have seen, as a natural performer he very much did. Therefore, dividing his business and personal lives between the very public Queens and the very private Langside made absolute sense; it was a masterstroke, even.

As an environment in which he could be on display whilst meeting friends and influencing people, the Queens could not be beaten. Self-publicity, after all, is a chief tool of any public figure's trade, and where better to propagate an image of dynamism and popularity than in the public areas of a busy city-centre hotel? Equally, if ever he grew weary of all the fuss, there was a peaceful, ready-made bolt-hole back in Bramhope. Whether it was arrived at via a deliberate policy or not, the arrangement would be a particular mercy during Eddie's twilight years, when, in the grip of a desperately upsetting illness, the very last thing he would need was to be pestered by hordes of fans, critics and journalists, all desperate for a piece of the man the press and BBC still insisted on calling 'Mr Rugby League'.

All that, however, was for the future. As a thrusting young journalist and broadcaster himself, there was a career path waiting to be trodden, and 'King Eddie' wasted little time in assembling a companionable little group of courtiers to help him on his way. If ever there was a master of the art of delegation, it was Eddie. Anyone who could assist was hauled into service. Son Tony telephoned reports through to the *Sunday Mirror* copytakers in

Manchester. Nephew Harry was called upon to bring urgently required pieces of archive information. A collection of local reporters were employed to write match reports for the games that Eddie could not personally attend. The revolving hotel doors swung to and fro with a constant procession of club officials, all providing information to be taken in and recycled for the following Sunday's paper or the next BBC match commentary. Meetings with the press, RFL officials and broadcasting bigwigs were also held there, routinely curtailed at some point by a Tannoy announcement calling upon the great man, or maybe a waiter or hotel manager with a very important telephone call on hold.

'Eddie would invite us over for coffee or a meal,' recalls one such former Rugby Football League official, David Howes, one of many to benefit from his host's penchant for useful little aphorisms such as: 'Always carry a tie, you never know when you are going to need it. You can always take it off.'

'He taught me, always sit with your back to the wall and look outwards,' Howes smiles, doing exactly that. 'That way, you can see who is coming in and who is going out. At every meeting, the concierge would come over and say that the editor of *Grandstand* was on the phone or the head of BBC Sport or someone. Maybe he was, but you got the impression that half of that was showbiz.'[10]

Harry Jepson recalls the scene with affection. 'Every Friday night in the '50s and '60s, Eddie held court in the Queens Hotel, at a bar he used to frequent and gather at with all his cronies. People like Hunslet's Hector Rawson, Ronnie Teeman of Bramley and Leeds' Jack Myerscough, good friends of Eddie's, would ring him up, or he would ring them, and they'd drop in with the titbits he needed for Sunday. He was a very hard-working man, Eddie. Success like he had didn't come by messing about. He had to really get down to it and do some real work. It came across in the way that he wore his trilby and flash overcoat that he was a bit of a fly-by-night, but he wasn't. He was a shrewd, incisive commentator who felt for the game.'

Stella Hirst, wife of the late Leeds and Yorkshire official George

Hirst, who took over as secretary-manager at Headingley shortly after Waring's 1946 departure with the Indomitables, recalls: 'He [Eddie] had a column in the paper called "Bouquets and Brickbats", for success and failure. When George and I were married in 1955, amongst our wedding telegrams was one from Eddie saying, "All bouquets and no brickbats." I remember when George and I were coming back from some function or other in Lancashire. When we got out of Leeds station, Eddie was just coming out of the side entrance of the Queens. He always came over for a chat. He would say "Owt?", meaning did George have anything to tell him, and George usually replied "Nowt". He was a very extrovert and warm man.'[11]

Moving in Eddie's journalistic circle, meanwhile, were the future *Yorkshire Post* correspondents Trevor Watson (husband of Dewsbury historian Margaret) and Raymond Fletcher. Along with his lengthy spell as chief rugby league writer on the *YP*, in tandem with David Howes Fletcher would also co-edit the *Rothman's Rugby League Yearbook* over the course of that much-missed title's 15-year run. Nowadays, he acts as the RFL's official statistician. As a young wannabe hack operating under a mop of blond hair and the rather swashbuckling nom de plume Ramon Joyce, he recalls: 'Eddie took a bit of interest in me and put one or two matches my way for the *Sunday Pictorial*. That was how I first started, with Eddie giving me matches to do. I had been doing stuff for the old *Rugby Leaguer* and things like that, but nothing national. I always wanted to be a journalist, but I started very late. I didn't have any qualifications and when Eddie took an interest I was way down the list of rugby league correspondents. I called it freelancing, but I didn't have any work at all until he put it my way. He had another man helping him out, a full-time journalist named Tom Hardwicke, who acted as his subeditor on the *Look North* television reports we provided for Saturday teatimes. Tom was another one who helped me a great deal. Between the two of them, they kept giving me that bit extra until I finally made it. I will always be grateful for that.'[12] ·

Then there was a man who, from the mid-'60s, would become perhaps Eddie Waring's closest working ally of all. His name is Dave 'Nosey' Parker, the last of the true rugby league newshounds, whose current byline in the trade paper *League Weekly* says it all: 'If you have nothing to hide, you have nothing to fear.' As Parker himself is first to admit, his unparalleled knack for breaking the stories that others would rather keep hidden has landed this former apprentice draughtsman in trouble more than once. In the 1960s, his success in generating *Sunday Mirror* exclusives irritated Eddie's fellow national journalists so much that on one occasion, according to Parker, he narrowly avoided potentially fatal consequences.

'The first time I met Eddie Waring, I was 18 years of age,' he says now. 'Bill Hughes, the former secretary of Halifax, had asked me to write for their match-day programme, following the opening of the floodlights at Thrum Hall. He knew I did the amateur rugby league round-up in the *Green Final*, which was part of the *Halifax Courier*. So, I started doing this and Halifax were chosen for a television game. Eddie took the programme home and saw the snippets and news pieces I was providing. He rang Bill up and told him he could use some of this stuff in his Sunday newspaper column. I was invited to help him with a television game at Odsal but couldn't go as I was working in Scotland, so my dad stood in for me instead. Next thing, I was invited to a BBC2 Floodlit Trophy game at Headingley.'[13]

In the years ahead, Dave Parker's presence would prove invaluable in sustaining Eddie's reputation as 'Mr Rugby League', in whichever area of the media he operated. 'I used to get some cracking stories for Eddie, which really upset the rest of the press boys,' Parker continues. 'I was absolutely getting scoops. Once, my dad and me were going to a match at St Helens, a television game. Jack Bentley, Joe Humphreys and someone else were in a car alongside us, and we were coming off under a bridge on the M6 where there was a concrete run-up. If we hadn't taken that, they would have run me into the pillar. Anyway, we got to Knowsley Road and my dad went straight up to them. He said that if they ever did anything like that again, he would flatten the three of them. We aroused quite a bit of jealousy, and they used to play hell about me. Jack McNamara [the veteran *Manchester Evening News* reporter] couldn't stand me – he had me kicked out of the Swinton press-box because I wasn't an NUJ man. To be honest, I felt that Eddie left me a bit exposed. Then again, very early on when I was getting him the news, he told me: "I need you on the telephone now, I can't be having you ringing me back all the time." He paid for me to have a telephone, and that was in the days when it was one phone for every ten houses. I used to sit religiously for him every Friday night from half past five to half past eight. I would spend Saturday mornings before we went to a match either for the *Sunday Mirror* or television gleaning the best news I could. Whatever he didn't use, what was worth recycling, the *Rugby Leaguer* got the benefit of. That's how I began to build up my "Nosey Parker" gossip column. In the 15 years we worked together, I would have done anything for him.'

Back at the Queens Hotel, meanwhile, as Eddie's media profile rose, so did the frequency of visits from national newspaper journalists. And though there was usually little in the way of personal revelation – 'twice when I chided him about his privacy,' wrote one *Guardian* journalist in 1971, 'he did perk up for a split second and exclaim: "That's Eddie!"' – a read of those clippings produces a wonderfully evocative picture of the man in his Leeds City Square surroundings.

Writing in the 26 September 1968 edition of the *Radio Times*, for example, the journalist Brian Finch reveals:

Catching Eddie Waring for an interview these days is a bit like waiting for a last bus that may already have gone. One doesn't arrange to see him. One finds out his route for the day and lies in wait. And as good a place as any for an ambush, if he happens to be in the country at the time, is the American bar of a certain Leeds hotel which has come to be known as Eddie Waring's unusual 'office'.

The word 'office', writes Finch, is actually 'a private joke', 'but the fact remains that if you want to get a message to the man you couldn't try a better place'.

When Eddie arrived, opening a wad of fan mail, he had just got in from Germany, and was making rapid arrangements to go to Brussels. Before leaving again, he had a Rugby League match to cover for *Grandstand*, a newspaper column to assemble, proofs of his latest book to correct, a Christmas book to negotiate, and his personal involvement with a forthcoming documentary to be ironed out. Mr Waring – who used to earn £3 a week on a Yorkshire journal and whose idea of a good tune is still to join in one of those Yorkshire choirs in a spirited rendering of 'Messiah' – is these days, one gathers, Big Business.

An even more particular account, published in the *Sunday Times Magazine* in 1968, came from the typewriter of that fine Northern sportswriter, among much else, Arthur Hopcraft. After revealing how Waring made about 50 personal appearances at cinemas, church meetings and Rotary clubs every year, Hopcraft wrote:

Eddie received us at his customary spot at one end of the cocktail bar in the Queens Hotel, Leeds, which is a British Rail massif. He likes to stand just inside the bar counter, with the gate up, where he can see who is coming in and going out and where the two-inch step-up from the rest of the floor level lifts his grey head to the height of most other men's. He is short and stocky. People wave and nod at him and shout out hellos across the room in proper, unceremonious Yorkshire style. The hotel is across the road from his office and he uses it like his club. The staff fuss over him in a mixture of deference and his own loud-hailing affability.

In fact, if he had chosen to do so, Eddie could just as easily have worked out of at least two offices, belonging to his newspaper and to the BBC, in both Leeds and Manchester. There, though, he would have been just one among many journalists, out of view of the public, and to Eddie, for most of his life anyway, mixing with 'real' people was vital. Not only was he on first-name terms with just about every employee in the hotel, he knew the names of all the staff in the train station next door too, not to mention the taxi drivers out front, who would be called upon to drive him off to games while he brushed up on his pre-match homework in the back. 'The Queens Hotel seems to revolve around Eddie Waring,' wrote Michael Wale, in another issue of the *Radio Times*, published some three years after Brian Finch's article.

> Barmen automatically pour a cider (a drink he alternates with bitter lemon) without being asked. Foyer staff rush forward with messages. Then we are in his pale blue Jaguar going up the hill to the BBC offices. There are more exchanges with doormen and other non-executive members of the Corporation. 'Are you going or coming, Eddie?' someone asks. Into the canteen for tea: 'You know we are always open for you, Eddie.'[14]

Peter Black of the *Daily Mail*, with a perhaps dubious use of analogy, told of the stir caused when Eddie arrived even in London, beginning from the moment he walked into the Great Northern Hotel, just off the train from Leeds:

> The porters and desk clerk greeted him as an old friend; and at the sound of his large, piercing voice the ladies and gents waiting in the nooks of the hotel's lounges for the train to take them back to the North raised their heads like animals at a waterhole who hear from the nearby forest the roar of one of their own kind . . . London taxi drivers say to him, 'Where you goin' today then, Eddie?' He was on the *Simon Dee Show* the other week.[15]

It was, wrote Arthur Hopcraft in November 1968,

the life of a local Big Wheel abruptly projected into the national consciousness by the conversion of image into presence. The strutting walk, the generous tipping and the curly brown hat are the characteristics of a resilient jauntiness. He is a North Country act, more aware of his special comicality than his audience imagines.[16]

And by now, thanks to one particular piece of heartfelt commentary at the end of the previous season's Challenge Cup final, that audience was bigger than it had ever been before.

Part III

CLARITY

Seven

MAKING A SPLASH

'He's in tears is the poor lad.'

Watersplash. A famous name for a famous game. In hindsight, Saturday, 11 May 1968 would have entered rugby league folklore anyway. As the dark skies opened high above Wembley's old twin towers, producing freak conditions more suited to water polo than rugby, no one had ever seen anything like it. Come kick-off, great pools of water covered the pitch. The players, trying doggedly to beat the elements, aquaplaned through puddles the size of Lake Windermere. The saturated and slippery ball went to ground with frustrating regularity, where it stuck stubbornly to the sodden surface like a crouton on soup. On any other day, the match would have been postponed. This, though, was the Challenge Cup final. London's Empire Stadium was booked and paid for. Some 87,100 paying customers, including fans of the competing teams, Leeds and Wakefield Trinity, had made their pilgrimage south for their sport's annual day in the sun. The journalists were in the press-box, the commentators at their microphones. And nationwide, thanks to the presence of the *Grandstand* BBC TV cameras – their 11th year of covering the event – a television audience of millions sat waiting in their living rooms. Torrential rain or no torrential rain, the show must go on.

In such atrocious conditions, it was a miracle that the teams put on as entertaining a show as they did. In terms of open, running rugby, the game was by no means a classic – how could it be? – but the performance of one particular player stood head and shoulders above the rest. His name was Don Fox, as tenacious and versatile a footballer as ever pulled on boots, with skills forged in the small West Yorkshire coal-mining village of Sharlston. The middle son of a league dynasty in which his even more famous younger brother Neil, the free-scoring centre, and straight-talking older sibling Peter, a future Great Britain coach, also loomed large, Don Fox had begun his professional playing career as a 17-year-old scrum-half at nearby Featherstone in 1953. It was in a 12-year spell there that he scored a club record 162 career tries before leaving Post Office Road for Wakefield, where, alongside brother Neil, he reinvented himself as a sharply intelligent loose forward-cum-prop.

By 1968, Don Fox was already moving towards 500 career appearances, had served both his county and country with honour and was widely regarded as being a credit to the sport. Playing in his first Challenge Cup final, he was simply sensational, packing down at blind-side prop but popping up everywhere. Though his 32-year-old legs had seen better days, Fox gave a towering display that belied the extreme conditions, prodding and cajoling his teammates towards what would – and should – have been a famous victory. His tactical kicking and organising influence put Leeds time and again on the back foot. Indeed, so heroic was his contribution that the assembled ranks of the Rugby League Writers' Association, when asked to vote upon the man of the match, awarded him the Lance Todd Trophy. Then, as the seconds ticked down on a remarkable contest, came an incident that would both unfairly define the career of Don Fox and produce one of television sport's most memorable commentary moments.

The 68th Rugby League Challenge Cup final had not been a high-scoring affair. In terms of ability, the teams were pretty much inseparable, with favourites Leeds having finished first and Wakefield second in the league. That story continued when, after splashing about in swamps that made sidestepping and swerving all but impossible, Leeds full-back Bev Risman – son of Gus – and Fox traded penalties as Leeds built an early 4–2 lead. And suitably, when the first try arrived after 12 minutes, there was an appropriate note of farce about it. The fall guy on this occasion was Leeds winger John Atkinson, who slipped while trying to keep Fox's upfield kick to touch in play, allowing Atkinson's opposite number, Ken Hirst, to intercede, dribble the ball over the line and touch down. Fox's glorious and now long-forgotten touchline conversion gave Wakefield a 7–4 half-time lead, to which, somehow, they managed to cling until one of the most controversial refereeing decisions that Wembley has ever seen, ten minutes from time. The trouble began when Barry Seabourne's speculative kick from just inside his own half came to rest with a plop somewhere near Wakefield's 40-metre line, completely wrong-footing the Trinity defence. This time it was the alert Atkinson's turn to hack the ball towards the Trinity line at the very same time as Wakefield's other winger, Ken Battye, raced across to cover. With around ten yards to go, the two fliers converged, Battye on the deck, Atkinson on his feet, spraying great plumes of water as they went. When the ball squirted forward, Gert Coetzer, the Wakefield centre, also joined the scrap for possession. In the resulting melee, Coetzer's attempted clearing kick scudded into the in-goal area, where it was collected by the fourth member of Trinity's three-quarter line, Ian Brooke, who looked to have relieved the danger as he raced back into the field of play. To widespread bewilderment, York referee J. Hebblethwaite decreed that Atkinson had been deliberately pushed off the ball and awarded Leeds an obstruction try, which Risman both converted and added a penalty goal to, one minute from time. At 11–7 to Leeds, the game, it seemed, was up.

Except it wasn't. For just as Trinity's Ray Owen was preparing to kick off from the restart, Don Fox once again took matters into his own hands, or, more accurately, feet. Pushing in front of his own scrum-half and ignoring the waiting forwards on his left, Fox hoofed the ball out towards Leeds centre Bernard Watson, who tried to trap it underfoot. Unhappily for Watson, he missed the ball completely and it skidded away to the side, where the uprushing Hirst fly-hacked it on towards the posts. Risman, Atkinson and the rest all tried in vain to cut him off, but a combination of Hirst's searing diagonal inside run and the slippery surface meant that the winger held a formidable advantage over the floundering defenders. Racing through, Hirst toe-poked ahead and touched the ball down under the posts, missing the dead-ball line and a passing photographer by inches. The winning conversion and an astonishing 12–11 victory were a formality, surely. Yet fate had one more trick up her soggy, mud-spattered sleeve.

Watching black-and-white videotapes of the latter moments of the Watersplash final today can feel like intruding on personal grief. Don Fox, whose legs must have been wearier than most, goes down on one knee, arranging the turf for what will surely be the match-winning kick. Normally, Trinity's skipper, Neil Fox, would be the one taking a shot at goal, but the Great Britain centre is absent with an injured groin, and anyway, his brother Don could back-heel this one over in his sleep. There is, however, something about Fox's body language that suggests he is not entirely comfortable in the situation. He takes a little too long in his preparations and after having apparently settled himself, picks the ball up like a nervous golfer lining up a putt, before placing it tentatively on the rough-hewn mound of damp earth. Meanwhile, looking down from the heights of the Wembley commentary box, and trying to make sense of it all for the viewing public at home, is Eddie Waring.

'Forty minutes gone and if he kicks this goal . . . some of the Leeds players won't dare look,' says Eddie, while the camera cuts back to reveal those same players standing with hands on hips or, like John Atkinson, crouched with their backs to the field. 'It's not a hard shot, but it's always a hard shot when the match depends on it,' continues Eddie. 'And in this weather, he is taking all the time in the world because he's allowed to kick it, he [the referee] can't blow time until he's kicked it. It's all on the goal. What a grandstand finish this is.' And then, as the ball, horrifyingly, is sliced wide: 'He's missed it, he's missed it! He's on the ground

. . . he's missed it! Well, and there goes the whistle for time. What a dramatic . . . everybody's got their head in their hands . . . and he's sure in tears, he's in tears is the poor lad . . .'

Later that same year, in an interview with Waring in the *Sunday Times*, Arthur Hopcraft wrote:

> The stadium and the players were stunned; the culprit covered in shame. Eddie remembered: 'I just shouted at the top of my voice, "He's missed it". And then straight away I said, "The poor lad". Now at a moment like that I could 'ave said anything. I could 'ave said he was a clot or he was anything stupid. But I just came out with "poor lad", and I think that's because I reckon I am not a bad sort of bloke. I was giving a decent bloke's reaction.'[1]

Certainly, Waring's instant empathy was appreciated by those closest to Fox himself. 'His brother, Neil, called Don all the names under the sun,' said Eddie, in a *Radio Times* interview some 13 years later, 'but when he rang home, obviously in tears, his sister and mother said, "Well, don't worry, you've got all the sympathy of the village, because Eddie Waring said, 'poor lad'. We all felt sorry for you and we all cried."'[2] Soccer has Kenneth Wolstenholme's 'they think it's all over'; rugby league has Eddie Waring's 'poor lad'.

* * *

On the back of just a few seconds of off-the-cuff live commentary, for Eddie Waring an already productive career path took an even more astonishing turn. In tandem with a then little-known show called *It's a Knockout*, in which Eddie had begun to appear as a judge the year before, Watersplash set forth the wave that would carry Eddie to the light-entertainment heavens.

In hindsight, of course, Eddie Waring's incomparable commentary style was always likely to attract attention. How could it not? For one thing, there was his distinctly odd way with proper nouns, wherein unnecessary emphasis would be placed on the final syllable – WarringTON – as though that was the point at which he was no longer fearful his false teeth would drop out. Then there were the gaps, the hesitations, the yelps of excitement, the rolling of consonants and the strangling of vowels, as in his trademark 'Rrrrregby leeeggga' or, putting one in mind of a camel-coated Tony the Tiger, 'Grrrrreeeeaaat BrrrrrrriTAIN'. To Eddie, although rules should be explained for the uninitiated, dry tactical analysis and statistics were best avoided, with an emphasis on player personalities and small human stories to the fore. But that, as the BBC producer Bryan Cowgill put it in 1966, was just 'the sort of thing which helps make Uncle Ed so happily and gloriously unique'.[3]

Eddie himself always insisted that the idea of rattling off light-hearted tales of players' hobbies and family lives did not come along until later. As he told the *Daily Express*:

> I do remember one match and it was terrible; nothing happening. And I thought of all these millions watching. I could see them turning off the sets and somehow or other I started making comments about the game, perhaps humorously, and it came off.[4]

Nevertheless, right from the start, Eddie's approach could hardly have been described as conventional.

In July 1951, some four months before that first national broadcast at Swinton, Eddie, now giving his address as The Rowans, Bramhope, wrote to the head of outside broadcasts, Peter Dimmock, to remind him of an earlier visit to London during which he had watched 'three RU matches being televised for experience'. In view of 'the northern invasion of TV', he wondered, had the BBC yet considered its plans in relation to rugby league football? 'The ban on the Cup final caused terrific upheaval both in official and unofficial circles of the league and the matter is being further discussed at a meeting today,' he told the BBC man. Dimmock's response? While the BBC had not yet made any definite plans concerning television outside broadcasts this season, he said, they were certainly eager to obtain some rugby league games when its units moved north, 'and perhaps you would keep in touch with me from time to time so that I can let you know should there be an opportunity to use you as one of the commentators'. As quick on his feet as ever, Eddie was already making himself indispensable.

With the first nationally televised game out of the way, rugby league coverage on the BBC settled into a pattern of irregular broadcasts punctuated by the odd outright camera ban and bout of anxiety from the clubs of the Rugby Football League. One game which most definitely was televised, allegedly resulting in the aforementioned drop in domestic attendances, was the final of the 1954 Rugby League World Cup – the first such tournament to be held in either code of rugby, and one of the first-ever sporting events to be broadcast live by the BBC via Eurovision link. Staged at the Parc des Princes in Paris, the game, in which Great Britain beat France 16–12, was shown live as part of the *Sportsview* programme, home to the majority of the BBC's national rugby league activity at that time. Commentator-in-chief was Alan Dixon, assisted by Alan Clarke, with Eddie employed as an 'inter-round' summariser. For this, Waring received three guineas less than the others because, as he helpfully told the BBC, the *Sunday Pictorial* would otherwise meet his expenses.

Whatever the payment, the signs are that Waring continued to have his critics within the organisation. Another letter to Peter Dimmock on 24 November 1954, 11 days after the events in Paris, began:

I am sorry I have created the impression of camera hogging – unintentionally I assure you. I have always been extremely conscious of the importance of such matters as timing, building up the interviewee and making them feel at ease. Possibly the fact that some of the people I have interviewed recently have been of the 'hard', heavy types I have, in attempting to 'soften' them created the wrong impression.

And Waring later confided to Arthur Hopcraft that there were

> one or two people [within the Corporation] saying 'Why can't
> we get someone to do this job who talks like we do?' But my
> producer used to tell them: 'You can. But you've only got one
> Eddie Waring.' I thought about taking speech training lessons,
> quite seriously, but I never did.[5]

Then, in 1955, came the birth of Independent Television – the BBC
had a direct competitor at last. For Eddie, of course, this was very
good news. It increased his market value at a stroke, especially
when ITV immediately began to court his services. In the autumn
of that year, the fledgling commercial broadcaster, keen to flex
its sporting muscles, signed a deal with the Rugby League to
broadcast a midweek floodlit tournament exclusively from London.
The final would be staged at the Loftus Road ground of Queens
Park Rangers, but otherwise it was an entirely Northern affair with
four top Yorkshire clubs (Huddersfield, Hunslet, Featherstone and
Wakefield) joining Lancashire quartet Leigh, Oldham, Warrington
and Wigan in playing for the Associated Rediffusion trophy. Won
by Warrington – 43–18 victors in the final over Leigh – this short-
lived quirk in sports broadcasting is now all but forgotten, but one
thing is for sure: its commentator was not Eddie Waring. Stung into
action by the thought of Eddie being lured away, the BBC's head
of sport, Paul Fox, set about tying his man, thus far employed on
an ad hoc basis, to a longer-term exclusive two-year contract worth
210 guineas per season. During that time, Eddie was guaranteed
14 fortnightly television appearances in the winter months and at
least 6, in some other sporting capacity, during the summer.

Although he was happy to tease the BBC with the possibility of
his being 'poached' – the 'commercial people', he said, were very
interested in his 'five-a-side football proposal' – it is equally clear
where Eddie Waring's true loyalties lay. For one thing, though he
was nonconformist to his bones, as a patriotic Brit, he was also
hugely impressed by national institutions. Nor was he a fool. Why

risk contacts and good faith painstakingly developed throughout a fast-changing decade on an enterprise that might very well fall flat on its face? By now, Eddie had begun to form friendly relationships with an increasing number of people within the BBC and they with him. He had a growing insight into how the wheels of the Corporation turned. If he had an idea – and he had a great many – he knew the very people to drive it along. One such was the outside-broadcast producer Barney Colehan, who sent an internal memo to the producer of current-affairs show *Panorama* in January 1955, recommending that a discussion might be arranged between Waring and the vehemently anti-rugby league journalist William Wooller on: 'Why in the two codes of rugby – amateur and professional – is there such antagonism when soccer, cricket etc. allow professionals and amateurs to play in matches together?'[6] Barney Colehan's role in Eddie Waring's career was by no means over yet.

After he wrote to ITV confirming his decision to remain with the BBC – 'I felt in all fairness to all concerned I must do this at once' – Waring's avalanche of extracurricular programme ideas continued to flow unabated. Several, such as the live five-a-side soccer tournament already mentioned, though outlined in some detail, came to nothing. 'The BBC were looking at all-in wrestling too,' says Eddie's son, Tony. 'They set about putting together a pilot, and so as not to let the cat out of the bag to ITV, made it in France. Owing to his interest in wrestling, my father went over and did the commentary. They showed the results to various interest groups to gauge the reaction but I don't think it was ever televised. My father used to receive telegrams and letters from the likes of Paul Fox all the time. "Eddie, can you get Fred Trueman for an interview?" and so on. He was a man who was expected to sort things out.'

On another occasion, in Wales, Eddie even got to broadcast from a horse-trotting trial. 'My father was never a great horse man,' says his son, 'but he had been doing interviews and they persuaded him to have a go himself. They assured him that it was a very steady horse, although he wasn't so sure about it. Anyway, they put him in a carriage which they called "Steady Eddie" and off it went like a rocket, while he hung on.' To some in the BBC, it seems, Eddie Waring's appeal was already moving far beyond mere sports commentary. In this open-hearted, good-natured Northerner, they had unearthed a ready-made figure of fun.

All that, however, would develop over time. With various sporting bodies including the Rugby Football League playing hard to get, the BBC's more immediate concern was simply to get sport – any sport – on the screen. From October 1956, at the behest of a man with whom Eddie would forge a lengthy and productive professional partnership, the outside-broadcast producer Ray Lakeland, Waring was appointed sports editor of *Sport in the North*, a five- to ten-minute Saturday-night programme broadcast from Manchester. Initially, that meant the preparation of programme contents, organising and delivering guest contributors and writing links between the show's different segments. He would not normally be expected to appear in front of camera, said his original offer of employment. But this was Eddie Waring, right? There was more chance of him sweeping the floor at Batley Variety Club. Needless to say, by the following year Eddie's duties had expanded to include introducing the programme and carrying out interviews.[7]

Although Waring's involvement with *Sport in the North* ended in February 1961, his Manchester-based regional BBC work continued throughout the '60s on both television and radio. In *Rugby League Extra*, Eddie provided a filmed report on the match of the day and interviewed a leading rugby league personality. Other regional opt-out television programmes in which Eddie took part included a half-hour programme called *World of Sport* (no relation to the later ITV effort featuring Canadian log balancing, Venezuelan newt bothering et al.), produced by Alec Weeks, and the London-produced *Sports Special*.

In October 1958, other buds were beginning to sprout too. One such was *First Return*, a documentary produced by Barney Colehan about the refurbishment of Leeds railway station, which Eddie narrated. Then there was the early-evening current-affairs show *Look North*, which, in those days, was broadcast right across the north of England. Whatever the vehicle, though, the attitude of some in rugby league towards television remained ambivalent at best. 'Eddie got a job doing a Saturday-night programme for BBC North,' recalls Harry Jepson, 'where he would quickly review the afternoon's rugby league games and give out the results. I don't know why, but no one would supply the BBC with the scores. So Hector Rawson said to me: "Eddie's having trouble. You hear the results in the committee room after the match, will you ring him with them before six o'clock so he can use them on the BBC?" So I did.'

By the time the *Look North* franchise split in two with the launch of another major Northern BBC studio east of the Pennines some ten years later,[8] up-to-date news and results were no longer a problem. Invited to become 'journalistically involved' in a Friday-night sports slot by the producer of the new Leeds-based *Look North* in January 1968, Eddie's first contributions came on 25 March, almost immediately after the new service began. Soon, he was a regular presence on other days of the week too, particularly Saturday, when the pre-existing system of delegation that had served him so well on the *Sunday Pictorial* and *Sunday Mirror* also assisted in fulfilling his small-screen responsibilities.

'We had a structure in place for his Saturday teatime results for *Look North*,' confirms his old journalist ally Dave Parker. 'We had Ray Fletcher helping us, who worked in the library then of the *Yorkshire Post*. There was Tony Metcalfe, father of the cricketer Ashley Metcalfe, who worked on the *Yorkshire Evening Post*, and Arthur Haddock too. Arthur's son, Neville, used to do match reports for Eddie in the early days as well. We all worked together to get the results and scorers in and Eddie would sit in front of the cameras and read it all out.'

A well-oiled machine, then, and it needed to be. For by now, Eddie Waring was very much a celebrity, primarily on account of a certain other programme also broadcast on a Saturday afternoon.

Its name was *Grandstand* and, over the previous decade, with its trademark 'boom boom' signature tune and knack of rallying the nation around big sporting occasions, it had all but rewritten the rules of the genre. From 1958 until its sad but inevitable demise in January 2007, *Grandstand* introduced the Great British public to events and personalities that might otherwise have passed them by. One of the sports to benefit was rugby league – until *Grandstand*'s appearance a sporadic presence on BBC television but afterwards a reliably eccentric little house guest, guaranteed to enliven many a Home Counties sitting room.

* * *

Ask the now-retired outside-broadcast producer Ray Lakeland how it was that Eddie Waring was first given the job of BBC rugby league commentator on *Grandstand* and his answer is unequivocal: 'The earlier commentators didn't cut the mustard. Eddie did, it was as simple as that.'[9] That may well be the case, but there were quite clearly other factors at play also, not least contractual obligations and Eddie's own political value as a go-between. More contentiously, there was also the thorny issue of just what sort of image the BBC wanted to project.

As we have seen, although BBC television was a regular broadcaster of rugby league, on and off, for some seven years nationally before *Grandstand* came along, its coverage was on the whole haphazard. Thanks mainly to the intransigence of rugby league itself, from 1953, Challenge Cup-final broadcasts had been largely confined to radio and the North of England Home Service, where in 1956, for example, Eddie took on the role of Wembley summariser. In fact, the vast majority of his pre-*Grandstand* work followed a similar pattern. On a programme like Bryan Cowgill's *Sportsview*, for instance, Eddie would record interviews in the BBC Manchester studios, while also sharing second-half commentary duties on a rugby league game to be shown later in the week, between eight and nine o'clock at night. In the Rugby League Championship final of May 1954, he provided summaries and interviews at Maine Road and, around a year later, gave his usual 'assistance with commentary' on the second half of a televised game at Salford.[10] What with a regular supply of Home Service wireless work since March 1937 at least, which had, by December 1955, progressed to providing the words for the third Great Britain versus New Zealand Test match, for Eddie Waring the broadcaster, the 1950s were an extremely productive decade, whatever the medium. And however the opportunity arose, all that experience and foundation-laying served him well when the time came for his first official solo *Grandstand* commentary, Wigan versus Hull, played on Saturday, 15 November 1958, the fifth Saturday after the programme began.

Although the very first presenter of *Grandstand* was Eddie's old correspondent Peter Dimmock, the anchorman role soon went to the slick one-time *Stockport Express* journalist and keen amateur runner David Coleman. Along with his fellow BBC presenter, the former Oxford University footballing blue and *Sportsview* presenter Frank Bough, Coleman – who seemed to enjoy his rugby league – would become perhaps the on-screen presence most readily associated with Waring's *Grandstand* career, right until the end. Yet while neither he nor Bough would be strangers to ironic media ribbing themselves in the years ahead, for many in the North the pair's knowing studio links to Eddie reflected the BBC's somewhat patronising attitude towards rugby league itself.

'On one occasion, someone persuaded my father to sit on the goalposts at Headingley,' recalls Tony Waring. 'Usually when they did the old scene-set at the top of the programme, when they would go to the presenter at each of that day's venues, it would just be a case of him sticking his heel in and saying, "The pitch is firm, they'll need long studs," or whatever. This time, they opened up on a really tight shot of my father, looking as though he was standing next to the posts. Then, when they pulled back, there he was sitting on the crossbar, halfway up!' For Eddie and his producers, it seems, this was merely a way to lighten the winter gloom. For others, it smacked of disrespect. Was the BBC laughing with Eddie Waring or at him? It remains a question to which there has never been a completely satisfactory answer.

'There were one or two commentators in contention for the job,' says Ray Lakeland, who worked with Eddie on *Grandstand* until his own retirement in 1975. 'Alan Dixon, who also did it for radio; Harry Sunderland; Keith Macklin – they all had a go but Eddie was head and shoulders above them. Where Alan Dixon would say "The ref's blown for some infringement in the scrum," Eddie would tell you what the infringement was. That was a big difference. He could also read a match and tell you which way it was going.' Quite clearly, his first game went OK because he was back again a fortnight later for Wakefield versus Hunslet live from Belle Vue. Then it was St Helens versus Leeds, followed, a few days before Christmas, by Oldham versus Wigan, and so on and so forth for the next 20-odd years. But why, if the BBC thought rugby league a second-rate sport, as some suggest, did it bid for the 13-a-side code at all?

'The BBC wanted something to fill the afternoon and they couldn't have soccer,' reveals Ray Lakeland. 'Alan Hardaker, secretary to the English Football League, turned us down. So we went for rugby league and union instead. We were better able to get on with Bill Fallowfield, the secretary of the Rugby League. He was amenable, and Eddie acted as a liaison man.'

The aforementioned Keith Macklin, meanwhile, although turned down for the top job proper, continued to work on BBC radio and acted as Waring's unofficial television understudy from that point hence, a role that, despite its longevity, turned out to be hardly the most demanding of positions. 'I did my first radio commentary at Headingley in 1956, Leeds versus Oldham,' recalls Macklin, now a doyen of the game's journalistic fraternity. 'From there on, I commentated on rugby league for BBC radio until the early '80s, when I moved to commercial radio. In the '70s, I was also soccer network commentator for Yorkshire TV and did rugby league on Sundays. During all that time, I was regarded as Eddie's understudy, but I only did four games in total. Even then, Eddie couldn't help himself. He went into hospital with an extremely painful ear condition and had to have a serious operation, losing part of his hearing as a result.'[11]

In fact, the episode in question occurred in February 1960, during which time Waring was hospitalised in the Leeds General Infirmary with the same deteriorating condition that had kept him out of the wartime armed forces. Even then, he was determined not to be forgotten. In a letter to the BBC's Paul Fox sent from his hospital bed, he wrote:

> My dear Paul, you have down St Helens v Whitehaven on the 26 March. On that day Great Britain are to play France at St Helens. I don't know what the position will be apropos covering this but I would suggest you have a word with Bill F about it. I spoke to him this morning . . . It is obviously no good doing a league match if the International is on.

Business dealt with, Eddie then got chatty. 'I am now in dock,' he reported.

> Got a good room and feeling fine. Only trouble is my 'lug' and the cost of the place. I am down in the morning for the 'op'. The 'prisoner' ate a good breakfast this morning. I hope to be able to give you a ring or write later in the week. I gave Macklin all the help I could on Saty [sic] so he starts with some knowledge. Hope all well. See you soon (I hope). Luv, Eddie. P.S. Told Ron I was fixing the best nurse for you lads.[12]

Despite his obvious reluctance to take a back seat, Eddie's offer of encouragement towards Keith Macklin seems to have been genuine. In Eddie's absence, the younger man managed just two televised league games, one World Cup match and a seven-a-side tournament at Headingley. Upon Eddie's return, things carried on exactly as they had before.[13]

'I suppose it's natural human instinct not to welcome too much competition and Eddie was no different,' Macklin says. 'He was always friendly and helpful when I met him. But he was very proud of what you might call his iconic status and most unwilling to let go of the commentary reins – even for the odd game. To be fair, he was the perfect man for the era and immensely knowledgeable about rugby league in all its patterns. I didn't bear him any resentment and was quite happy with my busy lot in other spheres. Anyway, the BBC didn't want a standard-English-speaking commentator with a neutral accent. They wanted a commentator who fitted the image of rugby league: a quirky Northern game administered by blunt-spoken and cloth-capped Cumbrians, Lancashire lads and Yorkshire tykes. Eddie fitted that stereotype perfectly.'

Once back on *Grandstand*, though, Waring did continue to help Keith Macklin – and others – in their careers. 'I was young and inexperienced then, but for a time, at Eddie's instigation I gather, I was given the chance to conduct live Challenge Cup-final interviews on the Wembley pitch,' Macklin goes on. 'I remember standing next to Derek Turner in 1960 as Wakefield were waiting to go up for their medals, and Eddie cueing me in for a live interview with the winning skipper. I was grateful for that. Eddie got some justified criticism, but he also received an awful lot of totally unjustified criticism. He was a total original. People could mimic him, but they could never get inside his voice and his personality. He was a strange mixture of deeply knowledgeable fan and comic turn, who, more often than not, used the English language like Les Dawson played the piano. Like most television personalities, he enjoyed his fame and milked that for all it was worth. But underneath was a deep love and loyalty to the game of rugby league.'

* * *

Away from the microphone, meanwhile, thanks to his various career balancing acts, for Eddie Waring there remained the possibility of a political upset around every corner. In the months before *Grandstand* began, the BBC's assistant head of television outside broadcasts, Alan Chivers, wrote to Eddie – c/o the Queens Hotel, Leeds – to chastise him about a story in the *Sunday Pictorial* in which he had exclusively revealed that the Corporation was about to resume its televising of the Challenge Cup final. The revelation had caused both the BBC and the RFL considerable embarrassment, Chivers wrote, before adding that 'with a less co-operative body than the Rugby League, we might have lost this contract'.

Mortified, Waring sent back a three-page letter of explanation, which began:

Let me first of all make it clear that my knowledge that the Rugby League Cup final was likely to be Televised came from Rugby League sources, not from the BBC. Furthermore because of my attachment and association with the BBC, I kept the publicity about the Televising of the final back from appearing in newspapers. In October 1957, it was decided subject to certain conditions to Televise the Final. This decision was made at a meeting of the sub-committee concerned. I knew immediately of this. In fact I informed Mr Dimmock through our Manchester office of this RL decision. On December 21st 1957, it was agreed that the fee for Televising the final be £2000.

Along with pledging his care and discretion at all times, Waring then goes on to outline how this information was contained in the Council's own minutes – 'available to many people' – and add that the story was about to be broken by other newspapers anyway.

As the years progressed, the issue of verbal credits on the BBC for the *Sunday Mirror* would provide another tricky roadbump although, as usual, Eddie's own diplomatic intervention settled the matter quite amicably.[14]

On the whole, however, as his continued employment on *Grandstand* suggests, Eddie Waring was never long out of favour with the BBC top brass. In May 1958, Paul Fox wrote to the BBC's man in Australia, James Mudie, asking him to assist the touring Eddie Waring in his search for stories that might suit *Sportsview*. The BBC, Fox said, was interested in film coverage of all three Australia–Great Britain Tests but would only show the third game if the series remained to be won – a stipulation it is hard to see the Corporation imposing upon any other major British sport. Mainly, though, Fox was interested in Eddie being able to provide a preview of the MCC cricket tour – preferably including an interview with Don Bradman – material on 'any new Aussie cricketing sensations', a preview of the Empire Games and anything about tennis. 'Perhaps,' he asked, 'you'd be kind enough to put Eddie in touch with whoever runs these things at A.B.C.'[15] And even when Waring's long-term BBC contract was not renewed upon its expiry in 1960, as a result of the slow-burning demise of *Sport in the North* and the reduction of Eddie's contributions to the same, leaving him once again engaged on an ad hoc basis, a number of those in power at the Corporation were far from comfortable at that unsatisfactory turn of events.

Largely at the behest of Paul Fox, it seems, Eddie's lost earnings were to be topped up by a 'consultation fee', on the basis that, as one North Region programme executive put it, 'his activities on our behalf behind the scenes had to be recognised'. In short, if the BBC's 'Mr Fix-It' was to be kept sweet, his reduction of income and lack of contractual security would have to be compensated for in some other way. The arrangement, once it was noticed by the bean counters in BBC accounts, both rattled a few financial cages and produced a flurry of internal correspondence, which often referred to Eddie's importance to the BBC in the most explicit terms. The consultation fee, said one such memo, was simply a means of retaining 'Waring's services over and above any commentating he might do for Rugby League, as a contact man, fixer and observer of inside and advance information'.[16]

Eddie's own reaction to the lack of a fixed contract – or, perhaps, given his usual fairly relaxed attitude towards all things monetary, that of his 'business manager' Mary – was to find himself an agent who could undertake all the sensitive financial manoeuvring on his behalf. Acting as his agent from September 1962 was London-based Bagenal Harvey, whose clients also included Colin Cowdrey, Fred Trueman and Bobby Charlton. Again, the move did not go down well with some at the BBC. One such individual, the organiser of television outside broadcasts, Jack Oaten, declared himself dismayed and branded Harvey's organisation, which also represented Frank Bough, David Coleman and the legendary cricket commentator John Arlott, a 'circus'. The most ominous prospect of all, however, was that with 'Mr Ten Per Cent' now pulling his strings, Waring might yet be persuaded to jump ship to ITV. Oaten claimed Eddie had already been approached by David Southwood of independent TV company ABC but had turned the offer down flat. 'Southwood might now try through Harvey,' he worried.

Around seven years old and growing fast, Independent Television did have increasingly bold plans for the British regions and, for a short while at least, courted rugby league accordingly. Most innovatively, ITV in the North had begun to broadcast amateur Under-17 and Under-19 matches every Sunday lunchtime, and, remarkably, the commentator-in-chief was none other than the RFL secretary Bill Fallowfield. This, at least, allowed Jack Oaten to console himself with the thought that

> Waring and Fallowfield now seem to be daggers drawn; that ABC use Fallowfield and, we believe, it is due to him that they got some Rugby League; that Waring is not popular with the R.L. people as a commentator because they do not like his peculiar humour. On the other hand most of us believe that R.L. would have no public at all in the South and Wales except for the fun of listening to Waring's cracks![17]

In hindsight, Oaten had nothing to worry about. Eddie Waring's loyalty to the BBC was absolute, and with the birth of Yorkshire Television in 1968, he went so far as to provide Paul Fox – now no longer a mere head of sport but the controller of BBC1 – with a personal report on the fledgling organisation's first faltering steps.

'Yorkshire Television are having many problems and as yet have not got off the ground,' Waring wrote.

> They recently entertained the heads of other commercial companies. They were unable to do this in their own buildings so hurriedly had to try and arrange a special banquet at the Queens Hotel, Leeds. This was not possible and they had to take a nearby clothing factory building to put on the facilities for the meeting.

After describing how the new television service was not at all popular with the locals, Waring added: 'They are to make a special attack on sport, I shall be reporting details to Bryan Cowgill on this.'

In any case, if the employment of Bagenal Harvey was intended to railroad the BBC into coming up with a new, longer-term offer as per Waring's original contract, it worked. Even though Harry Middleton, the head of outside broadcasts, initially continued to resist pressure exerted internally at the BBC by the likes of *Sportsview* editor Ronnie Noble, implicitly accepting Oaten's argument that for ITV to drop Bill Fallowfield as its commentator would be political suicide – particularly so, Middleton said, because 'Waring is not well thought of by the Rugby League who consider that he guys their game in his commentaries' – it wasn't long before he was persuaded to change his mind.

The U-turn, when it came, was the result of a direct offer of employment from commercial television. 'Waring has been, and is being, a very loyal servant to the BBC,' Ronnie Noble had written in November 1962, to little effect.

> Although there may be no danger of his going to the opposition, I would have thought that this loyalty would at least have justified the security of a minimum earning in the next 12 months. Apart from being a good comedian, why is he receiving different treatment to the rest of our commentators?

Some six months later, with Harvey having clearly been active in the interim, another internal memo, from Bryan Cowgill this time, had a more pragmatic impact entirely. Commercial television, Cowgill said, would continue to cover rugby league games next season, in competition with *Grandstand*, and, what's more, they wanted Eddie to front the show. The upshot was a two-year deal, dependent on the BBC actually winning the rugby league contract, which embraced all of Waring's current BBC activities, such as: 'live or filmed commentary of Rugby League matches; interviews; advisory work on the selection of matches; appearance for sports programmes, either in the North Region or for network, and any work he may be able to do in contacting personalities to take part in those programmes'.[18]

Whatever Bagenal Harvey's own role in sealing the deal, he continued to push his client's financial cause aggressively. In December 1965, Peter Dimmock penned an internal BBC memo advising that Waring was again under 'slight pressure' from ITV to leave when his current contract expired in May 1966. The response from BBC2 controller David Attenborough was: 'I intend at the moment to repeat our RL relays in Autumn 1966. Thus I have no hesitation in supporting the increase of Waring's guaranteed fee that you suggest.'[19] Eddie didn't go, of course, and by December 1968, he was putting pen to paper on a four-year contract, commencing 1 July 1969. Yet come February, Eddie Waring and Bagenal Harvey had gone their separate ways.

The crux of the split seems to have resided in Eddie's fear that while, thus far, Harvey's constant badgering of the BBC had been financially beneficial, it might also, one day, prove counter-productive. As correspondence between the pair confirms, the agent was not best pleased at this turn of events, but Eddie valued his ties with the BBC, and in his eyes that relationship still had a considerable distance to go. Indeed, several of the Corporation's most influential figures were now firm friends. He was godfather to Bryan Cowgill's children, for example, while, as Ray Lakeland explains, 'There was a friendship outside of work too. Eddie and

Mary used to come to our home in Cheshire, and he would sing songs at the piano with my wife, Muriel.' The Warings weren't completely done with agents – from April 1969, the Johnnie Riscoe Agency would look after Eddie's 'showbiz' activities. But when it came to rugby league, all BBC correspondence would henceforth be sent directly to Bramhope, allowing Eddie and Mary to negotiate all future contracts personally.[20]

* * *

Although the BBC expected Eddie Waring to be present before and throughout each individual match, more often than not his live input took the form of second-half commentary only. In fact, with the exception of Cup finals and the occasional Test match, the BBC didn't begin showing rugby league games in full as a matter of course until 1985, when, impressed by that year's cracking final between Wigan and Hull, the Corporation belatedly realised what a colourful sporting spectacle a rugby league match in its entirety could be.

ITV viewers, meanwhile, had been awakened to that fact as long ago as 1969, when the newly launched Yorkshire Television began to broadcast Australian games throughout the summer. According to Harry Edgar's *Rugby League Journal*, the BBC were not best pleased at this turn of events and invoked their monopoly contract with the RFL. Writing in 2005, Edgar noted that:

> Many British followers (cynics that we were!) hinted that the BBC's stance in trying to stop coverage of a competition that was not part of their agreement and shown at a time of year when they had no interest in broadcasting any Rugby League, might have been influenced by the fact that the Australian television coverage presented the game in a totally different light to the image the BBC themselves seemed intent on cultivating and maintaining.[21]

To be fair to the BBC, however, it had some four years earlier introduced a revolutionary new Tuesday-night rugby league programme of its own. From its birth in 1965 and throughout a subsequent 15-year run, the BBC2 Floodlit Trophy would not only double the amount of rugby league shown by the national broadcaster, drawing midweek viewing figures of around 700,000 as opposed to an average Saturday-afternoon audience of some 3.6 million, it would play a major part in transforming the game of rugby league itself.[22]

Again, other than a brief highlights round-up, only the second half of matches was shown, leaving the dangerous possibility that a game could be as good as over by the time Eddie Waring got to the microphone. Ray Lakeland, who produced the Floodlit Trophy broadcasts along with his *Grandstand* duties before relinquishing the job to Nick Hunter upon his retirement, recalls how the concept came into being. 'I was having a chat after one match with the secretary of St Helens,' he says. 'He was telling me that, nowadays, the club had floodlights. Later, I found out that one or two more teams had floodlights too. So I went down and sold the idea to David Attenborough, who was controller of BBC2 at the time. I sold him the Floodlit Trophy, as well as a bit of crown green bowling.' In fact, Bradford and Leigh were rugby league's earliest floodlight pioneers, and during that first year of the BBC2 competition, only eight clubs took part.

More relevant to the BBC, perhaps, was the fact that BBC2 itself had only been in existence for just over a year. In that regard, such a competition would be a perfect guinea pig upon which to test its own outside-broadcast operation. Yet, whatever the impetus, there is no doubt that the Floodlit Trophy proved to be a hugely significant development. In October 1966, the competition provided an opportunity to replace the current unlimited tackle system with a new four-tackle rule, intended to encourage livelier games through a more even spread of possession. So well received was the experiment that, just a few weeks later, four tackles became the norm across every competition until, in 1972, that system too was superseded by the six-tackle rule that remains in place to this day. Over the next two years, a further seventeen clubs had floodlights installed so that they too could get a slice of what was swiftly proving to be a very attractive cake.

For Eddie Waring, the birth of the Floodlit Trophy meant that he now came under the gaze of the rugby league public around twice as often as he did before. Writing in the now-defunct *John Player Yearbook* in 1973, he noted:

> Many followers of sport, both men and women, would like to be a commentator of some sort, and a surprising number of people write to me asking how they should go about [it]. One attribute is necessary as far as Rugby League and the North is concerned – you must have a sense of humour of some sort.

The advent of colour television, too, brought as many technological problems as it solved. 'The popular BBC2 Floodlit series is an expensive project for which special lighting [has] to be mounted,' Eddie went on to explain.

> No club in the Rugby League has lights strong enough to take the amount of power required for colour cameras. That is why some Saturday Rugby League games necessitated a 2.15 p.m. kick-off. This factor brought criticism and comment, but it affected both Rugby Union and Rugby League coverage and was due solely to the light.[23]

Whether working on *Grandstand*, the Floodlit Trophy or indeed the coverage that, later in the 1960s, would become a staple ingredient of Wednesday night's *Sportsnight with Coleman*, it must have seemed to Eddie, and to the rest of the BBC outside-broadcasting team, as if the critics weren't happy unless they were finding some reason or other to put the boot in. As long ago as 1959, shortly after the initial contract was signed allowing the BBC to televise regular rugby league matches on *Grandstand*, Ray Lakeland wrote in issue one of the *Eddie Waring Annual* that:

It is always exciting from a producer's point of view to televise a new sport – new, that is, to the viewers. Sometimes we are accused of pandering to the expert and being too technical in the treatment of the sport – other times we are accused of concentrating too much on the spectacle and not enough on the finer points of the game. Fortunately, these two criticisms tend to cancel themselves out and it seems to be true to say that more people are watching Rugby League both at home and on the grounds.

Lakeland continued: 'It will probably surprise you to know that 28 people are directly involved in televising a match.' These included a producer, commentator, stage manager and secretary, plus sixteen engineers and a team made up of three cameramen, a sound supervisor, an assistant, technicians and riggers. 'In addition,' said Lakeland,

eight microwave engineers control the links. These men are usually on each hill top where a microwave is needed. The producer does his work from a 'scanner', which is a van away from the actual site of the broadcast. From this van he controls the camera men on the site and the commentator.

Contrast that situation with today, when, as the outside-broadcast chief of satellite channel Sky Sports' rugby league coverage, Chris Sandeman, reveals, matters are considerably more hi-tech. 'We have seventeen cameras covering the matches, of which three do the studio, two the dressing-rooms and the rest are on the pitch,' Sandeman points out. 'Our scanner van has a footprint on the ground of about six metres, when extended, and around seventeen people work in there during the game. At the commentary position – or gantry – we have three cameras with three camera operators, and four commentators or summarisers in comparison with Eddie Waring's one. There is a fifth person there too – Ian Proctor, our researcher, who talks to whoever is describing the game and updates them on relevant statistics. Two more people input player details and a couple of guys operate the sound. On Grand Final day, I have 20 people on the main camera position; I would have 22, but Manchester United won't let me put any more people up there. All in all, there are several million pounds' worth of trucks and equipment, goodness knows how many miles of cable and 75 people working on each broadcast. The BBC, back then, would not have dreamed of such a thing.'[24]

* * *

Given the relatively basic conditions in which he discharged his duties, then, it ought to be no great surprise that player identification was not one of Eddie Waring's strong points, particularly as the years began to catch up with him. As anyone who has ever commentated on so much as five minutes of a rugby league match would confirm, instantaneously summing up this fast and furious sport can be a daunting task indeed, and a challenge frequently underappreciated by those who have never stood in that particular firing line themselves.

'Eddie's style changed over time and he became, in his later years, a caricature of what he used to be,' says Martyn Sadler, the editor of the weekly trade paper *League Express*. 'But in his earlier days he was an incredibly fluent and good commentator. Often, he had no co-commentator, no instant replays and just the odd camera covering the action, yet he was able to create an incredible atmosphere. In those days, Eddie Waring used language quite precisely and had certain things going for him. To start with, he understood the game thoroughly. He understood its tactics and personalities and brought them to life. He also had a tremendous sense of humour and a wonderful way of defusing tension, meaning he could interject in the duller parts of a game and make you smile. That's a valid thing to be able to do.'[25]

Certainly, when contrasted with the levels of technological support available to modern-day commentators such as Sky's Eddie Hemmings or the man who eventually replaced Waring on *Grandstand*, Ray French, Uncle Eddie's willing little team of helpers begin to look like something out of an Ealing comedy. The first time Dave 'Nosey' Parker and Eddie worked together on the Floodlit Trophy for example, at Headingley in the 1960s, the first-named gentleman remembers that he 'realised that the windows in the Perspex box in the South Stand there were scratched and dirty. So, having worked in the sheet-metal industry and not being afraid of heights, the first thing I did was clamber outside onto the roof where, to calls of "Fall, you bastard", I cleaned his windows with a couple of hankies. During the commentary, I realised that he could probably do with a bit of assistance, so I pointed things out and wrote quick notes as the game went along, shoving them in front of him. After that, he asked if I'd like to help him out on a regular basis. In those days, we were doing over 40 matches a year.'

And though the personnel changed down the years, the system remained pretty much the same. 'When I joined up, we had a chappie called Bill Smith on the touchline,' Parker continues. 'He was a former player at Bradford and backroom boy. Everybody used to class me and Bill as Eddie Waring's stringers, which is a posh word for lackey. But we weren't bothered, because we were doing something we liked doing and rugby league was our life. We used to talk to Bill over an old cranking telephone. We had no walkie-talkies, or Stornos as they call them now, just the phone. You'd pick up the receiver and talk away. I used to make a note of leading try-scorers, basic stats and things and present them to Eddie. I'd even send him some stuff in the post in advance. I did my utmost for him. As I got to know more, I'd pull his headphones back and whisper into his ear. He was good at taking it all in as he was going along. I would stick notices written in big felt-tip pen up on the windows all around. It wasn't that Eddie had frailties or wasn't up to the job, not at all. Compared to reporting on soccer, rugby league is so quick. Most commentators have statisticians now, and Eddie needed that assistance back then too. As the sport moved on a bit and new players came in as he grew older, he needed a bit more help. All the way through, if you thought of something that was good to use, we'd work it in.'

A valuable source of such information was the Carnforth shopkeeper Norman Graveson, eventually brought into the team as a replacement for Bill Smith. 'I brought in Norman, who was a director at Barrow,' Parker continues. 'He used to slip me bits of news for Eddie's newspaper column. When he joined us on the BBC, Norman came onto the bench instead of Bill. He was a shopkeeper by trade, but he had a talent for stats and was great for Eddie. Norman had lost a leg in the war and eventually it became a bit hard on the bench for him, so we swapped over. Norman went upstairs and I went down to the touchline. That's how it stayed until Eddie finished with the BBC.' Norman Graveson had his other uses too. Whenever the commentary team ran out of drawing pins, he would simply roll up his trousers and remove the one holding up the sock on his wooden leg.

Eddie's match-day routines would become the stuff of legend. Having more often than not arrived at the stadium by taxi, the royal procession would wend its way through the crowds with the bag-carrying BBC floor manager Dennis Montague in tow, amongst others. Once settled at his commentary position, Eddie would open his customary bag of fruit, intended to lubricate his vocal chords. 'He was a magnetic personality,' says Dave Parker. 'People liked to be seen with Eddie and talk to him. At Odsal, for example, you could set off from the dressing-rooms at the top and take the same walk as the players through the crowd, and down to the commentary position in the speedway hut. On the way down, there would be a programme seller, a half-time draw seller and a Bradford *Telegraph & Argus* seller. They'd say, "Will you be having one, Mr Waring?" and Eddie would say, "Yes, see to him, David." You'd get to the bottom and you had forked out a quid on all three. He'd say, "Put it down on your expenses," but we didn't get expenses, we just got a set fee from the BBC. There were lots of times when you'd do something for Eddie and get into a bit of a hole by doing it.'

Perhaps the venue where this sense of theatricality was most on show, however, was Headingley. For it was there, smack in the middle of the ground's notoriously riotous South Stand, that before every televised game Waring and the team would ascend a vertical steel spiral staircase: a feat, Eddie joked, that was like 'climbing the steep steps to heaven (to quote the hymn "midst toil, peril and pain . . .")'.[26] And, given the foresight of the Leeds board in installing undersoil heating, guaranteeing that more televised games were staged at Headingley than just about anywhere else, it was a trip he would undertake with great regularity.

In 1971, in the *Radio Times*, Michael Wale gave his readers an insight into this process when he coat-tailed the great man during a Tuesday-night Leeds versus Hull Kingston Rovers BBC2 Floodlit Trophy game. After a quick stop-off at the Queens to check for messages, writes Wale,

> [Waring] arrives a good hour-and-a-half before the game. He likes to have an hour to himself before the kick-off. As soon as we arrive, he sends his bag up to the commentary point and walks briskly to the Leeds boardroom, where on a white-clothed table the programmes are neatly arranged in the shape of a V. The previous night he had done his homework about the teams and he spends his time now sipping a bitter lemon and reading the evening papers to glean further information. Then it's time to climb the precarious metal ladder straight up into the night to the commentary point on the roof over the terracing. It's such a shock to the system that several players and officials have declined the climb to be interviewed. He is to commentate on the second half. It is bitterly cold and he eats grapes and has a warming cup of coffee. Then he is on the air. He has wound a scarf around his neck and put another coat over his knees.[27]

* * *

There are sports commentators and sports commentators; and then there is Eddie Waring. Just how does a writer get that extraordinary voice down on the page? Words like 'unique' and 'peculiar' scarcely do it justice, and though many a journalist has tried down the years, most have failed to get anywhere close to capturing its idiosyncratic rhythms.

Using varying degrees of creativity, the majority of feature writers have charted a path between imagination and cliché, with results guaranteed to raise the hackles of the most thick-skinned northern Englander. Writing in the *Daily Express*, for example, Geoffrey Mather declared: 'To the five basic vowel sounds of the English language, Mr Edward Marsden Waring has added several more of his own choosing,' before adding, 'they all trip readily from his lips equipped with tiny clogs.'[28] Arthur Hopcraft, in the *Sunday Times Magazine*, heard Eddie's dulcet Yorkshire tones as a 'West Riding coarse weave, flecked with strands of pulpit oratory, alternately emphatic and neglectful with aspirates, a thing of substance and attraction'. In the *Express & Star*, Gerry Anderson said that while Eddie had dismantled the English language into a large heap of syllables, 'he has rebuilt it nearer to the heart's desire, screwing the pieces together into memorable Meccano phrases, and despatching kangaroo sentences that flow and pounce and lurch'. Anderson even attempted a written impersonation: 'Well . . . er . . . here we are in, ahaa, LEEDS, in the Queens Hotel, which is oop and under from the . . . er . . . RAILway Station . . . so to speak.'[29]

For this writer, while there is something in all of the above, it is *The Listener* columnist Jack Waterman who comes closest to finding the Eddie Waring so often lost in translation. Weighing up the Waring style, Waterman decided that 'there is a cartoon element . . . accentuated by the indefatigable bounce of the delivery, and the voice – with the random harvest of aitches and odd mispronunciations – that sounds like a good, earthy turn from the old Argyll, Birkenhead, trying to be slightly pound-noteish'.[30]

And there the thing is in a nutshell. For, whatever else it is, Eddie Waring's accent is by no means your traditionally flat and dour West Yorkshire monotone. In and amidst all those unexpected verbal tics, mixed metaphors and offbeat nuances, lurching along as if pitched on the waves of a faulty tuning fork, tonsils clanging back and forth like the clapper on an old chapel bell, is the unmistakable twang of social aspiration. This is a voice clad in its Sunday best. It rises and falls like the Dewsbury hills of Eddie's boyhood. Its tones are those of a run out to Ilkley or Harrogate and afternoon eclairs in Betty's tea shop, of excitable, yapping little Yorkshire terriers and what Alan Bennett's class-conscious 'mam' might well have described as having 'a bit too much off'. It is the heightened and almost feminine sound of essential decency, dignity and harmless decorum, and of a perhaps subconscious yearning for escape.

Maybe that's why all those middle-aged ladies in Brighton and Basingstoke loved Eddie so much. Rare was the newspaper feature that did not, in its opening few paragraphs, allude to Eddie Waring's appeal in areas of British society where such a rough, tough activity as rugby league might not more widely be expected to thrive. 'Little old ladies who hear his TV commentaries have found a corner of life they never knew existed,' wrote Geoffrey Mather in 1979. In 1967, meanwhile, the *Daily Mail* writer Peter Black reported that:

> A viewer once rebuked him – 'you talk too posh' – but most of his letters are friendly, a surprising number from Southern ladies who confide secret yearnings – to have played in Rugby League. 'They mostly want to be forwards, I don't know why.'

Arthur Hopcraft thought that Eddie's vocal talents

> would be adequate for a racecourse bookie, polished up a bit for the silver ring, or for drowning the din at one of our more violent secondary mods. It speaks of virility to middle-aged mums in the Home Counties and suggests elocution lessons to the uncompromising kind of Yorkshiremen who talk about making money as 'getting some wool to yer back'.

Those closer to Eddie, meanwhile, offer a more prosaic insight. 'This "arrrrr" business, was just Eddie's way of giving himself time to think, linking players and so on,' says Dave Parker. 'There might be a new face on the field, and that's where I and, later, Norman came in. As well as watching the game live, Eddie had two monitors and in that second of looking up he might miss something.' Ray Lakeland adds: 'With the best will in the world, dark nights in the wintry north of England don't always make for the best black-and-white television pictures, so Eddie's coverage made a big difference to the popularity of the Floodlit Trophy. As a team, we tended to keep it light. If the match was getting dull, I'd say to him, "We'd better sharpen it up a bit." I would accelerate the cutting and he would speed up his commentary.'

Plus, of course, there was Eddie's tendency to favour an individual's quirky characteristics over descriptions of play. He christened the referee Eric Clay 'Sergeant Major'. He publicised Keith Hepworth's apparent predilection for pigeon fancying. And if it wasn't he who branded diminutive Hull KR scrum-half Roger Millward 'Roger the Dodger', then he certainly became the commentator most associated with doing so.

As Millward himself put it in his 2005 autobiography, *Roger*:

> Eddie in most people's eyes is the man who christened me 'Roger the Dodger' when commentating for the BBC during my early appearances for Castleford. I have got no reason to dispute the fact, but of course just about every other newspaper and TV reporter soon used it, so there was always a question mark against who actually said it first. But I am happy to think it was Eddie. He did as much as anyone to promote my career.[31]

'Eddie enjoyed making personalities of the players,' confirms Dave Parker. 'It was an example of him doing his homework on a game that was, in those days, very much part time. The players were miners, policemen, market traders and so on. One story concerned the mother of Jack Gamble, who played for Castleford and later Halifax. She was a market trader and Jackie used to help her out on the stall. But she was also a clairvoyant who held seances. She would warn Jackie, "The moon's in this quarter, the tea leaves are there." He would then ring Cas or Halifax and tell them he wasn't playing that weekend. That's where Eddie's phrase "the moon men from Castleford" came in. Those tales were Eddie's form of stats.'

Another player championed by Eddie, and whose image appeared on the back cover of his book *Eddie Waring on Rugby League*, was Allan Agar, who, as a player, won the Challenge Cup with Hull Kingston Rovers in 1980 and coached Featherstone to Wembley success over Hull FC in 1983. 'I met Eddie three or four times and did an interview with him after the 1980 Challenge Cup final,' Agar recalls. 'Eddie made you welcome, he was a great bloke and he loved the game. There were people who knocked him, but how people can criticise a guy who gave so much to the sport is beyond me. He was popular with the players because he would give his time up for them and spoke well of them in commentary. To Eddie, if they took to the rugby league field they were heroes.'[32]

That said, Dave Parker points out how the storytelling approach could have its problems too. 'Once,' he says, 'we got into trouble with the father of Halifax captain Gordon Baker, a well-known band leader named "Bunny" Baker who led the backing band on ITV's *Junior Showtime*. Bunny came to a Floodlit match at Thrum Hall and he had a monkey on his shoulder. We got the cameras to pan onto him and Eddie said, "There's Bunny Baker from *Junior Showtime*, the father of Gordon, and he's got a monkey on his back." Well, we got all sorts of complaints. Apparently, in those days, to have a monkey on your back was an American term for being a drug user.'

One rugby league star whose personality needed little in the way of embellishment, on or off the field, was Alex Murphy. One of several coaches, administrators and players who at various stages and upon Waring's recommendation found extra work as rugby league summarisers (including Eric Ashton and the Welsh international David Watkins), Murphy sat next to Eddie in the commentary box for over a decade. Indeed, he quite quickly earned a reputation for having a colourful way with language himself: 'There's no excuse for pace,' he once memorably told the nation.

Today, Murphy insists: 'People took Eddie the wrong way. He would never have described himself as the best commentator in the world, but he wanted people to watch rugby league outside the chosen few. Eddie didn't take the game too seriously and that meant he was accused of making the game a laughing stock. I don't think he did. He was too proud of rugby league to do that. I tell you what he did make it, though: he made it a household name.'

Although Waring's comical approach was enjoyed greatly by viewers who knew little of the code's tactical intricacies – i.e. well over half the population – increasingly, many in his Northern homelands took his wisecracks as a personal affront. Having passed his lips, such straightforward descriptive terms as the now immortal to the point of cliché 'up and under', a phrase already in use to describe a lofty kick to the skies by the time Eddie made it his own, were reinvented as national catchphrases. He became synonymous with all manner of other quirky sayings too. Although doubtless apocryphal in some cases, they included: 'He's limping – so he must be all right'; 'Well, well, well. What's a Frenchman without his trousers'; the quaintly philosophical 'You'd never think these lads will be buying each other pints in 15 minutes'; and, referring to a player in a two-man tackle, 'Eeeh . . . look at this. Which half do you want?' He even originated the odd catchphrase himself, most notably 'early bath', the fabled place to which players were sent in disgrace after high tackles or all-in brawls, preceded no doubt, by another of Eddie's famous quips: 'They've got to keep their hands warm somehow.'

In fact, Waring's sardonic and almost casual treatment of violence, such a paradox in a sport that otherwise prides itself on attracting family audiences, might be seen as one more attractive and comforting ingredient where his own widespread popularity is concerned. Certainly for those of a more reserved disposition, perhaps more used to nibbling on cucumber and watercress sandwiches than incinerating their tongues on Wigan meat pies, without the intervention of friendly, avuncular Eddie to make light of the situation, the sight of 26 mud-spattered behemoths knocking the seven colours of nutty slack out of one another might well have appeared alien and even a little frightening. 'From Hull in the east to Barrow in the west lies the land of rough, tough, northern acres where the brutal and barbaric (as opposed to Barbarian) sport of Rugby League football is licensed, practiced, and made perfect to the last thick ear and gobful of broken teeth,' wrote Jack Waterman, with tongue only partially in cheek, in 1975.

> No primaeval ooze could have harboured creatures of a more terrifying aspect than that of the muscle-bound, professional heavies who slosh their way off the pitches at Widnes, St Helens, Salford, Hunslet and Rochdale in drizzle all one with industrial murk: maimed, perhaps, but still alive with animal glory and pungent with the reek of ammonia, phials, liniment and steam off the scrum.[33]

As described by Eddie, any such dark and uncivilised threat was neutralised completely, replaced by a less foreboding vision of Northern masculinity. In reaction to one particularly messy brawl, for example, he is said to have burst into a stirring rendition of 'Fight the Good Fight'. As Geoffrey Mather put it: 'When Eddie Waring referred to mayhem going on in deep mud, he was merely reflecting for disbelieving southerners what the north accepts as natural.'[34]

'Rugby League is essentially a game which arouses violent emotions . . . if I'm not stirring up those emotions myself I'm not doing my job properly, am I?' asked Eddie himself in 1968.[35] And as early as 1947, while on the Indomitables tour, he related a saga of one particularly fiery off-field encounter in terms that were hardly censorious. 'Sitting near me was a very loudmouthed Aussie – and they can be very loudmouthed if they want to – who had doubted the legitimacy of almost every member of the English team,' he wrote, after describing how a British ship had docked at Newcastle, NSW, allowing everyone on board to come and watch the game.

Now one British sailor did not like this so he quietly told this Aussie supporter to keep quiet. It had no effect, nor had a second censure. At the third attempt, this laddie thought it was time for action, so without further ado he administered a beautiful uppercut that placed the spectator on his back, out to the wide. Few people saw it done, it was so neat and effective, but the English team had no further trouble from this particular individual.[36]

Or, to put it another way, how about the jacket notes on Waring's 1969 book *The Great Ones*?

It's as North as Hot Pot and Yorkshire Pudding . . . It's as tough as teak . . . It's Rugby League – a man's game if ever there was one. Gentlemen have played Rugby League. Gentlemen still do. But the hard core of Rugby League players, with their cauliflower ears, their broken noses, their busted and bruised bones, would far rather be called, to use a three letter word, MEN. There is nothing gentle about Rugby League! It's a down-to-earth game played by down-to-earth people. Good people. Solid people. To use that word again, MEN. From the pits, from factory floors, Rugby League players emerge each Saturday afternoon to provide entertainment and excitement to a critical public. To the men – and women – of the North, Rugby League is more than a game, it is a way of life.[37]

Eight

SEND IN THE CLOWNS

'That's St Helens' Frankie Barrow tackling Leigh's
Leatherbarrow . . . no relation.'

If Watersplash was the zenith of Eddie Waring's rugby league
broadcasting career, there is little doubt about its nadir. It came
during a televised Challenge Cup first-round tie between Leeds
and Halifax, on Saturday, 11 February 1978, when a particularly
tenacious dog invaded the Headingley pitch.

Ironically, owing to the freezing winter conditions, the Leeds
fixture was the only rugby league game played that weekend.
Even more ironically, Leeds greyhound track was frozen off
too. And, when the cheeky black-and-white collie made its first
incursion into the proceedings, most of those present – doubtless
relieved that the game was being played at all – merely saw its
appearance as a bit of a giggle. Then, after being chased away from
the playing area, the dog came back. Once again it was removed,
once again it returned. And again. And again. And again. And
not only did the hound wish to scamper about on the grass, it
seemed to want to take part in the match too. Players, in the
midst of an attack, were forced to sidestep the stubborn mutt as
it snapped at their heels. In fact, wrote Raymond Fletcher in the
following Monday's *Yorkshire Post*, 'Leeds [were more] worried
by the dog which roamed the pitch for the entire match than
by any Halifax player.'

Even then, the matter might well have been quickly forgotten about had the *Grandstand* outside-broadcast team not decided to get in on the comedy act themselves. For sure, it is difficult to see how their cameras could have ignored the intruder entirely, but the relish with which the producers fell upon the incident simply confirmed in the minds of many what they had suspected all along: the BBC thought rugby league was a joke. Using on-screen graphics to christen the hound 'K-9', in reference to the robotic dog currently accompanying the science-fiction timelord Doctor Who, no opportunity was missed to cut away from the sporting action and make light of this peripheral sideshow. Players valiantly giving their all became little more than a support act – an attitude of the utmost disrespect according to those for whom the game meant everything. Yes, professional sport was supposed to be fun. But, as this incident symbolised absolutely, where rugby league was concerned, for reasons best known to themselves, the BBC seemed more often inclined towards frivolity. Stuck in the middle as usual, with a brief to supply words to the pictures on his monitor, was everyone's favourite Aunt Sally, 'Uncle' Eddie Waring.

'Dog set back game's image three years', ran the headline above Raymond Fletcher's news report in the *Yorkshire Post*, in which the then Rugby League chairman Harry Womersley agreed that the matter had reduced the game to the level of farce. 'The referee and the home club could be reprimanded,' he said, 'if it is felt they are to blame.' For his part, Fletcher defended the match official, Mr Ken Spencer of Warrington, stating that 'he did send off the canine three times, but each time it returned. Short of ordering it to be shot, what else could he have done? On a day when referees' match fees were raised £1 to a paltry £15 it is ridiculous to expect him to be a dog-catcher as well.'

When asked whether the police ought to be responsible in cases like this, Mr Spencer himself offered the suggestion that 'Once I had got it off the field somebody should have taken it outside the ground. I understand a police constable did make some effort to get the dog but he was told by a superior officer that it was not his responsibility.'

Leeds chairman Jack Myerscough, meanwhile, 'particularly wanted the dog caught before the TV cameras were turned on for the second half. We had someone make a leash with boot laces and wanted the game stopped while the dog was rounded up. It would have been locked in the Pools office.'

In a back-page article marked 'Talking Point' in the same edition of the *Yorkshire Post*, Trevor Watson, who along with Raymond Fletcher had for so long assisted Eddie in his journalistic duties, assessed the implications of the debacle's effect upon television's watching millions. 'The constant appearance of a dog during the Leeds v Halifax RL Cup-tie may have provided light relief for television viewers who don't care how they obtain their amusement,' Watson wrote,

> but people with Rugby League at heart will question whether it was really so funny. The delight of the BBC at the intruder, even to the extent of showing an incident on national news at night, underlines the belief that TV still regards the professional game as a comic time-filler. Fortunately this was a tie when the outcome was decided from the early minutes but it could have been Leeds v St Helens with a good deal at stake and a frustrated player might well have lashed out with his boot to bring down the fury of a doting public.

He concluded: 'It is a pity that amid all the laughter a little more note was not taken of the fact that Rugby League had beaten the weather to provide a fixture when other sporting outfits had given up the ghost.'

Rather more vociferous in his condemnation was press officer David Howes, who, since his arrival at the RFL on a dream ticket with Bill Fallowfield's replacement David Oxley in 1974, had with great success set about trying to overturn more traditional representations of rugby league as a dour, post-industrial slugfest and drag the sport into the modern era. 'I watched the match and the dog's antics on TV until I could stand no more,' Howes told the *Yorkshire Post*.

It has taken us three years to present a better image of the game, but this held us up to ridicule. It was the sort of thing that might have been expected a few years ago but I thought we had got well past that stage. [The] BBC made the most of it by constantly referring to the dog and flashing its name on the screen as K-Nine. But I am not blaming them. It was a comedy situation that could not be ignored, just as the Sunday papers followed it up with pictures. It was a natural light-hearted story for the media. I am angry that it was allowed to happen.[1]

* * *

Only Eddie Waring himself could come close to challenging the dog on the Headingley pitch as a symbol of rugby league's dismay with the BBC. Yet in truth the situation had taken its most serious turn for the worse some eight years before, in 1970, when a Manchester-based management consultancy agency, John Caine Associates, was asked by the Rugby League to find ways of reversing the fall-off in attendances that had gripped the sport throughout the previous two decades.

The paper subsequently produced by that organisation in 1971 became known as the Caine Report, and within its pages, amidst an array of other recommendations that dealt mainly with the way in which the sport was being hampered by its then secretary Bill Fallowfield, sat another little landmine. The BBC's strategy of coverage, it said, was detrimental to the well-being of the 13-a-side code. Furthermore, the Corporation's choice of commentator – i.e. Eddie Waring – was 'unfortunate'. Eddie Waring might well be 'immensely entertaining and amusing, but the laughter is patronising, and lends support to the view of rugby league held by midland and southern watchers'. The report went on: 'The direction of the cameras and overall style of the programme is obviously designed to nourish the image of rugby which matches the commentary. We recommend urgent talks with the BBC.'[2] Although the statement in question took up just half a single page in a total of 30, in a sign of just how big a celebrity its target had become by now, the national newspapers fell on those particular findings with glee, especially when the Rugby League Council publicly promised to act upon the report's recommendations.

'Eh oop, lads. Eddie Waring, the Rugby commentator with an accent as flat as a Yorkshireman's cap, came in for a flying tackle himself yesterday,' declared *The Sun*. 'His dry sense of TV humour earned him a right Northern blasting – from a team of consultants called in by the Rugby League to improve the image of the game.' At the other end of the spectrum, Harold Mather in *The Guardian* revealed that:

> The report said there was 'little doubt that the game is widely held to be a sport for Northern heavyweights with a leaning towards brawn rather than brains, played against a background of pithead slag heaps in a steady drizzle and watched by a sparse, flat-capped crowd whose occasional comments are made in a nasal Eddie Waring accent.'

When contacted by *The Sun*, Eddie's own reaction was to deny having seen the report, 'but going on what people have told me, I might have to take action'.

Instantly, Waring's friends and colleagues at the BBC rushed to his aid. The following day, a press conference was convened in Manchester in which Eddie – accompanied by his solicitor friend and Queens cohort Ronnie Teeman and Derek Burrell-Davies, producer of that first-ever nationally televised match in Swinton and now head of the BBC's Northern network production centre – declared himself 'hurt and astounded' by 'the attack'. He said:

> If I have been criticised for mentioning cranes at Barrow-in-Furness, well, you have shipbuilding there, and if I see a picture

of those on the monitor, I shall talk about them, and I don't think this is deprecatory to Barrow. Neither is there anything wrong if I talk about trains going past with coal on them at Castleford. For many years there used to be a pit wheel behind the ground at Hunslet. I could not by any stretch of imagination convince people it was the big wheel at Blackpool. I tell the truth about a particular image. I am using the language of the north of England. The BBC would not be employing me if they did not think I was doing that.

Speaking both as 'an old friend' of Eddie's and a representative of the BBC, Burrell-Davies added that: 'Eddie Waring is not just a commentator. He is The Commentator, and the five million viewers prove it.'[3]

To strike a balance, a number of papers included an assortment of supportive Northern vox pops too. 'He knows what the game's all about,' Salford truck driver John Elliott told *The Sun*, 'and the women love him.' That was a point backed up by Manchester Post Office clerk Mrs Millicent Cleaver. 'I'm not a rugby fan,' she said, 'but I watch it when he's on.' In fact, up to and including the publication of the Caine Report, and beyond, it would be easy to overstate the extent to which Waring was disliked in the North. For although much of the published public comment relating to him leading up to this time and afterwards was predominantly negative, as ever, the feelings of the vast majority are not quite so easily gauged.

As Jack Williams has pointed out, while the Caine Report undeniably gave voice to the feelings of a substantial portion of the game, once published it also had the effect of inducing a closing of the ranks. Ken Ashton of the *Rugby Leaguer*, for instance, dismissed the report as 'waffle', calling it 'a nasty sideswipe at Eddie Waring', and 'inaccurate and unfair'. Ashton wrote, 'I don't like Eddie's style either – but he is and always has been a serious interpreter of the game as a player, manager, writer and broadcaster and it is unfair . . . to pillory him.'[4] Jack

Williams also points out how a report covering four weeks of the BBC2 Floodlit Trophy in 1971 'found that between 76 and 89 per cent of the viewing sample had thought Waring's commentary excellent', while Michael Groves in the *Yorkshire Evening Post* decided that Waring was 'not one of the "jamp orff" boys, but he is a straightforward commentator with a style of his own . . . who else could make a collision between, say, Batley and Rochdale Hornets, compulsive viewing on the TV screens of the benighted South?'

In grappling with this tricky North–South phenomenon in 2002, Williams wrote:

> Responses from rugby league to the Caine Report's criticisms of Waring indicate the sensitivity within the sport to criticisms from outside. Whilst some thought that Waring had belittled the game and caused it to be mocked by Southerners, there was clearly a feeling that rugby league had to protect one of its own against criticism from outside.

These twin impulses, Williams asserts, can be seen as two sides of the same coin, or as 'expressions of a Northern insecurity in the face of an imagined Southern sense of superiority. Defending the distinctiveness of rugby league and particularly its Northernness was defending Northern achievement and traditions.'[5] In other words, we can criticise ourselves – but outsiders better not start.

It is an attitude that remains prevalent in rugby league to this day although, in this instance, used to support an argument that ignores the fact that John Caine Associates were actually based in Manchester. Then again, the BBC had a reputation as a totem of the upper-middle-class Establishment and the compilers of the report presumably wore suits, and rugby league's grievances – real and imagined – were always rather more about class than geography.

* * *

It seems clear that although Eddie Waring was the butt of much personal and public criticism, that can be at least partially explained by the way in which: (a) his was the voice and face at the front of the BBC coverage; (b) brickbats are an inevitable occupational hazard for any well-known broadcaster; and (c) when gorging upon any story, the media – and particularly the tabloid media – prefers to take potshots at personalities rather than try to unravel the more complex and meaningful underlying issues.

As early as 1962, writing in the *Today* newspaper under the headline 'Would YOU Like to Kick Mr Waring?', Norman Smithson wrote: 'Either you love him or you hate him. But you can't ignore him. He is Eddie Waring, BBC television's most offbeat sports commentator.' Waring's comments, said Smithson, brought Eddie fan letters 'from all over country, along with lots of abuse . . . particularly from within the borders of Yorkshire, Lancashire and Cumberland – the home of Rugby League'. It was in these counties, the journalist noted, that

> many Rugby League fans would like to get Eddie Waring in a scrum – as the ball! One highly critical viewer told me that he switches off the sound when Rugby League is on and just watches the pictures. 'I just can't stand the voice,' says Tom Crossley, of Armley, Leeds, in blunt Yorkshire fashion.

In the *Sunday Times*, Arthur Hopcraft quoted one unnamed retired rugby league international forward thus: 'I think most people up north would cow-'eel Eddie. Round our way when he's on TV people switch the sound off and just watch the action. He's shouting and laughing away there. He makes it a circus level.' Yet it wasn't until the formation of an organisation called the 1895 Club in 1975 that discontent amongst the game's supporters firmed up into anything more substantial.

'Fans Slam TV Eddie', screamed one of many such reports in *The Sun*, after the 1895 Club, founded in St Helens, delivered a petition bearing 11,000 names – roughly a quarter of the total average paying rugby league audience per week – to the BBC on the morning of the 1976 Challenge Cup final. In fact, superficially at least, the thrust of the petition was more openly aimed at Waring's employers. It demanded greater pre-match coverage, a better results service and improvement in camera angles. It also appealed for fewer soccer scorelines to appear on screen during rugby league games and was intended, according to the 1895 Club press officer, to be 'the strongest possible protest against the BBC for the way they abuse, exploit and misrepresent the game of rugby league'.

That, however, was not the bit that interested the papers. Lamenting the fact that rugby league was apparently the only sport to have had the same BBC commentator for 25 years, the petition also described the image projected by Eddie Waring as 'inane' and unpopular with fans. And comments attributed to the 1895 Club secretary, Michael Hevey, went much further. Hevey reportedly revealed that some fans had offered to sign their names in blood if that would get rid of the man in the trilby hat. 'His commentaries are an insult . . . they are turning the game into a music hall joke,' Hevey said. 'He's a nice lad and his heart and soul are in the right place but he's a bloody awful commentator and here in the North we loathe the sound of his voice. Mr Waring has done marvellously for himself, but very little for Rugby.'

Phil Pennington, the 1895 Club president, told of how people had queued up to sign the petition at Leeds Supporters Club, and said that many more signatures could have been collected if there had been the time.

As before, the BBC refused to buckle to the protests, insisting that the petition actually contained 2,000 signatures, not 11,000 as claimed. The London-based national media, most notably *Daily Mail* columnist Ian Wooldridge, sprang to Eddie's defence too, although in terms not altogether helpful. On 7 May 1976, he wrote:

At 10.30 tomorrow morning, a privately raised petition allegedly bearing 10,000 signatures will be handed in at the BBC Broadcasting House, in London's Portland Place. Its object, while lacking the guts to say so specifically, is to get Mr Eddie Waring sacked. This is not only a nasty thing to do but a pretty stupid one as well. The offices of Mr Waring's immediate employers are eight miles further down the road in Shepherd's Bush.

Tsk, those simple Northern yokels, eh? Fancy not knowing their way around London. In any case, wrote Wooldridge, the petitioners were due to be disappointed. Quoting head of BBC Television Sport Sam Leitch, he revealed: 'No Eddie Waring, no new TV contract.'

Whatever his public resolve, privately it seems that the 1976 petition cut Eddie Waring deeply. Dave Parker has said that from that moment onwards, Eddie retreated into his shell. 'He could be a little bit wary of the fans,' Parker reveals. 'Most supporters warmed to him, but with others there was that element of jealousy. I used to stick to the side of him like glue. As I got to know him more, if anybody would have a go at him, I would have a go back. There were times when he would come on the phone and pour his heart out a bit, over various comments and complaints. It upset him.'

Eddie's nephew Harry Waring, meanwhile, recalls that 'The Eddie we saw on television was the same one we saw off it, without a doubt. It wasn't an act, he was just being himself. He didn't like making enemies, and, of course, you make a few enemies in the television commentary game, don't you? He tried to dismiss the critics, but they did hurt him. He felt that he was doing his best and the right thing for rugby league.'

Eddie Waring's modern-day successors in the commentary hot seat are also willing to pitch into the debate, offering views both on Eddie's capabilities in the role and on the reasons why the viewing public seem to take their efforts so personally. 'My first memories of Eddie were as a young lad in St Helens, when he used to come around the Northern towns with his *Sunday Pictorial* roadshow,' says Waring's heir to the BBC throne, Ray French, a former dual-code international and St Helens legend, who in 2007 commentated on his 27th consecutive Challenge Cup final, surpassing Eddie's own long-standing stay at the top. 'Then, of course, I met him when I signed on at Saints. He was a very friendly man and I had good affection for him. In his commentaries, he never said anything hostile about you and that made him popular with the players. If you wanted something, people would say, "Ask Eddie. Eddie will do that for you." That was how he was.'[6]

Little did Ray French know, but one day he too would be in a position to take the sport into the living rooms of a nation. And although the advent of multi-channel television has rather diminished the ability of the modern-day rugby league commentator to make a mainstream name for himself – the very notion of Ray French treading the boards with Ant and Dec seems a wild one indeed – when he took over the mic, the stinging barbs of public criticism were seldom far from hand. 'As a commentator, you have to be human and you have to be warm,' French says. 'You have to engage with every viewer, not just those who live in the north of England. Of the people watching, 85 per cent aren't from rugby league country. The biggest proportion comes from down south or in Wales or Scotland or wherever. When you are commentating on the BBC, you are talking to somebody's mum, their granddad or a couple who just happen to be watching on a Saturday afternoon. So you've got to be a bit wider. You've got to explain rules, you've got to give background to personalities and say who these people are. And one of the big problems, if you have come through the traditional backgrounds, is dealing with the game's own public. People have said to me, "Ray, why do you always say players come from such and such a place?" It's because people don't know. You might know in Wigan or Warrington that he's from St Pats, but nobody in Hackney Wick knows that, do they? Rugby league people can actually be quite bigoted. They fire at the Southern media, they fire at rugby union, but at times they are as bad as anyone. I take flak and, on Sky, Eddie Hemmings and Stevo take flak. Yet outside the traditional boundaries, you take very little. In fact, it's non-existent. Rugby league folk tend to want to destroy their own for some reason, I don't know why, and that's the way it was with Eddie. What people didn't appreciate is that rugby league was one of the first sports to be shown live on television. It had to sell and promote itself, and Eddie was the ideal man for that at the time. He did a great job.'

The commentator presumably destined to follow Ray French and Eddie as the BBC's voice of rugby league is Dave Woods, whose views on Waring's legacy are also based on childhood memories, this time in Wigan. 'Watching the Floodlit Trophy would be my earliest memory of hearing Eddie Waring on TV,' he says. 'We actually had a colour television set in our house, so Mr Smith, who lived back-to-back to us and was the father-in-law of Cliff Hill, the Wigan stand-off, used to come round to watch the game. I remember they only showed the second half live, so by the time the programme began, it was often:"Let's go across to Headingley, where it's Leeds 68 Hunslet 0."I remember once that Wigan were playing Leeds in the Cup. Leeds were winning and Eddie Waring was going: "Arrr, Leeds are in the draw for the next round." Next news, Green Vigo scores a long-range try: "Arrrr, tickets for the replay," and then, before Eddie had finished the sentence almost, Vigo goes in again! I remember thinking: "That's stuck it to you, Eddie!"'[7]

Nowadays, a more mature Woods thinks that those who judge Eddie as a poor commentator have got it all wrong. 'I would disagree with that because as a commentator you are always looking for a line,'he says.'Some people have preconceived phrases and know what they are going to say if a certain situation arises. Eddie was confident enough to trust in his natural ability to come out with great lines exactly when they were needed. If you look at some of them, most famously"poor lad" in the 1968 Watersplash final, they sum up the situation beautifully. The economy of words and that preciseness of meaning is just what you look for as a commentator.'

Jack Dearden, meanwhile, of Manchester-based Channel M television and the presenter-in-chief of BBC Radio Manchester's popular *Rugby League Hour*, emphasises the part that Eddie Waring's Northern tones played in transforming the medium of television completely. 'His distinctive style may not have been everyone's cup of tea,' says Dearden, 'but it certainly helped to put regional commentary, as well as rugby league, on the map. Nowadays, regional accents on the BBC are encouraged, but it hasn't always been like that. You had to speak "properly" or you wouldn't get the opportunities. Eddie Waring was a forerunner in overturning that. He was absolutely unique and helped to turn all that stuffiness upside down. Modern-day broadcasters have a heck of a lot to be grateful to Eddie Waring for.'[8]

Though not a rugby league man himself in his youth, Sky Sports' Eddie Hemmings also considers much of the criticism unfair. 'I wasn't that concerned with rugby league in my formative years, I was a Liverpool fan,' he admits. 'But I always remember the Challenge Cup on Saturday afternoons and hearing this peculiar sound coming out of the television set. At the time, I didn't think he was much of a commentator, to be honest, but looking back he kept the game in the public consciousness for all those years, when it was scratchy, grainy black-and-white television and they were rolling around in inches of mud. A lot of people claim he held the game back, but I wouldn't say he did. He told people in the Home Counties South about a quirky little game called rugby league. If there's any tragedy at all, it's that here in the twenty-first century, with the game evolving as it has, some people are still stuck in that time warp. They still think it's flat cap and whippets, pint of Guinness before they go out and sherry and raw eggs.'[9]

If any modern-day commentator can be said to have assumed Eddie Waring's mantle as the man rugby league fans love to hate, it is his fellow Dewsbury product and one-time Great Britain international hooker Mike Stephenson, Hemmings's on-screen partner.

'The first piece Mike ever wrote was in the *Dewsbury Reporter*,' reveals that paper's former assistant editor Margaret Watson. 'I remember him saying to me before going on tour to Australia: "I'd like to write some stores and send them over, would the *Reporter* publish them?" I said of course we would. There are a lot of parallels between Mike and Eddie. I would say that Mike would have admired Eddie for finding a way to incorporate another income and another job into his rugby career. Mike had the confidence to go on television too. As a young lad from Dewsbury, he must have thought at some stage, "Well, if Eddie can do it, I'm sure that I can."'

'When I was a young lad, a lot of people associated with rugby league didn't like Eddie,' says Mike Stephenson himself, a World Cup winner with Great Britain in 1972, who worked as a painter and decorator, glazier and restaurant owner before going on to enjoy a hugely successful professional playing career in England and Australia. 'They felt that he ridiculed the game, but I was never so sure that was true. For one thing, I knew the amount of work he put into the game before then. Eddie was a smart cookie during the war years to realise that people needed entertainment, and he showed his prowess not only as football manager but also an entrepreneur. He wasn't this buffoon that was portrayed on TV, he was a very switched-on bloke. I've realised since coming into the industry myself that a lot of the criticism you attract is down to jealousy.'[10]

Along with coming from Dewsbury, the other parallels that can be drawn between the pair are numerous. Both have attracted fan mail and vitriol in equal measure whilst, away from the television limelight, busily organising a variety of good causes intended to ensure the ongoing health and vitality of a sport they love. Where Eddie Waring had his roadshows, Stevo took his own personal collection of historical rugby league artefacts on a tour of Australia, where, since signing for Penrith in 1973, he has lived on and off ever since. 'We went around New South Wales in four railway carriages in the mid-'80s,' he told the April 2007 issue of *Sky Sports* magazine. 'I did it for two years. Sometimes they even let me drive the train.'

Thanks to his duties with Sky, since 1990 Mike Stephenson has spent half of each year in the UK. In 2005, he was the prime mover in launching a long-overdue museum for the code – the Gillette Rugby League Heritage Centre – at its Huddersfield birthplace, the George Hotel. Both he and Waring developed larger-than-life reputations that were, in many ways, bigger than the game itself. Both are seen as controversial comedy figures and both have been routinely considered, by some, not to be Yorkshiremen at all. 'A lot of people think I'm Australian, but I'm a West Riding lad,' said Waring in 1962.[11] 'I don't think you'll ever hear me drop into a broad Yorkshire accent; some people think I'm an Australian,' says Stevo today. Then, Stephenson goes on to point out, there is the question of personal financial gain. 'I get people coming into the [Rugby League] Heritage Centre at the George and they'll say, "Aren't you making enough money?"' he says, aghast. 'This is a non-profit organisation! It's my gift back to the game. Some of them have their tongue in their cheek, but others are quite vicious with it. But you get that anywhere. I get abused by crowds all over.'

The links extend to other, more light-hearted areas too. It is a standing joke in Dewsbury that just about every family boasts at least one member who claims to have been to school with Eddie Waring. As usual, though, the irrepressible Stevo can go one better than that. 'My mum and Eddie were childhood sweethearts,' he says. 'Mum and Dad have passed away now, but when I had been working with Sky for five or six years she just happened to mention it one day. She said: "It's amazing that you've become a commentator on television, a bit like Eddie Waring."

'"Yeah," I said, "I suppose it is."

'"You know that Eddie and I once had a crush on each other?" she said.

'"Oh," I said, "what age?"

'"We were about 11 or 12," she said. I found that a very fascinating story.'

But wait! There are more similarities still. 'Because you are elevated, people think you automatically change,' the London-based Stephenson continues. 'They invented a myth for Eddie that he had a specific room put aside at the Queens Hotel. The weird thing is, I actually do! That's where I stay whenever I come north – the Queens

Hotel. If my room is available, they try to give it to me every week. I'm a bloody good customer for them. I've done well out of the game, but I think I've been pretty good for rugby league too. I'd like to think Eddie was the same. I wear a trilby now, as well; not because Eddie wore one, but because I'm bald and my head gets cold. I also have a proper cashmere coat and look like an undertaker.'

But what about that allegation that Eddie Waring turned the 13-a-side code into a music-hall joke? Though the arrival of Sky Sports unequivocally raised the technological bar for televised rugby league, comedy continues to be a predominant feature. Many in the sport remain upset at how Hemmings, Stephenson and latterly their former GB international summarisers Terry O'Connor and Barrie McDermott play it for laughs at every opportunity. Not surprisingly, that is not quite how Mike Stephenson sees it. 'We never take the mickey out of the game,' he insists. 'We take the rise out of each other, but you'll never hear us pulling the game apart. I may have a go at the officials, the administration or players' performances, but that's what I'm paid to do. I defy anyone to bring me concrete proof that I take the mickey out of rugby league, because I don't. My love for the game is unbelievable. As for Eddie Waring, he created a style that worked, so why the hell change it? His accent was what the BBC wanted and he wasn't stupid enough to try and change that. Eddie Hemmings and I have been working together for 16 years and we have created a style too. Everybody loves Eddie Hemmings and they hate me. It's show business, isn't it?'

One of Waring's own summarisers, meanwhile, the former dual-code Wales international David Watkins, reveals that while Eddie was a players' man through and through, even there he could have his detractors. 'I came to Salford in 1967 and didn't know too much about rugby league, apart from the fact that I had been offered terms when I first played as a Wales youth international in 1959,' says Watkins, these days the long-serving chairman of Newport RUFC who, in 2000, was admitted to the Welsh Sports Hall of Fame. 'The first thing I ever saw of rugby league was the film *This Sporting Life*, and I knew little about it, apart from what

I'd seen on television. At Salford, I got to know Eddie quite well, so much so that he invited me to be his co-commentator. To have the opportunity to work with Eddie Waring was absolutely incredible. I think he chose me because I had a Welsh voice. I helped him at the Wembley final for several years.'[12]

Despite his obvious respect for Waring, David Watkins and other cross-code converts also felt a keen sense of frustration when they learned just how little respect rugby league was afforded in contrast with the rugby code they had just left. 'At the time, Eddie was the only rugby league face that union people ever recognised,' Watkins points out. 'League was regarded as a simple professional game that had no part to play in union at all. In fact, union people made fun of how it was play-the-ball rather than ruck and maul. When I went to play it, though, I found that it was probably the hardest and most physical game in the world. Eddie's commentary played up that fun element and was certainly different to that of Cliff Morgan and people like that, who all seemed so serious. With Eddie, it was all "Oops a daisy, he's taken a little knock again" and so on. He brought out the amusing side of the game, which a lot of people didn't like because they wanted rugby league to have equal status on television with rugby union.'

Then there was the notion that Waring's approach was selling the players short. 'Compared to the David Duckhams, Gareth Edwards, Barry Johns and Andy Irvines of the day, even though they were every bit as good and a little more dedicated, rugby league players were second-class citizens,' says Watkins. 'Of course, when you played rugby league as a professional, you played for money. The clubs had a bonus system where you got so much for winning and not so much for losing. Amongst the players, therefore, there was a strong emphasis on the seriousness of rugby league and a feeling that, in his latter years, Eddie didn't take the game seriously enough. I honestly do believe, and I don't say this lightly, that rugby league was diminished by some aspects of Eddie's later commentary. Some of the players, when they went out there on that field, were playing for their livelihoods and putting far more into it than any rugby union player. Some of the union players were noted only for international rugby, yet in rugby league, you had players who had played two, three or four hundred games at the professional level, where every week it was very hard and there was no quarter asked or given. That felt like an injustice.'

Of course, it could be argued that such a blatant lack of even-handedness would have existed within the BBC anyway, whatever Eddie Waring's input. And David Watkins insists that there was never any personal animosity between the pair. 'Although in the early days he wondered if I was ever going to make it and so on, Eddie was very complimentary to me,' he says. 'What helped most of all in that regard, even though I say so myself, was my ability in sevens rugby. Seven-a-side was something I could play with some skill. When the BBC began to televise rugby league sevens in 1968, Salford played in the first six tournaments and won every one. He called us the "Sevens Kings" and was very complimentary about the side. There was never any bad feeling between us; there couldn't have been for him to invite me to work with him on the BBC. Eddie was a cult figure who, if he advertised you on the likes of the BBC2 Floodlit Trophy, could really set you up. It was solely through his invitation that I got to work on the BBC, and that projected me as a player and made me feel more welcome in the game. Working with Eddie gave me a better status.'

Meanwhile, back among the ruins of the 1895 Club petition, the journalist Ian Wooldridge reported that: '[Eddie's] eyes were showing the strain yesterday and his hand trembled slightly. "I'm probably more upset than I really care to admit," he said.' At 64 years of age, wrote Wooldridge, Eddie was at 'a time of life when many Northerners are ready to renounce the struggle and sneak south to raise hollyhocks around some retirement bungalow in Bournemouth'. Eddie, though, was going nowhere. 'I'll accept criticism when I know it's justified,' he told Wooldridge. 'But in this case I don't really know what the criticism is. Really, there are only a few hundred thousand who understand Rugby League and I've always seen my job as having to make ten million people enjoy it.' In any case, as Eddie told the *Express & Star* journalist Gerry Anderson in 1978,

> commentators are always the butt of jokes and criticism. Everybody fancies themselves as a commentator but why are there so few of us? Because it's the hardest job in the business, and those who don't believe that should try listening and talking at the same time. Only women can do that.

After concluding that Waring's image was all about 'slagheaps, Tetley's ale, black puddings, Lowry paintings, busted noses, huge white thighs and players who talk precisely as he talks,' Wooldridge had something else to add. Presumably, he said, this attempt to get rid of Eddie was

> all part of the Rugby League's 'New Image' campaign which recently led them to appoint a very personable young public relations officer, a charming new secretary with an easy manner and Oxford arts degree, and inspired them to come to London only the other day to entertain lots of us to lunch in the dignified ambience of the Garrick Club. It emerged then, that Eddie Waring embarrassed them. Well, that staggers me.

* * *

The 'personable' and 'charming' gentlemen in question were the two Davids, Howes and Oxley, a couple of Hull natives who had arrived at the Rugby Football League's Chapeltown Road headquarters on the outskirts of Leeds in 1974, intent on waking a struggling sport from its slumber.

A supporter of Hull Kingston Rovers since the age of eight, the rugby league-loving David Howes began his working life as a journalist, first with a year's training in Darlington and then with his home-town paper, the *Hull Daily Mail*. In the early '70s, Howes, aged 23, alarmed at the state of the game and blithely unaware of the inner politics, wrote to the RFL to offer his views on how this most inward-looking of sports needed, as he saw it, to embrace a wider audience or face the potentially disastrous consequences.

'At that point, without being too dramatic, the game was dying,' he says now. 'Rugby league was lacking in inner confidence and failing to attract the outside public.' To his great surprise, the RFL replied that there was indeed going to be change and held open the possibility that Howes might take part in the process. Bill Fallowfield's reign was over, it seemed, whilst Brian Snape, the Salford chairman with a background in cinema and bingo halls, had emerged as the game's latest power broker. Favourite to run the game now was Gus Risman's son, Bev, an intelligent and eloquent former Great Britain international in his own right and a veteran of the Watersplash final. But as things turned out, with the findings of the Caine Report still ringing in its ears, the Rugby League Council chose a different route entirely. In July 1974, the Oxford graduate David Oxley was appointed secretary general before, some three months later, Howes too arrived on the scene as rugby league's first-ever public-relations officer.

'To be fair, both David and I came in as complete and utter virgins, totally naive, but with no political baggage,' recalls Howes, whose career since has included spells as chief executive at St Helens, managing director at Leeds, promoter, publisher, agent, media man and after-dinner speaker par excellence, among much else. 'Bev Risman was the favourite for the secretary's job, but "Ox" came in from public-school teaching and wowed them with his personality. I knew little of the business world but had a raw passion and love for the game. A lot of what we did in that first year was simply injecting that passion into other people, lifting them up again.'

Despite his gathering years, one man never deficient in the enthusiasm stakes, of course, was Eddie Waring. The Fallowfield era might be over, but Waring's political clout remained substantial, especially where all things BBC were concerned. Eddie didn't quite sit in on the television contract negotiations themselves – such meetings were generally held behind closed doors in London, Leeds or Harrogate, with the irrepressible Tom Mitchell at the helm for the Rugby League and Cliff Morgan and/or Jonathan Martin representing the BBC – but otherwise his presence continued to be felt everywhere.

'When David Oxley and I came in, there were no structures in place or anything,' says David Howes. 'Part of any PRO's job is dealing with the media, but the only reference we found to that subject was a law book belonging to Bill Fallowfield, which opened at the libel pages whenever you touched it. That went in the bin. We wanted to improve rugby league's image in the media, and the biggest projector of the game at that time was the BBC. In their eyes, Eddie was still "Mr Rugby League". He liked to broker the deals between the BBC and the RFL and would tell you how he'd had an influence on the early contract talks, whether they were going to be renewed and at what level and so on. He did oil the wheels, there's no doubt.'

For Eddie, then, far from signalling a retreat to the sidelines, the arrival of new blood meant new friendships to cultivate and a latest opportunity to extend his already sizeable sphere of influence. And again, while the more cynical may detect an element of self-preservation in such social manoeuvrability – in Yorkshire parlance, anyone so adaptable must surely be 'up to summat' – it is equally likely that the open-minded enthusiasm shared by the two Davids would have fired Waring's own. Eddie may well have been at a time of life when most in his position would be contemplating bus passes rather than press passes, but nobody needed to know his real age, did they? Impressed, no doubt, by Oxley's friendly and cultured urbanity, it was to the new RFL secretary that he became most closely attached. The pair became good friends, forging a loyalty that, despite Ian Wooldridge's claims to the contrary, would remain unshaken by all future criticism. As Oxley himself told the *Yorkshire Evening News*: 'The BBC wouldn't tell us who should referee the Cup final and we wouldn't tell them who should do the commentary. It's their affair and I think Eddie does a good job.'

At the time, however, Oxley's number two, David Howes, was not quite so reticent when it came to voicing criticism. 'I became the bad boy, which, looking back, in view of the fact that I was employed by the Rugby Football League, was totally unprofessional of me,' Howes says now. 'At the same time, we were in an era when the game needed organising, particularly from a promotional point of view. For me, the criticism really came home when we had the K-9 thing at Headingley. That took everything off at a tangent and took the mickey out of the game. I reacted poorly and the *Yorkshire Post* carried a big piece, which Eddie came out of very badly. In effect, quite fairly, the BBC told us: "That's your contract, that's your commentator, behave yourself." We got the odd letter from the BBC asking us to calm the criticism, and we did have our wrists tapped a few times. But I felt very strongly, as someone who loved the game, that they were taking liberties with us that they wouldn't have taken with anyone else.'

In many ways, of course, Howes was merely echoing the views of the wider rugby league fraternity in which he moved every day. 'One of the things we always prided ourselves on at the RFL was that we mixed with the public,' he goes on. 'We went out to dinners, went to matches, and, to be fair, you did have your finger on the pulse, because you talked to everyone in the game. You became a bit of a sponge. Definitely, a large strand of opinion targeted our main problem as the image that we had. Rugby league needed recognition of the talents of the players and coaches, not just to be seen as a bunch of Northern lads having a bash around on a Saturday afternoon. I don't want to portray myself as the brave man who went out on a limb, because I am not. My criticisms came purely out of a raw passion for the game and business naivety. In the modern world, I would probably have been sacked for not toeing the company line, but one of the main reasons I didn't get the push was that there were a lot of people in the Rugby League Council chamber who shared my opinion.'

In any case, according to Howes, the professional relationship between the pair remained amicable. And after penning a tribute to Waring – aka 'The Talking Trilby' – published in the game's celebratory centenary brochure in 1995, the former RFL man has been alerted by hindsight to the more positive impact his one-time bugbear actually had on the game. 'I never fell out with Eddie,' Howes says. 'Our relationship was always top-surface and all right. We were moving the game into an era of greater professionalism and people were putting in huge amounts of effort, so there was a rawness at the way we were still being portrayed. It was only in writing that later article, though, that I came to realise just how entrepreneurial a figure Eddie Waring really was. There are only a few people of whom you can use the phrase "ahead of their time". In rugby league, Roy Francis was one, using coaching methods for which, these days, you would get a sports science degree. Weight programmes were unheard of until Vince Karalius brought them over from America. Eddie was a marketing guru, more through instinct than anything. Nowadays, we are probably more sophisticated in our sense of brand awareness and so on, but back then the only person with any sort of marketing expertise at rugby league HQ was Eddie. We look back with fond memories on people like Harry Sunderland, but there's no doubt about it, Eddie Waring was far more productive.'

At its most mundane level, Waring's productivity on behalf of the game and its chief broadcaster frequently extended to the simple matter of getting matches played at all, often no mean feat in the depths of a northern English winter. If that meant arranging for gallons of freeze-busting chemicals to be surreptitiously poured on the pitch, phoning on ahead to ensure the field was adequately covered with tarpaulin or, if all else failed, simply slipping the match-day referee an illicit fiver to give an otherwise doubtful game the nod – as, according to Waring's old mate Dave Parker, happened once at Workington – then so be it. Whatever the weather, once the *Grandstand* cameras were ready to roll, the show had to go on.

Eddie's widest-reaching contribution to the off-field commercial fortunes of the sport, though, came with his impact on a new area of activity altogether: sports sponsorship. 'In Bill Fallowfield's day, Eddie, Bill and Tom Mitchell were rugby league's three main cogs,' confirms Parker. 'The three of them would decide which matches should be televised, Eddie would take it back to the BBC and they would do it. So, at the end of the day, what Eddie said went. Then, with the arrival of the '70s, sponsorship started to take off in a big way and companies like Mackesons, the brewers, and the tobacco company John Player started to come in. Eddie got very closely involved and gave the day-to-day running of this side of things to Tony Metcalfe, who, I think, was looking to scale down his journalistic work. During the week, Eddie and Tony would place you at a fixture with a Players No. 6 personality girl and it would be your job to pick the man of the match. We also had the Mackeson top ten tries. Those three, Fallowfield, Mitchell and Waring, and later it was David Oxley, David Howes and Eddie, sorted the sponsorships out between them, but Eddie was the main attraction.' Thanks to his celebrity status, rugby league didn't need a commercial manager with Eddie Waring around.

'Before it became our job, the idea of sponsorship was absolutely brand new, and Eddie was instrumental in bringing John Player into the game,' David Howes continues. 'People from agencies would go to Eddie and ask "How do we get into rugby league?" or "How do we get on the BBC?" Being the entrepreneur that he was, Eddie was prepared to broker the deal. He acted as a consultant for people coming into the sport and introduced big companies to rugby league. He pioneered the John Player Trophy, and in time they became the game's longest-running sponsorship, over 25 years. If Eddie Waring had been around today, he would have had endorsements coming out of his ears. He was certainly approached by several firms to advertise their products, including hair-gel people, but at that time the BBC wouldn't allow such a thing. He knew he had a value in a commercial way that he was never fully able to exploit. Even now, though, you don't make a lot of money in this game. If it was all about money you would choose another sport. To stay loyal to rugby league comes with a financial cost.'[13]

* * *

Of course, the one accusation to which Eddie Waring's critics would never submit is that they themselves might be culpable in propagating the Northern rugby league stereotype. For weren't the same people who put the boot into Waring's Wembley commentaries the very ones who, year after year, made the great 'pilgrimage' south, clad in comical fancy dress, giving the London-based media its annual chance to roll out those 'friendly invasion of the Northerners' features, thereby reinforcing the 13-a-side code's image as a purely parochial concern? 'So what?' they might quite reasonably reply. 'We can't do anything about that. Why should we be governed by what the London media thinks? What matters is that we are being true to ourselves and having a good time while we are at it.' To which Eddie Waring would unquestionably have responded: 'Well . . . er . . . quite SO.'

Yet it cannot be ignored that many Northerners – especially those steeped in rugby league – have long felt deprived of accurate representation. And that way frustration lies. Whenever the BBC made a serious documentary about the game – almost always with Eddie Waring's involvement – they were most often downbeat, dreary affairs of the 'doomed sport, all about money' persuasion. In the 1966 production *Gone North*, for example, the opening shot was of a St Helens glass furnace, whilst further scenes featured backdrops of industrial chimneys and aqueducts, smoky canals and players lining up for pay cheques in a grotty club office. Three years later, as part of the Tuesday Documentary strand, the cross-code move of Michael Coulman from Moseley to Salford was tracked in a programme entitled *The Game That Got Away*. This time the opening scenes came courtesy of a Wakefield cemetery; after panning across one or two gravestones, the camera cut to a scene in a cobbled Leeds back street, hung with line upon line of washing. For many with the code's best interests at heart, it felt as if the BBC was intent upon restricting their favourite game to a stereotypical Northern working-class ghetto, leaving it to fight the good fight with one arm tied behind its back.

'People were suspicious of the BBC and felt that Eddie was doing their dirty work for them, playing up to the stereotypes with the trilby and all that type of stuff,' says RFL historian Tony Collins, who, born in Hull in 1961, was taken to his first game by his dad in 1969. 'There was this perception that he would tell you stuff you didn't want to know. To many people, Eddie presented an image that was detrimental to the game.'[14] And worse, while the rest of the nation tuned in for its weekly dose of friendly Uncle Eddie, for many in the North his high-profile presence brought to mind another kind of uncle entirely.

'Fundamentally, the problem with Eddie was that he was perceived as having gone native,' Collins continues. 'To his critics, he lived up to all the clichés and, certainly by the early '70s, he was seen as an Uncle Tom character. It would be a mistake to make too much of this, but to an extent there are certain parallels between the Northern working-class experience and the treatment of black Americans. The jazz musician Louis Armstrong, for example, was always very keen on having a white manager. He realised that if there was any trouble, a white manager would better be able to sort the situation out; the power structure at that time was about white people. Financially, Armstrong would get a better deal if he had a white manager than a black manager. There's an element of that in Eddie. He kind of played it safe and went along with the status quo because, outside of social struggle and mass protest movements, that's the way individuals advance. Eddie would have said that his light-hearted approach was taking rugby league to more people than ever before, but ordinary supporters might well have seen that as selling out. And the hostility blinded people to all the good things about him.'

Martyn Sadler, the editor of *League Express*, has another interesting take on all this, particularly bearing in mind Eddie's background as both a Congregationalist and a radical rugby expansionist. 'Rugby league is a minority game, and following it is a bit like belonging to a minority religion,' he says. 'If people convert to your religion, then they tend to take it pretty seriously. It's the same sort of thing as saying, I suppose, that Roman Catholicism was a minority religion in this country for a number of years and the people who practised it were probably more dedicated than people who were part of the established church, who didn't feel themselves to be under any sort of threat. Rugby league has always attracted a group of people who are fiercely passionate about it and who believe that it is not being given its proper due.'

Nor should it be ignored that, upon occasion, many in the North do give the impression of enjoying nothing better than a good moan for moaning's sake. Take the viewer to whom Waring refers in his piece, 'The Trials of a Television Commentator', for the 1973–74 *John Player Rugby League Yearbook*:

> In last season's Yorkshire Cup final between Dewsbury and Leeds the Dewsbury colours of red, amber and black looked quite different to the blue and gold strip of Leeds. To spectators at the match and viewers watching colour TV, that is. The four million viewers watching black and white couldn't tell the difference. One official at the game was asked if he could arrange a change of strip. But his answer, which I'm sure he believed, was 'I can easily tell the difference.' I had to try to save the match for the black-and-white viewers by talking about light stockings, numbers on shorts, and constant identification of teams and individual players. This prompted one irate viewer to write: 'Why keep telling me which team is which when I've known them both since before you were born?'

Indeed, so important to them is their chosen sport that not a few rugby league supporters seem in permanent danger of losing all sense of wider perspective. One particularly amusing example of this tendency came in a piece by the reliably excellent rugby league writer Stephen Bowes in *Rugby League Journal*. Recollecting his family's excitement at the news that their beloved Workington Town were to be featured away to Castleford on a 1968 episode of *Grandstand*, Bowes recalled:

A couple of things stand out in my memory about that one besides the result, a 20–6 victory for the home side: Eddie Waring pointing out the difficulty in identifying the Town players because the numbers on the back of their shirts had become washed faint by too many launderings, and the fact that the coverage was interrupted, not by the racing from Newmarket, but to go for 'live' pictures from outer space, where Apollo VII was circling the moon. I was annoyed at the time, but realise now that it was one of those utterly surreal moments unlikely ever to be repeated in my lifetime.[15]

Now then, let's see. Manned spacecraft orbiting the moon or 26 blokes chucking a ball about at Wheldon Road. Tricky one that. Trust the flamin' Beeb to head straight for the stratosphere.

But what about the BBC's actual attitude towards rugby league? To the disappointment, no doubt, of conspiracy theorists everywhere, after hours of extensive research, by both this author and Tony Collins, smoking guns betraying definite BBC bias against the 13-a-side code have been notable only by their absence. 'It's not that there's a BBC conspiracy against rugby league in favour of rugby union,' Collins says. 'It is more that the BBC had – and indeed still does have – a particular view of its own role as the national broadcaster. People fit into that in particular ways. It follows, therefore, that if you are talking about the north of England and a sport identified with that region, you want someone who, in their eyes, is emblematic of the place.'

It is a theory that even the most cursory glance over the BBC's sports commentating roster of that period – and beyond – backs up absolutely. Cricket? John Arlott and his crusty, colonial mates, easily imagined quaffing port in the Lords Long Room. Rugby union? The double-barrelled Nigel Starmer-Smith and authoritarian Hawick PE teacher Bill McLaren. Motor racing? Bit of a petrolhead, voice like screeching tyres – Murray Walker. Swimming and athletics? The games teacher-esque Ron Pickering in his tracksuit. Golf? The supremely clubbish and a bit too pleased with himself Peter Allis. Tennis? How about the very posh Dan 'Ooh, I say' Maskell? And soccer? The egalitarian, apparently classless Kenneth Wolstenholme and, later, John Motson.

The saddest irony, of course, is that in taking their anti-Waring stance, his critics were entirely misrepresenting the views of the man himself. As we have seen, few in rugby league had done more to promote the sport across every class and race than Eddie Waring. 'I like to think I have helped to make Rugby League known on a national level and to make it respectable,' he told Norman Smithson, writing in *Today*, in 1962.

> For many years it was known mainly as a working man's game, cloth caps and mufflers and that sort of thing. But now it has progressed. It attracts a lot of professional people these days as players and spectators, including many university men. It is certainly more respectable than it used to be.

Indeed, even at the height of the criticism, Waring never missed an opportunity to champion the cause of the sport in universities and polytechnics where, once upon a time, the very notion of playing rugby league had been an impossibility. 'There is a Southern amateur rugby league, of which I'm the president, and there are many universities which play rugby league,' he told Roy Plomley on *Desert Island Discs* in 1974. In later years, Eddie spoke at the Oxford Union about the game, and in his 2006 autobiography, *Born on the Wrong Side*, the former Hunslet and Workington player Cec Thompson recalled how, after he had taken on the role of 'president and coach of the first official Student Rugby League club in the world' at Leeds in 1966, he

> at once took on the task of raising funds, and asked Eddie Waring to chair a quiz and film show at the university. Though we charged 7s 6d a head we managed to fill the largest lecture hall. Eddie refused payment. 'I'm only too pleased to help,' he told me in his famous growl. 'I just hope you and Andrew

[Cudbertson] are successful in getting Student Rugby League off the ground.'[16]

One of the first black players to represent Great Britain at rugby league, Cec Thompson also told of how, in 1951, Eddie wrote in the *Sunday Pictorial*: 'If Cec Thompson is not chosen for the Great Britain squad, the selectors must be racists.'[17] In fact, in a society where skin colour and race offered far greater potential for stigma than, perhaps, they do today, Waring's own attitudes to race reveal him again as a man ahead of his time. Writing about Billy Boston in *The Great Ones*, for example, Waring notes admiringly how the Wigan favourite, who had once flown home alone while the rest of his fellow GB tourists travelled on to play a handful of missionary games in South Africa, stood up frequently to 'crowd comments about his play and colour'. It was Eddie who first noticed the talents of the Fijian star Joe Levula, who eventually signed for Rochdale in 1961, and it was Eddie who, rather ingeniously, arranged the transfer of Jamaican sprinter McDonald Bailey to Leigh in 1953, resulting in a crowd of 15,000 as the club switched on its floodlights for the first time with a game against Wigan.[18]

Politically, though a free marketeer by instinct, Eddie Waring might well be seen as New Labour before such a thing existed. As his son, Tony, explains: 'Although he was never actively involved in politics, my father thought that people should have the opportunity to make the most of themselves. I think that perhaps, later on, he was conservative with a small "c", but then most people are as they get older. Overall, he was very much a democrat.' In 1967, the *Daily Mail* writer Peter Black described Eddie as 'a loyal Tory and disciplinarian', perplexed, said Black, about Britain:

not sure what's gone wrong but [who] thinks there are a lot of unhappy people about, worried over their jobs and their future. He thinks the accepted image of young ones is unfair to them and, though he dislikes the Hippie clothes, he doesn't mind the long hair, when it's clean. 'When it isn't,' he said wistfully, 'I'd like to send them into a scrum. They'd soon have it off 'em. I'm a nonconformist and I like people to be different. But today I think we have a kind of mass nonconformity and not enough real individuals or rebels.'

Waring's appeal, said Peter Black, was that of the ordinary chap writ large:

> He hates unpunctuality and bad driving and not being told why the train is late. He likes crime and travel books, used to sing in the mighty Yorkshire choruses of 'The Creation' and 'Messiah', his heroes are men of 'purpose and reliability': his father, Churchill, Kennedy and Lord Birkett.

His job on television, said Eddie, was 'to be there, keep it friendly, never let it get out of proportion', before adding less than convincingly that rugby league was 'only a game'. As Eddie Waring knew better than anyone, in reality, it was anything but.

* * *

Most definitely only a game was the classic BBC TV series *It's a Knockout*, which began, with Eddie Waring as referee, in 1966. As a mainstay of Friday-night viewing over three decades, *It's a Knockout* and its European counterpart *Jeux Sans Frontières* were without doubt the shows that gained Eddie his biggest regular television audience, attracting numbers that dwarfed those tuned to his rugby league commentaries.

Described in some quarters as the 'Idiot Olympics', *It's a Knockout* was a madcap riot of sports-day-style mayhem, characterised by surreal costumes, bizarre missile attacks, lunatic physical risks and the deliberate whipping up of long-standing domestic and international rivalries. At its height, it proved hugely popular not only with some 19.4 million British viewers but with another 180 million right across Europe.

In its glory years, the programme's star turn was the Manchester-based news presenter-cum-sports journalist Stuart Hall, who, clad more often than not in striped blazer and straw boater, spent much of the show convulsed in fits of highly infectious laughter. Seldom has the sight of a refuse collector from Skegness struggling to fill a bucket with water on a slippery rotating turntable whilst clad in an outsized penguin suit been so amusing. Having handed over the refereeing duties to the retired FIFA official Arthur Ellis, meanwhile, the occasionally unintelligible Eddie's main responsibility was for the marathon, or *fil rouge* as it was known in Europe, where Belgium ('ha ha ha – here come the Belgians – ha ha ha!') always seemed to finish last and those pesky Germans would stop at nothing to secure victory. It all added up to an anarchic, light-hearted mix of rabid nationalism, civic pride and good clean family fun that all but the most pompous could enjoy.

Waring's involvement with *It's a Knockout* owed much to his friendship with the BBC producer Barney Colehan and the fact that, in its original form, the show was based exclusively in the north of England.'During the war, along with managing Dewsbury, Eddie organised Sunday-night concerts at the town's Empire and Playhouse music halls,' remembers Harry Waring. 'I think that's where he first met Barney Colehan. Barney would produce the shows and Eddie would organise, manage and direct them. So he was getting into a bit of show business even back then.'

By 1966, Barney Colehan, characterised by his curly handlebar moustache, was a BBC name to be reckoned with, and would have worked alongside pretty much the same outside-broadcast teams as Eddie. Most famously, he was the man responsible for creating and directing the long-running BBC show *The Good Old Days*, which, between 1953 and 1983, gave early career boosts to the likes of Ken Dodd, Hylda Baker and Morecambe and Wise, transmitted from the City Varieties music hall in Leeds. When Colehan, educated at St Bede's Grammar School in Bradford, came up with the idea of *It's a Knockout*, he knew exactly who he wanted as referee.

Jeux Sans Frontières kicked off a year earlier than *It's a Knockout*, in 1965, as part of a four-way battle not televised in Britain between Belgium, France, Germany and Italy; British competitors did not take part in the European arm of the show until 1967. Furthermore, in the first BBC series, directed by Colehan and presented by the seasoned broadcaster McDonald Hobley, only two English counties took part: Yorkshire and Lancashire. The venue for the first-ever *It's a Knockout*, broadcast live on Sunday, 7 August 1966, was the beach and promenade at Morecambe, where the home town, in tandem with neighbour Heysham, took on the might of fellow west-coast resort Blackpool. Alas, this debut outing ended in disarray. No one, it seems, had allowed for the tide coming in and swamping the three-legged football. The cameras had a lucky escape too.

As he told the *Radio Times* in 1976, however, Eddie's most vivid early memories were of the following week's contest, a face-off between Scarborough and Bridlington in Peasholm Park. Eddie explained:

> In this particular week, the idea was to build a pontoon bridge out of pit props across a lake, and then run backwards and forwards across it with balloons. It so happens that most of the contestants were paratroopers but, let me tell you, I've never seen men so exhausted. They were literally throwing up every few minutes on the bank. It was tremendous.

Sharing the master-of-ceremony duties throughout that first series were the comedians Charlie Chester in Lancashire and Ted Ray in Yorkshire. In a sign of things to come, Waring, who had in the late '50s already acted as referee in Colehan's town-against-town BBC talent show *Top Town*, was briefly joined in officiating the 1966 *It's a Knockout* grand final – played for the 'Tip-Top-Town Trophy' – by one Stuart Hall.[19]

In 1967, *It's a Knockout* spread its wings not only into Europe, but across the rest of the UK too. For this second series, McDonald Hobley was assisted by a new MC, namely the up-and-coming sports reporter David Vine. And while the opening programme was again based in the North (a clash between Lytham St Annes and Southport), by week two the programme had decamped to Colwyn Bay, Wales. Then it was off to Galashiels, Scotland, followed by more heats in Brighton and the town that provided Britain's first European finalists, Cheltenham. In 1968, Vine was given a new female assistant in the shape of former model and *What's My Line?* star Katie Boyle, although, happily for Eddie, she was not around for long. After suffering what Stuart Hall describes as 'a fit of the vapours', she departed ahead of the 1969 series and Eddie was promoted to co-presenter, a move, according to Tony Waring, that his father mulled over long and hard.

'He was conscious of a potential clash with his rugby league duties,' says Tony. 'In the end, though, he felt that his involvement in such a popular international programme provided further exposure for the game itself.'[20] Whatever the circumstances, once up front and centre stage Eddie made an immediate impact on viewers and programme makers alike. And when *It's a Knockout* appeared in colour for the first time in 1970, before the inspirationally eccentric Stuart Hall took over from David Vine in 1972, ushering in a thrilling new era of jet-propelled water hoses, 10-ft rubber giants, foam chutes, exploding electronic mice and a certain louche charm where interviews with beauty queens and female contestants in tight shorts were concerned ('Pulchritude has its place,' quoth the great man), Eddie Waring's passport to a still greater pitch of notoriety was assured.

'These days, you'd never get it through health and safety,' chuckles Stuart Hall, perilously close to a trademark laugh that calls to mind an asthma-attack victim choking on a cough sweet. 'The contestants were always getting dislocated shoulders, broken ankles, head injuries and God knows what. But back then, people took responsibility for themselves. There was no compensation culture. I played virtually every game you could think of and if I hurt myself, so what? It's my life and I'm the one risking it, so why bother?'[21] Speaking as a time-honoured

Knockout fan, Stuart, hear hear. And if anyone took a blow to the genitals, so much the better! Throw into that mix the added ingredient of Eddie Waring, whose contributions developed into a series of incoherent gurgles as the fever pitch rose, and how could it possibly fail?

'The problem for Eddie was that despite his brain whirling around, he could never quite formulate the words,' says Hall, who, in the course of a nine-year professional partnership, became Waring's close friend as well as colleague.'He would start a sentence in the middle of the previous one, and then go off at a tangent saying something else. He had a unique way with language. When we were abroad, for example, he would never realise that girls' names ended with"a" and boys' with "o". So the net result was that while the German presenter was called Camillo Felgen, Eddie always called him "Carmell-ah!"There was a lovely Italian girl presenter called Rosanna Vaudetti. She used to come to us for the English pronunciations. One week, we had a team playing from Thurrock in Essex. Rosanna came to our little cabin and asked how she should pronounce that. Eddie immediately turned around and said:"Therrrrock-ah!" So off she went and pronounced it like that herself.'

While the format of the UK heats changed structurally over the years, one constant throughout the most memorable period of its run was the interplay between the two main presenters. Stuart Hall seldom missed an opportunity to pull his colleague's leg, while Eddie, always up for a caper, seemed only too happy to play along.'We used to give him daft names and play silly jokes, but he knew what was going on,' says Hall.'Eddie took it in good spirit, but then he had to, didn't he? *It's a Knockout* is a fun show. If a custard pie comes your way, you take it in the face.' Even so, Eddie was clearly not entirely untouched by doubts. As Hall himself once admitted: 'One side of him wanted to make people laugh and the other side of him wanted people to think of him as a respectable commentator. I used to say to him: "Eddie, you've got something that is priceless. Your voice is absolutely God's gift.

People imitate you. They don't imitate Stuart Hall or anyone else. Whilst you're on, it's Eddie Waring – you've got everyone in the palm of your hand."'[22]

Whatever his private doubts, whilst working on *It's a Knockout*, here as elsewhere, Eddie was as popular off screen as he was on it, even if that complex personality of his proved just as stubbornly tricky to unravel. 'In many ways, Eddie was one of the most complicated men I have ever met in my life,' says Stuart Hall. 'When I joined *It's a Knockout*, I had heard that he was a bugger for protecting his position in rugby league. I said to him at the start: "Look, Eddie, all I want is for this to be a successful programme. I don't want Stuart Hall to be a star or anything, it's a team effort, and I don't want any backstabbing or messing around."

'"Arrr," he growled, "I wouldn't dream of tackling you." So we had a truce. I protected his corner, he protected mine and we formed a team.'

True to form, Hall has an unconventional explanation for Waring's tendency towards surreptitiousness too. 'Eddie was very secretive about everything,' he says. 'He was always suspicious of everyone and never took anybody on trust at all. His attitude was that everyone was an enemy until they proved themselves a friend. You would think he was being spied on by the Gestapo. Why was he like that? Well, he was a Pisces. If you look at the astrology charts, Pisceans are by nature inclined that way. They are suspicious, they don't trust people and they think a lot. Eddie thought too much about everything, really.'

Those foibles apart, Eddie's self-deprecating nature made him great fun to be around, and, though a reluctant swearer on the whole, it seems he was not altogether a stranger to Anglo-Saxon phraseology if the situation demanded. 'Whenever I was abroad, the Continental countries used to provide me with the fastest car in that country,' says Hall. 'Naturally, in Germany, I had a bright-orange Porsche 911 Carrera. We took off from Hamburg to go up to Kiel. Eddie, of course, was in the passenger seat. I put this thing into gear and in no time we were whizzing along. Eddie is looking at the speedometer, worried. I could hear his brain ticking over. I said, "Eddie, have you figured out what kilometres per hour is in mph?"

'"Arr, arr, of course I 'ave, lad," he said, through gritted teeth. "It's fucking quick."'

Nor were the *It's a Knockout* team spared Waring's penchant for aphorisms. 'Eddie had various sayings that he used to trot out,' recalls Hall. 'He was much older than I was, and he used to say: "I must cull the youth in you; I must make you toe the party line." When we were away with *Knockout*, we used to go to wild parties where I'd be pulling the night away. At about three o'clock in the morning, Eddie would tug on my sleeve and growl: "It's, er, time to go home. The whole of life's timing an' picking. The party's peaked and it won't get any better, now come on. Timing an' picking." He was always right. From then on, it was downhill. As we approached the end of every series in September, he used to say to me: "Beware the dark days of November when the knives are out." He was always looking over his shoulder waiting for the dagger to come between his shoulder blades.'

Often, it has to be said, with good reason. For while *It's a Knockout* enjoyed massive viewing figures, not everyone was a fan. Within rugby league, for instance, there was a collective sense-of-humour failure at how the show's pantomime image echoed the BBC's supposed treatment of the 13-a-side code. And in the crustier corners of the media, the more highbrow critics did tend to condemn what was an essentially harmless piece of Friday-night froth in terms not altogether unfamiliar to rugby fans north of Doncaster. *It's a Knockout* was, wrote the *Listener* columnist Jack Waterman in 1975, 'a simple-minded programme in which people are invited to chase Westphalian ferrets, or each other, through hoops and up greasy poles suspended over lakes of piranha-infested custard, or so it seems'. Another writer accused Waring of 'gargling with tripe'.

Such was the *Knockout* phenomenon that even Clive James felt compelled to get in on the act. Writing in *The Observer*, during his days as a television critic, James revealed:

Every week I watch Stuart Hall on *It's a Knockout* (BBC1) and realise with renewed despair that the most foolish thing I ever did was to turn in my double-O licence and hand back that Walther PPK with the short silencer. Some poor klutz running flat out on a rolling log with a bucket of Géricault in each hand is trying to spit greased ping-pong balls into a basket held between the knees of a girl team-mate bouncing on a trampoline with her wrists tied behind her back, and Hall is shouting: 'The seconds count, Robert. Are you going to do it? Are you going to do it? Ten seconds to go, Robert! Yes, YOU MUST DO IT NOW, because if you don't, you . . . OOH! Will you make it? AAAGH!'

Then, with a dip of the rapier, it was Eddie's turn. 'Cut to Eddie blaring at the marathon,' James continued:

Knockout's Augean Stables. 'Ahn eeh ahm da whey,' bellows Eddie, rocking from foot to foot like a man in the early stages of the hully-gully: 'Oom wah hoom there's still one more go to game.' Behind him, on a beam over a tank full of water, two shivering comptometer operators slug each other with pillows. The rain pours down.[23]

Ah, yes. The rain. 'As an antidote to all that secretive business, I have one particular memory which sums Eddie up perfectly,' says Stuart Hall. 'We were making a programme in Ashington in the North-east, where Bobby and Jackie Charlton were born, and had a rehearsal at nine o'clock in the morning. It was raining absolute stair rods. I went out, on my own, to rehearse with the teams. When I got back to the caravan, it had no heating and no facility to make a cup of tea or anything. Two hours later, I had to go out and do another rehearsal, by which time I had changed my clothes – I only had two sets. Again, I was on my own, apart from our scoregirl, "Nipples" Nolan. Back in the caravan, Eddie could see on the monitor that I'd had enough, and just as I am thinking "What am I doing here, on a Sunday morning, throwing it down with rain, soaking wet through?" and ready to quit, out he comes swathed in bin bags. He comes over to me at the scoreboard, where I'm rehearsing, and he starts to sing: "Underneath the arches, we dream our dreams away . . ." In the pouring rain, we did our Flanagan and Allen act and fell into one of those hysterical fits where you are so deep in despair that you either commit suicide or laugh like a hyena. We laughed and laughed while the rain belted down. Then Eddie turned to me and said: "I could see you were on the next tram home." That phrase lingers with me to this day. "You were on the next tram home." He completely restored my spirits, 5,000 people turned up and it was one of the best programmes we ever did. At a time of crisis, there he was.'

* * *

Given his lifelong theatrical inclinations, once the opportunities arose, the lure of a parallel career in light entertainment was always going to prove irresistible to Eddie. Thanks largely to the growing popularity of *It's a Knockout*, it wasn't long before shows unassociated with sport or physical endeavour began to covet this most idiosyncratic of personalities. Eddie's first major break in that direction came with the *Morecambe and Wise Christmas Show* in 1971.

Although yet to reach its greatest heights, owing to the winning charm of its eponymous stars and the considerable input of Liverpudlian comedy-writing genius Eddie Braben, *The Morecambe and Wise Show* was already a staple of mainstream British culture. In Eric and Ernie, the universal qualities of traditional northern English humour – an emphasis on the struggling little guy, the juxtaposition of the real and surreal, a recognition of the value of friendship in the face of the ultimate absurdity of human existence – were never better expressed. Mainly, though, Morecambe and Wise were just profoundly silly. Whatever your age or geographical roots, they were there to be enjoyed. Eddie Waring slotted into the pair's zany world as if to the manor born.

In both that 1971 festive outing and the even more rapturously received 1977 Christmas show, which, despite attracting a record British television audience of over 28 million, heralded an ill-fated switch to ITV for Eric and Ernie soon after, Eddie's own roles could not have been smaller. Even so, as part of the chorus in a pair of musical numbers choreographed by the great Ernest Maxin, like the trouper he was, Eddie all but stole the scenes. In the first, a Fred Astaire and Ginger Rogers parody, the actress Glenda Jackson, a Morecambe and Wise regular over the years, appears at the top of a flight of stairs, resplendent in ginger wig and red ballgown. Below her is a row of men, each with his back to the audience, dressed in top hat and tails. As Jackson descends, to a burst of the song 'You Were Never Lovelier', each of her suitors turns to the audience, miming the word 'lovelier' as he goes. First it's the celebrated BBC anchorman Cliff Michelmore. Then comes Frank Bough and third in the line, getting the biggest laugh so far, is his *Grandstand* colleague Eddie Waring. After Eddie come the xylophone-bashing astronomer Patrick Moore, a youthful Michael Parkinson and, finally, the cadaverous newsreader Robert Dougall. That done, arms akimbo, the dapper sextet advances towards the camera in single file, before floating individually off screen with a smile. At least, that's how most of them do it. When it comes to Eddie's turn, he can't resist dropping his arms and selling the cameraman a cheeky little dummy and sidestep.

Six years later, in one of the best-known Morecambe and Wise musical skits of them all, a parody of the musical *South Pacific*, Eddie and Frank Bough were back again, miming to 'There Is Nothing Like a Dame' in a group of sailors played by well-known television faces Michael Aspel, Richard Baker, Richard Whitmore, Barry Norman, Philip Jenkinson and Peter Woods. This time, there was rather more for Eddie to do. For not only did the sailors have to mime a particularly tricky set of lyrics, there was a dance routine to get through too. Although by now getting on a bit, Eddie did his best to keep up and even got to show that he still had a bit of rhythm. Of all the sailors, though, apart from Woods, who came on at the end to add the booming final touches, Eddie was the only one not to be included in a series of spoof aerial acrobatics. Even when it came to stunt doubles, there could only ever be one Eddie Waring.

If appearing alongside Morecambe and Wise did Eddie's light-entertainment career no harm, it looked, for a while at least, as if the surge in popularity of an imaginative Stockport-born impressionist named Mike Yarwood might be another matter entirely. Prior to Yarwood, mainstream impressionists had dealt almost exclusively in safe Hollywood film stars: John Wayne, Charlie Chaplin, James Cagney and so on. Suddenly, with the arrival of *Look – Mike Yarwood!* in 1971, here was someone impersonating contemporary public faces including, on one mildly controversial occasion, HRH Prince Charles. True, Yarwood's spoofs were affectionate rather than cutting, but at first, until people grew used to the idea, it all seemed rather revolutionary, especially on prime-time television. Politicians such as Labour Prime Minister Harold Wilson, his Chancellor of the Exchequer Denis Healey and Conservative leader Ted Heath were among the show's most frequent targets, while television personalities like the political interviewer Robin Day and *Some Mothers Do 'Ave 'Em* star Michael Crawford also featured strongly in an act where the attachment of at least one prop, physical or verbal, was of paramount importance. Just about every Mike Yarwood impression came complete with its own instantly memorable catchphrase and soon-to-be iconic wardrobe item. In Harold Wilson's case it was a pipe and Gannex raincoat, in Frank Spencer's a beret. Exaggeration was everything. So popular were Yarwood's characterisations that once he latched onto you there was really no point in arguing. As far as the Great British public was concerned, that was the way you would be remembered whether you liked it or not.

'At first, when Mike Yarwood began taking him off, Eddie wasn't all that happy,' reveals Harry Waring, 'but when Yarwood grew more popular, Eddie was a good deal happier!' Tony also recalls: 'Initially my father wasn't sure about it, but in time he saw it as quite flattering.' In fact, Yarwood and Waring became friendly. 'There was one occasion when my father was appearing at a player's benefit night in Wakefield,' says Tony. 'Mike Yarwood was playing Batley, or somewhere nearby, and some bright spark persuaded him to come along so they could both appear on the stage together. Mike always said, "It's a caricature, stand me next to him and they'll see the difference." But they did the double act anyway. It brought the house down.' In 1973, after Yarwood had impersonated Waring – along with Larry Grayson, Edward Heath, Jess Yates, Harold Wilson, Frankie Howerd, Malcolm Muggeridge, Clement Freud, George Brown, Robin Day and Hughie Green – on the previous year's *Christmas Night with the Stars*, the man himself turned up as a real-life guest on *The Mike Yarwood Christmas Show*.

As the '70s advanced, it wasn't just Eddie's stonier-faced rugby league critics who fretted over how this light-entertainment business had begun to impact upon his sports commentary. Some of those close to Waring at the BBC were also concerned that their man could be spreading himself too thin. Ray Lakeland, for example, admits: 'I must say, I wasn't very keen on him doing that. It didn't spoil his commentary, but I don't think it did it any good. I thought the entertainers weren't treating him very fairly and skitting him a bit. I didn't think they were being very nice to him.' Having decided to dive into that world, Eddie himself pushed fervently on with everything that came his way – whether it be prime-time national television appearances or opening a supermarket.

And why wouldn't he? At one level, this was exactly what the star-struck kid from Dewsbury had dreamed of all his life. As he himself put it in a 1962 interview with the *Today* journalist Norman Smithson:

I produced shows – mainly variety – for a good many years, and what I picked up then from working with people in show business is coming out now. I liked particularly the style of comedians like Jimmy James and Eric Morecambe. In similar style, my humour has been described as slow combustion.

Tony, meanwhile, has said: 'My father loved being famous and was always conscious of his image, but not in a poseurish manner.

He adored show business, courted meetings with famous people such as Laurel and Hardy, and treasured his appearances on the *Morecambe and Wise Show*.'[24]

* * *

As Eddie's fame grew, so did the prestigiousness of his contacts. 'We did a Floodlit Trophy match at Leigh,' recalls Dave Parker, 'and Eddie said he wasn't going straight home, he was off to a Wythenshawe nightclub. Princess Margaret was there and he was doing a charity night. Because he was dealing with royalty, there were two outriders to accompany his car.'

In an era when the nation had a choice of just three channels – BBC1, BBC2 and ITV – anyone with a television set was bound, eventually, to bump into Eddie Waring. Among other BBC programmes to be given the Waring touch were *The Generation Game*, on which Eddie appeared with Bruce Forsyth in 1976 and new presenter Larry Grayson in 1978, and Cilla Black's variety vehicle *Cilla*. In a 1973 edition of that latter show, via a live link from Elland Road, Eddie introduced the Lockwood Brass Band playing 'When the Saints Go Marching In' – rather incongruously given that the act before was Marc Bolan's T Rex. In 1974, Eddie gave his own vocal chords a workout on *Short, Back and Sides*, recorded at the City Varieties, in which he joined in with a chorus of 'Down by the Old Mill Stream', as sung by a barbershop choir. In 1977, he instructed *Blue Peter* fall guy John Noakes in the art of rugby league in an episode of *Go with Noakes*, filmed in Castleford. And at the close of the decade, in 1979, he was a panellist on the BBC quiz *Blankety Blank*, alongside Roy Hudd, Anna Dawson, Shirley Anne Field, Nicholas Parsons and Beryl Reid.

Tony Waring recalls how Eddie's workload and list of celebrity contacts grew in tandem with his mainstream profile. 'In 1966, he flew back from Australia and my mum and I went down to pick him up from Heathrow,' his son remembers. 'We went to see *The Sound of Music* and went backstage to meet Roy Hudd, who my father knew. Then we drove up to Morecambe for the first *It's a*

Knockout. It was straight from Australia and back to work. Another time, we were in London the night before the Challenge Cup final and had pre-dinner drinks in the Speaker's Room of the House of Commons. Selwyn Lloyd organised it. Afterwards, we went to the New Victoria Theatre, where we met Max Bygraves in his dressing-room. My father had all sorts of contacts in all sorts of areas. He had this idea of sport as theatre – another branch of the entertainment industry.'

Sometimes, the entertainment industry would visit Eddie. 'Eric Morecambe once came to our house when he and Ernie were doing panto in Bradford,' continues Tony, whose 21st birthday party guests included the comedian Dickie Henderson amongst others. 'I remember Eric doing archery in our garden. Then, on another occasion, my parents were having a party and Eric came over. It was during a polio outbreak or something and there was a lot of vaccination going on. People were queueing up for a serving of my mother's casserole and when it came to Eric's turn he said: "Can I have it in this arm, please?" My father had lots of contacts in Australia too. He knew Sir Frank Packer, Kerry Packer's father, for example. My father was very approachable and he liked interesting people, whether it be in sport, the arts, music or whatever. He had a lively mind and enjoyed other lively minds.'

Harry confirms his uncle's inherent sense of theatricality. 'Another of Eddie's favourite comics was Albert Modley,' he says, 'although I don't think he ever tried to impersonate any comedian in particular. It was just a natural Northern type of presentation that came out as humorous. He always told the story of how Eric Morecambe once paid him a visit at Bramhope, complaining, "It's all right coming up here, but the roads are so mucky that my car gets filthy."

'"Well," says Eddie, "the garage I use is just 200 yards down the road. Go and get them to wash it and charge it to me." Later, when he got the bill, not only had he paid for the car wash, he had paid for a service and a tank full of petrol as well. Another time, I remember driving him over to the filming of *Star Town* at the BBC studios in Manchester. When we arrived, the presenter,

Terry Wogan, was already there and the guest of the day was Tessie O'Shea, who would probably have been about 70 at the time. Barney Colehan was there too and we all sat down for a meal. I sat next to Tessie. She had a glint in her eye, did Tessie. She asked me if I would like to go for a holiday to Florida, where she lived. I said I remembered seeing her as a kid and told her how much I enjoyed her playing the ukulele or banjo. She said, "Would you like me to play it now?" I said, "I would, but obviously you can't." So she leans down and brings out this ukulele from under her chair and starts singing, "I'm Two-Ton Tessie from Tennessee." Eddie thought that was really funny.'[25]

Nor could Eddie be accused of being out of touch with the younger generation. 'He would tell stories of the time he spent the evening with the Beatles in Paris,' says Tony. 'They met in a hotel bar and he ended up in their suite or something. As a teenager, I was very impressed by that. He liked John and Paul the best, that was his line. He also spent an evening in Leeds with The Who, and I will never forget the time that I met Dusty Springfield in a Blackpool lift after we had gone to watch Morecambe and Wise play there.' Then there is the wonderful story – probably apocryphal but who wouldn't want to believe it? – of the time that Eddie and his friend the Leeds chairman Jack Myerscough were in the American bar at the Queens Hotel. 'Jack had a bit of an eye for the ladies,' reveals Tony Waring, 'and he spotted a slim figure across the way with long blonde hair. Naturally, he went up for a chat and asked: "Can I get you a drink, love?" When she turned around, it was Rod Stewart.'

In fact, Eddie frequently found himself in the sights of what might then have been termed the counter-culture. In 1966, he was spoofed on *BBC-3*, a topical satire show fronted by the two Johns, Bird and Fortune. In a now long-forgotten skit on sports shows, Eddie was played by Roy Dotrice, while other actors took on the roles of David Vine and Peter O'Sullevan. Later, Waring would be referenced regularly by the Oxbridge set. In one episode of *Monty Python's Flying Circus*, for example, he was impersonated by Eric Idle playing Julius Caesar –'Arrr, tota Gallia divisa . . . est in TRES partes

Wigan, HUNslet and Hull KINGston Rovers' – as part of the fictional gameshow *Historical Impersonations*, hosted by Michael Palin's Wally Wiggin. In a *Python* episode subtitled 'Whither Canada', a character sounding suspiciously like Eddie marks Genghis Khan, Richard III and Abraham Lincoln on the inventiveness of their deaths. There were other such occasions, too, and in the first show of his follow-up to *Python*, *Ripping Yarns*, Palin also referenced Eddie in his very funny introduction to 'Tomkinson's Schooldays' (1976). Impersonated by Graeme Garden, Eddie Waring was a frequent presence in the long-running radio show *I'm Sorry, I'll Read That Again*, and when Garden, Tim Brooke-Taylor and Bill Oddie re-emerged as the Goodies, Eddie Waring – and this time the real Eddie Waring – turned up there as well.

Indeed, if there is one television appearance in the 1970s that might be said to run Eddie's appearance on *The Morecambe and Wise Christmas Show* a close second, it is surely his brilliant cameo in the 1973 festive special *The Goodies and the Beanstalk*. In it, the trandem-riding Buster Keaton-wannabes are homeless and destitute in downtown Cricklewood. After selling their infamous bike at auction in a desperate bid to raise funds, Bill, to the dismay of his two friends, returns home with a tin of baked beans. Graeme plants one of the beans in the ground, from which erupts the fabled beanstalk. Upon answering an ad for *It's a Knockout* competitors – one of whose challenges is to climb said vegetation – the zany threesome head for the clouds, where, after having stolen a number of golden eggs from geese belonging to the vertically challenged giant, they are pursued by the disgruntled birds, who proceed to rain down eggs like bombs. At the foot of the beanstalk, meanwhile, is none other than Eddie Waring, looking for all the world as if he is about to present the *fil rouge* – or, to adopt the correct pronunciation, 'thee-ah feeleh roooge'. When one golden egg hurtles in his direction, Eddie catches it, displays a perfect hand-off and sidestep and races away to an imaginary try-line, where he punches the air in delight.

'I remember being with Tim Brooke-Taylor in the BBC club in London,' recalls Tony Waring. 'He seemed slightly shy and a bit worried that my father was going to knock him over. Alfie Bass and John Cleese were in that show too, and my father thought it was all great fun; he wouldn't have done it if he hadn't. His sidestep in *The Goodies* was always a family favourite.' Clearly, Garden, Oddie and Brooke-Taylor enjoyed his contribution too. In 1975, Eddie was invited back to play a television host in that year's equally ridiculous Christmas special, *Goodies Rule – O.K?*, in which the nation is taken over by puppets.

Along with this and everything else, in 1971 Eddie Waring also narrated *The Ukulele Man*, a BBC documentary investigating the appeal of that other great Northern icon, George Formby. And, like Formby, Eddie also inspired an appreciation society in his name, albeit, in his case, one grounded in the campuses of Britain's universities rather than Blackpool's Golden Mile.

The seeds of a group that – if newspaper reports are to be believed – spread right across the country seem to have been sown at Lanchester Polytechnic, Coventry. It is from that establishment that a letter was sent on 'Official Eddie Waring Appreciation Society' notepaper to Eddie on 5 April 1972, thanking him for his acceptance of honorary membership. 'We originally hoped to put a picture of you in some membership cards we were going to have made,' the letter writer claimed, before adding rather cheekily:

> we couldn't find a way of obtaining sufficient of adequate quality at a reasonable economic cost. We would still very much like to produce these membership cards so have you any ideas where we could obtain approximately 600 passport sized (or slightly smaller) pictures of you? This would be just sufficient to satisfy this and next academic year's membership.[26]

Whatever its basis in reality, the notion of an Eddie Waring Appreciation Society gained momentum. Indeed, the Northern club comic Nicky Martyn went so far as to cut a record aiming to cash in on the interest. In January 1974, the *Daily Mirror* claimed: 'Rugby fans at [Liverpool] university have won a grand for their new hobby – impersonating TV commentator Eddie Waring.' Some 25 years later, one former member of that group was revealed as none other than current Football Association chief Brian Barwick. The story, written shortly after the poaching of Barwick as ITV head of sport from the BBC, revealed how, in 1979, his original BBC job interview had been a bizarre one indeed. Barwick, said the report, had been a member of 'a hero-worshipping group of [Eddie Waring] fans featured on the now-defunct BBC *Nationwide* programme'. 'I told them I do the best Eddie Waring impression in Great Britain,' Barwick told *The Independent.* 'I said, if you do give me a second interview, I will do it all in Eddie Waring.'[27]

This knowing, ironic strain continued to be a feature of the reaction to Eddie right up to his retirement and beyond. Around 1971, the decidedly trippy prog-rock band Help Yourself recorded an obscure, if not half bad, extended guitar solo called 'Eddie Waring', written by Deke Leonard – the sort of thing that turned up as a matter of course back then on *The Old Grey Whistle Test.*[28] And in 1988, as part of a collaboration with Leeds band the Mekons, under the name Sportchestra, the communal agitpop anarchists Chumbawamba released a double album, *101 Songs About Sport*, number 83 of which was also called 'Eddie Waring'.

Meanwhile, back in the mainstream, the 1970s were also notable for Eddie's aforementioned appearance on *Desert Island Discs*, during which he revealed a talent for catnapping and admitted that although he played records a lot, it wasn't as often as he would like because his was the sort of a job where finding time was difficult. Once cast adrift, Eddie said, he would like the music chosen to remind him of the past, cheer him up, put him to sleep, rest him and, if he got lonely, allow him to think of 'someone else there that I knew'. When asked by Roy Plomley whether he would try to escape, Eddie replied: 'Not immediately. Not for quite a while. But I think eventually I might.' On television, Eddie's musical and religious interests merged as he twice presented *Songs of Praise*, when that Sunday-night religious show visited Thornton Cleveleys and Sheffield in 1973, an undertaking, according to Dave Parker, that left its temporary host 'chuffed to bits'.

* * *

Eddie Waring continued to work like a demon away from the broadcast media too. In Michael Wale's *Radio Times* profile of Waring in 1971, for example, the writer noted:

> When he isn't preparing for Rugby League games; writing his column for the *Sunday Mirror* (Northern editions) or working on *Knockout* with Barney Colehan, Eddie is busy rushing from charity event to charity event. Besides the *Songs of Praise* service on the Wednesday of the week I was with him he did a show for the Pakistani flood fund and visited a remand home outside Leeds where he showed Rugby League films, held a quiz in which he dressed each participant in an outsize, but real, international Rugby League shirt and staged an *Any Questions?* session.

In the evening, Wale wrote, Waring also attended a charity event in aid of cerebral palsy.

There were regular requests for charitable assistance in the post, too. 'Dear Mr Waring,' began one such, from a young Wakefield Trinity supporter named David McGill in 1978:

> My dad has been to every Rugby League Cup final at Wembley since 1946. Since I have been old enough he has taken me with him. But this year he has been ill and he is in hospital so he cannot go. He is very upset at not being able to go but he is letting me go with his friend. Will you please be nice and say you hope he gets well soon during your commentary of the final on May 13th?[29]

Sometimes, the letter writers drafted in celebrity back-up. 'Hi Eddie,' came one scribbled note from a certain Jimmy Savile OBE in November 1975. 'Could you do anything about this?' Attached was a letter sent to *Jim'll Fix It* by ward sister Margaret Pooley of

Tehidy Hospital, Camborne. 'I have a 17-year-old patient, Tony, on the ward who last July suffered brain damage in a motor cycle accident,' it began.

> He is now improving and aware of his surroundings, can understand all that goes on and that is said to him, but cannot communicate as he is unable to talk or move except for a slight nod or shake of the head. He has been offered cassette recordings of any books that he wishes to be read to him but all he wants is a recording of Eddie Wearing [sic] as rugby was Tony's love before his accident and he played for Cornwall in the under 23yr team.[30]

Although Eddie did appear on *Jim'll Fix It* the following February, it was to commentate on a pillow fight on a plank over a swimming pool between the boxer Henry Cooper and 20-year-old Louis Manning. That he did send the recording as requested, however, is apparent in a news story published in *The People* on 3 October 1976. 'The voice of Eddie Waring has helped save a life,' it began. 'For although his commentaries have irritated and outraged Rugby League fans his words were music to the ears of Rugby enthusiast Tony Calloway.' For days, the report said, Tony had lain in a coma without showing any sign of recovery. After the hospital's request for help, Eddie, with the aid of BBC producer Geoff Wilson, prepared a recorded message. 'Tony recognised the voice and . . . now he's out of hospital and making a slow but steady recovery.'

Tragically, the previously indefatigable Eddie Waring's own health was about to take a terrible and distressing turn for the worse.

Nine

BE NOT AFRAID

''Eeez goin', goin', still goin'... 'eez gone.'

According to many of his more sympathetic admirers, Eddie Waring's biggest mistake as a rugby league commentator was simply that he outstayed his welcome.

'My own personal regret is that Eddie wasn't managed to retire,' says one such, the former Rugby Football League PRO David Howes. 'As so often happens, you do one year too many and end up being measured on that, rather than all the years before. Somebody should have advised Eddie earlier that he had peaked.' In Howes' own 1995 tribute to Waring, meanwhile, his former RFL boss David Oxley mused that Eddie 'always maintained that he knew when the time would be right to call it a day'. In hindsight, things could not have been so predictable either way.

Listening to Waring's later commentaries now, it is painfully apparent how, from the mid-'70s onwards, his grasp of events on the field began to slip. In that light, his comically unsteady appearance on *The Morecambe and Wise Christmas Show* in 1977 takes on a more poignant air entirely. At the time, of course, it looked like a simple matter of age. The years were catching up with Eddie: no more to it than that. In journalistic terms, the writing had been on the wall for a while. When Eddie reached retirement age in 1975, the *Sunday Mirror* replaced him with another, lesser-known journalist named George Dowson. In the event, Dowson lasted just 18 months, but the man who took over after that, John Huxley, recalls how his predecessor-but-one's standards had slipped. 'I took over the job that Eddie used to have at the *Sunday Mirror* in 1977,' says Huxley, latterly a respected member of the RFL media department. 'Dear old Eddie had fallen out with the paper by then, but in his last few years he had struggled to produce his copy. Other people were doing his work for him, although it was still going in under his name. It seemed as though he was showing his age a bit.'[1]

Quite naturally, Eddie was less fluent with a microphone than he once was too, but wasn't that more than made up for by his still bubbly personality? Certainly, that is the way his employers, the BBC, appear to have viewed it, even if his critics, as evidenced by the 1895 Club's petition of 1976, took a contrary view. What no one – including Eddie himself – realised was that the situation was far more serious than that. Although his symptoms would not have been publicly described in this way at the time, and indeed still remain open to doubt where exact medical diagnosis is concerned, it seems clear that Eddie was in the early stages of what would now be widely recognised as Alzheimer's. Aged 66, the lively minded go-getter Eddie Waring, as prodigious a visionary as British sport has seen, had fallen prey to one of the most pernicious and cruel diseases of all.

In attempting to place Alzheimer's into some sort of medical perspective, we can perhaps do no better than quote the website of Britain's own Alzheimer's Society. According to that organisation, the disease is just one relatively common form of progressive dementia, more often than not associated with those over the age of 65. Its symptoms include loss of memory, confusion and problems with speech and understanding. 'Loss of short term memory is a common early sign,' a helpsheet published by the Society says. 'The person with Alzheimer's may forget about recent conversations or events. They may repeat themselves. They may be slower at grasping new ideas or lose the thread of what is being said. The person with Alzheimer's . . . may show . . . an unwillingness to try out new things or adapt to change.' In the middle stages of the disease, 'The person is likely to become increasingly forgetful, particularly of names, and may sometimes repeat the same question or phrase over and over because of the decline in their short term memory. They may also fail to recognise people or confuse them with others.' And finally, as the dementia runs its terminal course, 'the person with Alzheimer's will need even more help, gradually becoming totally dependent on others for nursing care . . . The person will also become increasingly physically frail. They may start to shuffle or walk unsteadily, eventually becoming confined to bed or a wheelchair . . . Although the person with Alzheimer's may seem to have little understanding of speech and may not recognise those around them, they may still respond to affection, to people talking in a calm soothing voice, or they may enjoy scents [or] music.'[2]

Spiritually, Eddie was well-prepared for the battle to come. For as he had told his viewers in that 1973 *Songs of Praise* broadcast from Thornton Cleveleys, just a tram ride away from his son's alma mater near Fleetwood: 'The first oratorio I took part in was Mendelssohn's "Elijah". My father was conducting it in Yorkshire. I was only a lad at the time, but there I was among the basses. There's one chorus from "Elijah" that's stuck in my mind ever since, and the words come back especially at moments of pressure or difficulty: "Though thousands languish and fall beside thee and tens of thousands around thee perish, yet still it shall not come nigh thee." So I'm going to enjoy listening to the choir here singing this chorus now – "Be Not Afraid".'

Nor did things deteriorate straight away to anything like the degree they did later. For his unknowing fans outside rugby league particularly, the apparently harmless effects of Eddie's advancing years simply added to the enjoyment of his comical and eccentric television persona. This, perhaps, is an important mitigating factor when contemplating how it was that Waring's BBC employers did not take charge of the situation earlier. For while it might be reasonable to accuse the BBC of putting its loyalty to Eddie and/or the desire to present rugby league in a certain way before the needs of the game itself, there is no doubt that Eddie himself was held in a great deal of affection by many within the Corporation. The BBC circles in which Eddie moved were not made up of cynical and faceless Establishment bureaucrats. Many of these people were Eddie's closest friends and would not have done anything deliberately to harm him. Sadly, as time went on, in a perhaps misguided bid to protect Eddie, they left him open to attack just when he was at his most vulnerable.

Of course, rather than acknowledge the complicating presence of real human beings at the levers of power, each with his or her own attitudes and emotions, it is far easier to view the motives of organisations like the BBC in monolithic black and white. If, for his increasingly voluble critics, the commentator himself was the problem, to others Eddie was merely an unfortunate dupe in a bigger and more sinister process. According to this theory, it was the BBC who promoted Eddie Waring as Northern caricature, ensuring that the wider world never got to appreciate all the positive contributions to the game he had made before. Yet while such a point of view is understandable and not a little comforting, it is also a rather patronising and fundamental oversimplification of the facts.

By and large, the complaints aimed at Eddie before the late '60s were merely of a type always aimed at broadcasters, whatever their hue. Frankly, the BBC could have put Sir Laurence Olivier in the commentary box and he would have been criticised too. When, as the '60s became the '70s, his career took a more pronounced swing towards showbiz, star-struck Eddie, blessed with theatrical roots, seemed only too delighted to play along – and why not? After all, he was promoting the game, and making people laugh is no crime; to be a comedian is an honourable thing. With the onset of old age and an initially undiagnosed illness, a television image that was always an extension of the five-parts-showman, five-parts-shy man off screen simply grew exaggerated. For that, at least, no one was to blame. Not Eddie. Not the BBC. Not the rugby league fans who sought greater respect for their favourite sport. It was life, fate, or whatever you want to call it, that's all, playing its unfathomable tricks.

* * *

As keenly as we may wish otherwise, none of us goes on forever. For Eddie Waring, the time to put away his bag of fruit and hand over the microphone came with the Premiership final of 1981, an all-East Yorkshire affair between Hull and Hull Kingston Rovers at Leeds. Suitably, his closing words, when they came, were more homely than historic, carrying echoes of that Watersplash final of some 13 years before. 'So there it is,' Eddie said. 'Back to David Coleman in the *Grandstand* studio. It's all yours, David, lad.' To which Coleman replied: 'The television presentation of the match was by Nick Hunter, summaries were by Alex Murphy and, for the last time in *Grandstand*, we say the commentator was . . . Eddie Waring.'

For many, however, the truly symbolic moment of Eddie's departure had already occurred, just two weeks before on Saturday, 2 May 1981. For it was then, at the 'Three Fives' Challenge Cup final between eventual winners Widnes and Hull Kingston Rovers, that the reality of the situation really hit home. Who could imagine Wembley without Eddie Waring? In the official match-day programme, priced 60p and boasting other such Northern notables as Cannon and Ball (leading the pre-match community renditions of 'Ilkla Moor B'aht 'At', 'She's a Lassie from Lancashire' and 'Abide with Me'), the flat-capped steeplejack Fred Dibnah and ostrich-riding Bernie Clifton, there appeared a personal tribute penned by Rugby League secretary general David Oxley. 'Today, some 11 million people will witness the end of an era,' Oxley wrote. 'Eddie Waring, the most famous voice in Rugby League, will be covering his last Wembley final.'

By 30 January 1981, the date of the official announcement of Eddie Waring's retirement, it was evident that for everyone's sake, not least that of Eddie himself, a change simply had to come. The

BBC, treading the trickiest of tightropes, with one eye doubtless on contractual obligations and the other on its employee's professional and personal dignity, agreed to let Eddie complete the season, but few were in any doubt as to the significance of the Wembley occasion. Once the news was out, the newspapers were full of admiring career obituaries, mostly supportive but always laden with catchphrases and acknowledging the controversy that had dogged Eddie's later broadcasting career in particular.

'Sports supporters of every persuasion (though some may feel that rugby league and *It's a Knockout* are not far removed),' wrote John Groser in *The Times*,'will be saddened to hear that Mr Eddie Waring, godfather of the oval ball, has decided to take an early bath.'[3] More tactfully, in the *Daily Telegraph*, Roger Heywood reported: 'Eddie Waring, whose down-to-earth comments helped to simplify the complexities of Rugby League for millions of television viewers in the south, is to quit as BBC commentator on the sport at the end of the season.'[4] Paul Keel, in *The Guardian*, said that Eddie's approach had 'provoked mimicry in the South and apoplexy in the North'.[5]

In fact, matters were rather more geographically complex than that. Also writing in *The Guardian*, the following day, the St Helens-born but London-based actor and screenwriter Colin Welland stated explicitly the case for the opposition. Though one letter writer to the same newspaper some four days later, the Very Reverend John Regan of Cathedral Church of St Paul, Dundee, described the timing of Welland's piece as 'unfair and ungracious',[6] it is nevertheless worth quoting at length because it so eloquently captures the complex emotions felt by many where Eddie's contribution to rugby league was concerned.

'When Eddie Waring announced his retirement, Rugby League heaved a sigh of relief,' Welland began.

> We all love Eddie. He's a really nice man. He's been to our house, his son lives around the corner from me in Barnes. Eddie used to get me tickets for the Cup final before I had a bit of pull myself. Consequently, it has pained me and the rest of us over the last

few years to see the disservice he was doing to himself and the game. For the blunt truth of the matter is that Rugby League has evolved beyond him, passed him by.

Although Eddie and the BBC had indeed made rugby league nationally popular, Welland insisted it was for all the wrong reasons. The sport portrayed in the television spectacle that the nation had 'built such a patronising affection for' bore little or no relation to the one found in reality. 'The game is more than a line of giant clowns rushing at each other and falling in heaps,' he continued.

> But the BBC have liked it that way. They have encouraged Eddie to develop his whole style towards presenting it as such and as a result have done the game a continuing disservice. They have made a most likeable man, who has Rugby League wholly at heart, synonymous with an image of the professional code which is woefully inaccurate.[7]

Supportive to the end, the BBC revealed that although Waring was indeed to step down from his main role, he would continue to be employed as the Corporation's 'Rugby League Advisor'. 'I know how much Eddie will be missed through the country,' said BBC head of sport Alan Hart, 'because he's done more than anyone else to develop the popularity of the sport he loves. However, we're all delighted that his enormous experience won't be lost to the BBC, and we will continue to benefit from his advice and guidance.' In a ready-made sound bite, Waring himself added: 'After nearly 30 years of doing commentaries, I think I should let someone else climb those steep ladders to the commentary points.'

As if to underline the extent to which, in recent years, Waring was more likely to shrink from a spotlight than bathe in it, as the announcement of his retirement was made, Eddie and Mary took themselves out of the way on holiday. 'As time went on, Eddie grew embarrassed about going into shops and being recognised,' recalls Dave Parker. 'On your way to meet him he would ask you to buy him some throat lozenges or pop or whatever.' Harry Jepson, too, recalls Eddie's increasing discomfort when it came to dealing with his extreme level of fame. 'When he was getting towards the end of his days as a commentator,' says Jepson, 'he suffered not a change in personality exactly, but he did seem to shun publicity. I remember once, at Leeds in the 1970s, Jack Myerscough asked if I would walk around to the commentary position with Eddie. He was nervous about walking through the crowd from the pavilion at Headingley to the South Stand, where he had to climb that famous old spiral staircase. He put the collar of his overcoat up and was wearing a trilby as usual. Everyone still knew it was Eddie Waring, of course.'

Such a reaction is all the more touching when one considers how, with the news of his imminent departure, the massed ranks of the everyday rugby league public seemed suddenly keen to swamp Eddie in affection. This particular majority could hardly be described as silent, but perhaps your average supporter had felt that way all along. Either way, in reporting how Eddie was received on his final appearance at Hull Kingston Rovers, the *Yorkshire Post* opened an illuminating window on the issue, reporting that:

> Evidence of [Eddie's] fame was all around him at Craven Park on Saturday when spectators young and old called out 'good luck, Eddie' and 'happy retirement'. The hardened, outspoken east Hull fans were obviously speaking from the heart and Eddie Waring – commentating for the first time since his recently announced retirement – was left in no doubt of his popularity. Eager young fans, showing obvious respect and admiration, sensed this occasion as they crowded round for him to autograph programmes – souvenirs they will no doubt treasure for years.[8]

With the arrival of his last Challenge Cup final, tributes continued to be published. Perhaps the best and certainly the most perceptive, written by Geoffrey Mather in the *Daily Express*, took Eddie's religious faith and devotion to music as its theme. 'As he climbed the long ladder to the commentary box at Headingley, Leeds,' wrote Mather, 'Eddie Waring used to sing to himself three verses of "Fight the Good Fight". When he came to the words "Faint not, nor fear, His arms are near," he knew he had at last arrived.' Once the famous last words were spoken, Mather continued, it would be 'like the removal of Nelson's Column. Life's steps are climbed. The good fight is fought. The monument can rest content.'[9] Meanwhile, in the *Sunday Times*, David May wrote:

> In the 30 years Waring has been broadcasting he has propelled rugby league from a grim and barely understood northern ritual into a television spectacular attracting audiences of up to 10 million viewers for BBC *Grandstand*. Since he announced his retirement . . . he has received thousands of letters wishing him well.[10]

Watch and hear so much as a short burst of the 1981 Challenge Cup-final commentary now, however, and despite the odd banner in the Wembley crowd bearing a goodwill message like 'Goodbye Eddie W.', it is on the whole a desperately sad experience. As the action speeds to and fro before him, the 71-year-old Eddie struggles to keep up as best he can. 'For those people who say, well, give us the score, it's 5 to 2,' he says at one point, before a sudden attacking break leads him to shout, 'And a chance, a chance, more than a chance, a try! A . . . very . . . good . . . try . . . indeed . . . by . . . Mick George.' 'This is a break, and the support, and a try, this is a break [pause] Andy . . . Gregory,' goes another such moment of non-revelation before, at long last, Eddie's final Challenge Cup commentary concludes with the words: 'Mick Burke has won the Lance Todd Trophy . . . is there going to be a late try? No, and there goes the final hooter.'

'How Eddie got through it, I don't know,' recalls his nephew Harry. 'He could no longer memorise players' names because he was ill. It was a tremendously brave achievement.'

* * *

On the eve of his Wembley retirement, Eddie was the focus of a BBC documentary, *Success Story*, his show in that strand sandwiched neatly between episodes devoted to prog-rock keyboard wizard Rick Wakeman and actor Anthony Newley.

And although his rugby league broadcasting career would soon be behind him, in the short term at least, there were further brief moments in the sun for Eddie to enjoy. In March 1980, for example he featured on BBC Radio 2's *Be My Guest*, in which, as on *Desert Island Discs*, he got to select some favourite pieces of music. Along with the theme tune to the Floodlit Trophy – 'Entente Cordiale', a brass-band piece 'which said to me: "Come on! Let's enjoy this game together"' – Eddie chose 'Deep Harmony', Peter Dawson's 'Maori Poi Song', 'Delilah' and, tellingly perhaps, something by Edith Piaf, another diminutive and geographically precise public figure who, in her day, was no stranger to the creative mingling of myth and reality. 'I know I could say, "I did it my way,"' Eddie told his listeners, 'which is in the same sort of mould, possibly.' But no, for Eddie, it was 'Non, Je Ne Regrette Rien'. 'We Sail the Ocean Blue' from *HMS Pinafore* was another choice, along with 'Eternally' from Charlie Chaplin's 1952 film about a faded vaudevillian, *Limelight*. Topping it all off was 'The Day We Went to Bangor', a song about a trip to the seaside performed by the folk group Fiddler's Dram.

Shortly before his last Challenge Cup final, meanwhile, the Rugby Football League formally recognised Eddie's contribution to the sport and made him a life member, an honour that brought him great pleasure. Then, in December 1981, came an even bigger boost. Edward Marsden Waring was to be awarded an MBE for services to rugby league. 'That was fantastic,' remembers Tony Waring, of the occasion three months later when Eddie joined fellow sporting superstars John Toshack and Bob Willis in receiving his award. 'We stayed at the Athenium Hotel in London, courtesy of the chap who had been the manager of the Queens in Leeds, Ronnie Jones. Ronnie said he would be honoured to have us as his guests, and it was very convenient for Buckingham Palace. The BBC laid on a Daimler Limousine to collect us, and off my father went to get his MBE from the Queen. Afterwards, they organised a special lunch at Television Centre. A lot of his friends and colleagues, including Ray and Muriel Lakeland, Cliff Morgan, Frank Bough, David Coleman, Alan Hart and Bryan Cowgill, were there, and there were speeches and congratulations and so on. Both my parents enjoyed and appreciated it. My father was always very loyal to the BBC, and they in turn were loyal to him. He looked very dapper in his top hat and tails.' Eddie told the *Evening Standard*: 'The Queen knew so much about the game I almost got tongue-tied.'[11]

Despite brief oases of hope, Eddie's health had deteriorated badly. While, initially, it was announced that Eddie would continue to participate in *It's a Knockout*, it soon became clear that even the light duties demanded by that show would now be too much. Even so, other than taking a week off for heat four in Luton – where his place was taken by guest presenters Paul Shane, Ruth Madoc and Su Pollard from the BBC sitcom *Hi-De-Hi!* – Eddie did complete the 1981 series as planned. To describe it as a bit of a slog would be an understatement. Showing great determination, Eddie battled on gallantly but, to the distress of colleagues and viewers alike, began to slur his speech and appeared unfocused; the old Eddie spark had gone. After one last domestic contest, recorded at the Derby Baths, Blackpool, came his final challenge: heat seven of *Jeux Sans Frontières*.

Although, as a result of cuts to the BBC budget, Eddie no longer travelled to the European heats, meaning Stuart Hall provided those commentaries single-handed, when *Jeux Sans Frontières* came to Britain, Eddie presented the *fil rouge*. Hall remembers his colleague's very last show, recorded in Sunderland on 25 August but shown on Friday, 30 October, as being particularly difficult. 'We were to pretend to have a stately home,' he says. 'Eddie was the master, I was the chauffeur and butler. Two days before the recording, we filmed in a Rolls-Royce Silver Ghost out on the hills of Northumberland. He murmured, "What am I doing?" and I said, "Not a lot. All you have to do is say yes, no and thank you." His mind was already going. On the night of the recording, we had the Rolls positioned in front of the stately home. Frankly, Eddie had no idea what was going on. So I opened the car door and told him that all he had to say was, "It's great to be here and I'm off to my marathon." Then I would reply, "Yes, sir, thank you. Delighted to be your servant." I didn't realise then how severe his condition already was, but I wasn't going to tell the producer that he couldn't do it, I was determined to shepherd him through. Eddie was a pal. We had been mates and conquered Europe together, there was no way that he was going down. As it turned out, he did get through it and that was the last programme we did.'

With the job seen through, as the show approached its closing credits Eddie raised a glass of champagne to the camera and bade everyone watching goodnight. He knew his time was over.

* * *

Around three weeks after the little white dot finally blipped on Eddie Waring's television career, the shadows of his predicament lengthened alarmingly when he was taken ill whilst on a well-deserved holiday in the south of France.

The British media, when it picked up on Eddie's turn for the worse, reported it as a heart attack. 'The 71-year-old Rugby League expert and star of *It's a Knockout* is expected to be flown home to Leeds by air ambulance today,' *The Sun* informed its readers on 18 September 1981. 'He was rushed to hospital on Wednesday after collapsing with chest pains. His condition is not believed to be serious.' As those closest to him realised only too well, events were of far greater significance than that.

As usual, though, Eddie and his family were determined to keep the gravity of the situation to themselves. As his old BBC producer Nick Hunter told the same newspaper: 'He has constantly strived to keep his public and private lives separate, and has been very successful at it. When he gets home and puts his slippers on he is a completely different person.' Eddie's return, when it took place, was on a special flight organised by the St John Ambulance

Brigade. Upon landing at Leeds Bradford Airport, it was reported, Eddie would be taken to the intensive-care unit at Wharfedale General Hospital, Otley. In the event, back in England the initial heart-attack diagnosis was downgraded to a 'heart rhythm defect'. By 21 September, Eddie was out of hospital and back recovering in Bramhope, with a message from his doctors: 'No more work – just rest.'

Along with Mary, Eddie had travelled to Antibes, a Mediterranean resort town on the Côte d'Azur, with nephew Harry and his wife, Pat. At first, says Harry, the holiday was progressing nicely. 'Sitting on the apartment balcony and having a cup of tea,' he remembers, 'we talked briefly about the Black Knights jersey he had given me as a child. He told me that when he was doing Floodlit Trophy commentaries he had suggested to the RFL, through Jack Myerscough, I think, that it might be an idea for rugby league to have a Barbarians-style representative side. They could play champagne rugby against leading sides during public-holiday periods, bringing good publicity. He even offered to get a team of stars together for the inaugural match. He said he wanted to call them the Black Knights.' Once the illness struck, however, there was only one thought on anyone's mind: getting Eddie home, as calmly and quickly as possible. 'When he first fell ill,' continues Harry, 'Eddie was taken into hospital in Nice. At first, he appeared to recover but then suffered a relapse and had to be flown home in a Lear jet. He was adamant he didn't want any publicity. When we flew into the airport, Pat and myself acted as decoys for the press because Eddie wouldn't get out until they had gone.'

Once back at Langside, Eddie settled into a period of what was initially hoped to be recuperation but which, in time, developed into circumstances far less hopeful. Even then, though, with friends and family rallying around, there were moments to lighten the gloom. 'I used occasionally to take Eddie out on a Saturday afternoon,' says Harry. 'On one trip, in October 1983, I took him to watch Leeds. We were in the room with the large windows overlooking the corner of the ground at the dressing-room end. About ten minutes before kick-off, Eddie walked towards the window. On seeing him, the spectators in the North Stand stood and applauded as though they were wishing him well and pleased to see him back at Headingley. Like a Mexican wave, it started there and went right around the ground. It was a spontaneous tribute from die-hard supporters of rugby league and one that gave him a tremendous boost at a very difficult time. It was a very moving moment.'

It was during these difficult times, too, that Mary, always a source of huge strength to Eddie, provided her greatest support. 'Before Eddie's illness, I used to call Mary "the Producer",' says former BBC producer Ray Lakeland. 'She used to tell him what he was doing wrong in his commentaries and how to get it better, and I used to have to put it right. But we got on very well with Mary. She was a great prop to him. She was everything to him, no doubt about that. He wouldn't have been anything without her. She had him sorted. When he had to go away to do a job, she would pack his bag for him and put little labels on his shirt – wear this shirt tonight and that suit tomorrow, and so forth. She really looked after him.' And no more so than now. 'Well, they do say that behind every successful man is a woman, and my mum was tremendously supportive,' confirms Tony. 'You can imagine how important it is when you are in the public eye to have someone who can look after you. My mother was a tremendous lady. She was advisor, supporter, guide and sounding board. Certainly latterly, when my father was poorly, she did a tremendous lot to help him.'

By July 1983, however, Eddie's deterioration had reached the point where, reluctantly, a decision was taken that he would be better off in professional care. At first, that meant a Quaker nursing home near York, where, according to his former employers at the *Sunday Mirror*, 'these days he tends to watch a quiet game of bowls with a couple of pretty nurses'. Well, Eddie did always have a thing for nurses. 'A far cry from the boisterous "up-and-under" of Rugby League,' continued the *Mirror*. 'We wish him well.' Quite quickly, though, Eddie returned home to Bramhope, where, shortly before Christmas, after being housebound for several weeks, his condition again took a major turn for the worse and he was admitted to High Royds Hospital, Menston.

Even at this point, most people within rugby league were oblivious to the real nature of the illness. Many, including several of those closest to Eddie, blamed his apparent downfall on sudden retirement after such an active career. Perhaps, back in those less enlightened days when the understanding of mental-health issues was less developed than it seems to be today, there was a simple, if misguided, fear of stigma. Either way, Eddie's by now complete absence from public view served only to heighten the air of mystery until, on 29 December 1983, the press were finally informed that the former 'voice of rugby league' was now very ill indeed. As one report in the *Daily Star* put it: 'TV personality Eddie Waring has been admitted to a psychiatric hospital after being taken seriously ill at Christmas.' It went on: 'His wife Mary said: "Obviously it has been a time of grief. But the support and affection shown by his friends has been overwhelming."'[12]

With Eddie an apparently permanent resident at High Royds, Mary, now living on her own, opted to sell Langside and relocate to nearby Ilkley. Although the move must have been heartbreaking, it was also appropriate in all manner of ways, some practical, some sentimental. Not least of which was the fact that, since Eddie's childhood, this small Yorkshire town on the banks of the River Wharfe had long been a favoured day-trip venue for the Warings. 'In Dewsbury, the family used to go on trips up to Ilkley Moor all the time,' says Tony Waring. 'It was one of the places they would go on Sunday school outings. My father always loved Ilkley. When we lived in Bramhope, we were up there quite a lot. I remember once when the BBC's Ronnie Noble, a Southerner, came up to Leeds and my father took him to Ilkley. Ronnie, a lovely man, couldn't believe it. He thought the North was all coal mines. My father liked that about Ilkley and the moors: that it was a side of Yorkshire that people were not necessarily aware of. He liked its character. Ilkley is a nice, genteel little place but it's also a bit of a frontier town, with people coming in from all over the Dales and so on.'

For Mary, therefore, the blow of losing the family home was lessened. 'My mother was very reluctant to let my father go into hospital,' continues her son. 'But it got to the point where, because he had some form of dementia, he needed the care of that environment. Nowadays, people tend to call it Alzheimer's, but they were never sure, and he came down to London for all sorts of tests. Whatever the diagnosis, the people at High Royds looked after him very well. When it became clear that my father wasn't going to be able to come home, my mum was still in this big house in Bramhope, with the fences being blown down in winter and that sort of thing. So she sold it and moved to a flat on the road up to White Wells, overlooking the moors. That worked well, because my mother suffered from arthritis and she was able to drive in underneath and into the garage where there was only one step up into the lift that took her up to her flat. Of course, it was very convenient for getting to the hospital too.'

Once resettled in Ilkley, Mary visited Eddie every day. 'It was a very difficult time and my mum was a real stalwart,' says Tony. As indeed were the massed ranks of close friends and former colleagues from both the Rugby Football League and the BBC who continued to offer support whenever it was needed. Eddie's old *It's a Knockout* partner Stuart Hall, for instance, remembers how, on one occasion, the Waring family brought Eddie out of High Royds for the day. 'I went along and he looked so young and healthy. His complexion was great and he carried himself well. But when I went over to him to say hello, he didn't know who I was. I said, "I'm your old chum, Stuart."

'"Oh no you're not," he said, "Stuart was a lot different from you."'

At Tony's request, old friends such as Jack Myerscough and Harry Jepson visited Eddie in hospital too – an attempt to jog his rapidly deteriorating powers of recollection. Given the merciless and ultimately terminal nature of the condition, it was a noble if futile task. Even a mind as bright and alive as Eddie Waring's was powerless in the face of such a devastatingly cruel disease. After over half a decade of the most debilitating, unforgiving personal struggle throughout what ought to have been the happiest of retirements, and a good many more years spent bringing sunshine to the lives of millions, the unforgettable Edward Marsden Waring MBE, boyhood soccer star, precocious youth coach, innovator, successful secretary-manager, campaigning newspaper journalist, intrepid international traveller, diplomat, facilitator, adorer of trains and music, players' champion, public showman, private family man, author, fund-raiser, comedian, entrepreneur, broadcasting legend and, most importantly of all, warm and decent human being, relaxed his grip on the harsh strains and cares of this life and, on 28 October 1986, ever the free spirit, embarked upon the greatest adventure of all.

* * *

On the day of Eddie Waring's funeral, held at St Giles' Church, Bramhope, the flagpole of the local working-men's club in Ilkley, within view of Mary's flat, flew the Union Jack at half mast. At High Royds, to show their gratitude at the way Eddie had been looked after, the Waring family set up a trust fund to buy a minibus for patients in his memory – an apt notion indeed for a man who once told Peter Black of the *Daily Mail* that his idea of a perfect day was 'a good, steady run into the country for a nice lunch, then slipping up to the coast to meet a few pals, and a nice quiet run home and finish with a good theatre show'.

As might be expected, for this, Eddie's final public appearance, the TV cameras were there and every seat in the house was taken. Among the hundreds of cards and flowers on display, from a vast army of well-wishers, was one bidding 'farewell to one of broadcasting's true originals, from all his friends in *Grandstand*'. The list of mourners passed 150 and included – apart from Eddie's own family – friends, former colleagues and their own wives and families. From the BBC came Bryan Cowgill, Cliff Morgan, Alan Hart, Keith Phillips, Nick Hunter and Jonathan Martin among others. Having ironically, in light of Eddie's earlier advice, now moved to

Yorkshire TV, Paul Fox attended too. Representing *It's a Knockout* were Arthur Ellis and Barney Colehan. Among the rugby league notables were Ernest Ward, David Oxley, Charlie Seeling, Arthur Clues, Dickie Williams, Jim Ledgard and, on behalf of the Australian Rugby League touring team, Tony Smith. Quite a number of rugby league journalists were also present, including John Yates of the *Rugby Leaguer*, John Morgan of the *Yorkshire Evening Post*, Raymond Fletcher of the *Yorkshire Post*, Peter Shaw of the *Sunday Mirror* and John Robinson of *The People*. There was even a Mr Gordon Hall in attendance, representing British Transport Hotels and the British Railways Board, while Steve Maslen was there on behalf of Queens Hotel managers and staff, past and present.

Oh, yes. One more young guest was on hand too: someone who, in true Eddie Waring style, establishes a delightfully direct link between the music of the past and that of today – not that anyone could have known it at the time. For, in honour of the occasion, the St Giles' Church choir was, for one day only, complemented by guest singers from Leeds Grammar School choir. In the congregation, meanwhile, was the Ilkley-based TV producer Geoff Wilson and his wife, the former scoregirl Glyn, colleagues of Eddie on *It's a Knockout* and parents of two boys, James and Richard, to whom Eddie was godfather. As a beautiful service neared its conclusion, and the curtain finally came down on Eddie's packed and fruitful life, choirboy Richard delivered a spell-binding solo performance of 'Pie Jesu', the memorable high point of an already emotional day. These days, that young choirboy is perhaps better known as Ricky Wilson, lead singer of the hugely successful Leeds band Kaiser Chiefs.

Quite rightly, despite the sadness, the funeral of Eddie Waring was as much a celebration of a life well-lived as a day of sorrow. Even the vicar himself, the Reverend John Raymond Ward, seems to have harboured secret end-of-the-pier ambitions: 'I am sure that Eddie will be going "up not under",' he quipped to reporters. For Mary, however, though proud of Eddie's professional achievements of course, the sense of personal loss was shattering. All the physical and emotional stress of guiding Eddie though his troubled last years, a task borne with seemingly endless endurance, had taken its toll. Just three short years after watching the light in Eddie extinguished before her, the demands of that struggle proved too great and Mary too passed away, broken-hearted.

* * *

Writing in *The Times*, days after Eddie's funeral in November 1986, the diarist Simon Barnes reflected:

> Eddie Waring died this week unregretted by many people in Rugby League. They felt his clowning commentaries – 'eh, there's steak pie in them legs, lad' – did great harm to their sport. 'It's taken us years to recover from that man,' a rugby league person once told me. The sport shows great ingratitude to the most significant populariser it has ever had; it was Waring who brought Rugby League into the consciousness of people south of the Wash and showed us what a marvellous change it is from the kick-bloody-kick of rugby union. The sport should give three cheers for the old up-and-under king.[13]

Or, to put it another way, as the London-based Welshman Huw Richards did so eloquently some 17 years later:

> there's a good reason why a strikingly high proportion of the league fans I know in London are also followers of non-league soccer. It is a taste for the authentic, the unfashionable and the grassrooted. It is the reason why so much league humour is dry and ironic, an appreciation that life does not always live up to its promises, but a warm appreciation of what is genuine and worthwhile. This is perhaps why Eddie Waring had such an appeal for those of us growing up outside league's heartlands in his heyday of the 1960s and 1970s. Eddie loved the game and cared about it deeply. But it was always a source of enjoyment and humour. It mattered, but not disproportionately.[14]

Even now, more than two decades after his death, the fascination with Eddie Waring remains strong. And if, these days, the term 'iconic' is bandied about rather too frequently, it is an entirely appropriate way to describe Edward Marsden Waring. An icon he was and, signs are, an icon he will eternally remain.

For his detractors in England's North, stewing in a brew of genuine grievance and insecurity, Eddie Waring was a canvas upon which to paint their own anxieties and frustrations. Yes, a clichéd and unimaginative representation of any region can be irritating to those who think they know better. And, yes, it would be nice to see rugby league taken more seriously from time to time. But as for the rest, well, as Dave Woods, perhaps the next man to follow in Eddie's footsteps, insists, rugby league-loving Northerners ought not to be ashamed of their background: the very opposite in fact. The word 'Northern' does not have to be pejorative.

'As Northerners, we are too embarrassed at hearing our own accent and think that in some way it demeans us,' Woods says. 'I don't think it does. We are as exotic as any Cockney, aren't we? There is no reason why we should be ashamed of hearing a Dewsbury lad talking about rugby league on the television or worried about being lampooned. If we are, then that has more to do with our lack of self-confidence than anything grounded in reality. If we are Northern, we should be proud of it.' In other words, how can your life be positive, fulfilling and worthwhile if you spend all your time worrying what the neighbours think?

In the end, for any professional sport, it does not matter why people are watching, just so long as they are. In television terms, thanks to Eddie Waring, rugby league never had so many bums on seats. If, by simply opening his mouth, chuckling at the wrong moment or thanking some maiden aunt in Eastbourne for the nice new pair of knitted gloves she'd sent him as Clive Sullivan crashed over unnoticed for a try in the corner, Eddie sparked resentment in a few over-sensitive souls, then just whose problem was that exactly? Yes, to some extent his commentaries were a performance, but a performer is what Eddie was to the core. If Eddie Waring talked about brass bands and hymns, it was because he grew up with brass bands and hymns. If he referred to shipyards, railway lines and coal pits, there they were in the background. If he preferred to dwell on characters, rather than on the sport's deceptively complex tactics, that didn't mean he had no understanding of how it worked: on the contrary, until those last sorry years, he knew more about rugby league than anyone. If Eddie seemed fascinated by players' lives, it was because he liked and admired them as people and would try to help them at every opportunity. Nor, despite his comfortable lifestyle, did the game earn him a financial fortune. In his published will, Eddie left just £75,182, a not inconsiderable sum in 1986 but hardly a treasure trove either.[15] Ultimately, did those throwing brickbats really think that rugby league's grim and muddy knock-'em-down image was entirely down to the antics of some happy-go-lucky chap in a camel coat and trilby? If so, just who was kidding whom?

Whether through intransigence, ineptitude or outside interference, throughout the Eddie Waring era and beyond, rugby league has, until very recently, shown every inclination to remain a big fish in a small Northern pond. To paraphrase the modern-day Northern comedy troupe the League of Gentlemen, 'This is a local sport for local people. There's nothing for you here.' Inexplicably, while simultaneously insisting that rugby league is and always will be 'just' a Northern game, a sizeable proportion of the code's administrators, players, supporters and journalists have bemoaned the lack of attention given to the game nationally. To knock the one man who, historically, had enough wit and practical resources at his disposal to break free of those shackles yet who never lost sight of the qualities that make rugby league worth exporting in the first place seems perverse to a ridiculous degree.

No, to adopt a suitably Waring-esque aphorism, if ever there was a prophet without honour in his own land, then surely it was Eddie. For if rugby league was shaped to an extraordinary degree by Edward Marsden Waring, it is equally true to say that the extraordinary Edward Marsden Waring was shaped by rugby league. Then as now, north, south, east and west, there is nothing wrong with being Eddie Waring.

POSTSCRIPT

'Those who drink the water should remember those who dug the well.'
'The mill will not grind with the water that is passed.'
– two of Eddie Waring's favourite aphorisms

Wembley: Carnegie Challenge Cup final day, 25 August 2007. After an enforced seven-year hiatus, rugby league's annual showpiece occasion is back at its spiritual home: in the shadows of what were once the twin towers, now an impressive yawning metallic arch, glinting in the late summer sunshine like the exoskeleton of some giant futuristic clam.

If ever there was a time to marvel at life's capacity for reinvention and regeneration, it is here today, in this marriage of the traditional and the new. Step out of Wembley Park tube station and the sight that greets you is as spectacular as ever before. Stretching right up Wembley Way and beyond, heading inexorably towards the gleaming white cathedral on the horizon, there shimmers a colourful, vibrant ocean of carnival and noise. Replica tops from just about every rugby league club on the planet abound, awash in a sea of fancy dress, beer, singing and hot dogs. It is a vision guaranteed to bring anyone up short.

Meanwhile, in the stadium itself, bathed in 28-degree heat, the presence of a marching brass band lends another note of familiarity. The trademark shiny red seats are here too, if in greater number than before, and helping to dress the stadium there is a perimeter banner boasting the names of clubs from Dewsbury to Wigan to Workington to London, each with the date of their first – and in some cases only – Wembley appearance.

For all the time-honoured custom, however, apart from the majestic new stadium itself, something about today is novel indeed. For while one of the competing clubs, St Helens, appeared in the very first Challenge Cup final, against Batley at Headingley in 1897, their opponents have only been in existence for two years. From Perpignan, France – where *rugby à treize* has faced a battle simply to survive this past 70-odd years – come Catalans Dragons, the first non-British team ever to play in the Challenge Cup final and about to run out in front of the biggest crowd – some 85,000 – ever to watch a French rugby team in either code. Hence the preponderance of *sang-et-or* flags, the thousands of excited Mediterranean-coast accents, the inclusion of the Catalan anthem 'Els Segadors' in the pre-match build-up and the hordes of sympathetic Wigan fans clad in berets and strings of onions, despite the fact that it was the Catalans who knocked them out in the semi-final.

It seems too that, perhaps fleetingly, the national press has awoken to the implications of this momentous occasion. Since the advent of open professionalism in rugby union and the dawn of summer Super League in 1996, rugby league is now played at least to an amateur level in just about every county in England, along with lumps of Wales, Scotland and Ireland too. Overseas, 13-a-side competitions in the likes of Serbia, the Lebanon, Jamaica, Russia and the United States are sprouting up like so many small acorns from which, one day, mighty oaks may grow. On the weekend following the Wembley final, though beaten 30–8, the Catalans team would be introduced to a 90,000 crowd at the Nou Camp, Spain, before a La Liga soccer clash between Barcelona and Athletic Bilbao. In the words of the *Guardian* leader column: 'This no-nonsense game, born in the industrial North, is becoming as globalised today as most others.' How Eddie Waring would have loved that.

In a sense, of course, Eddie Waring is still among us, in spirit anyway. Certainly, by introducing rugby league to such a wide national audience, he was at least partly responsible for laying the foundations of its exciting growth today. Nevertheless, meaningful official recognition for his pioneering achievements is negligible.

From 1987, the year after Eddie's death, the Rugby Football League, in association with the Waring family and the BBC, introduced the annual Eddie Waring 'Top Try' Trophy in his honour. Five tries were broadcast and viewers voted for their favourite, with the winner presented with the award on national television, at first by Mary Waring and then, after her own death, by Tony. When Rupert Murdoch's Sky TV all but laid exclusive claim to rugby league in the 1990s, the Beeb was left with little footage and the award was reluctantly discontinued. Since then, along with the naming of an unassuming residential cul-de-sac, Waring Way, on the site of the old Crown Flatt in Dewsbury, each Cup final has seen the presentation of an Eddie Waring Memorial Coin, tossed by the captains beforehand and kept as a memento of the occasion by the referee. It is a nice touch, but surely the game can do better than that.

Pre-match at Wembley in 2007, a number of former Lance Todd Trophy winners were introduced to the crowd, including such legendary rugby league figures as Dick Huddart, Neil Fox, Alex Murphy, David Topliss, Ellery Hanley, Joe Lydon, Andy Gregory and Martin Offiah. One of the most prestigious individual honours in the game, the Lance Todd Trophy was inaugurated in 1946 at the instigation of no less a figure than Harry Sunderland, who, along with Warrington director Bob Anderton and Yorkshire journalist John Bapty, dreamed up the idea when the New Zealander Todd was killed in a road accident in 1942.

Upon Harry Sunderland's own death in January 1964, a similar award was instigated in the little Australian's name, to be won by the man of the match in every Championship or Premiership final – known since 1998 as the Grand Final – at Old Trafford, Manchester. Is it not time that a similar recognition of excellence should be made in the name of the proud and pioneering Englishman Edward Marsden Waring, whose love and ambitions for rugby league never dimmed? Or could it really be that, some 21 years after his death, the game remains so insecure that it is still embarrassed by its most popular Northern son?

AFTERWORD

BY HARRY WARING

My earliest memories of Uncle Eddie are from childhood Christmases; when he walked into a room, it lit up. In Eddie's company, life was never dull.

As a boy, I listened in awe to his anecdotes of chapel trips to the Dales and Peak District, his triumphs as a schoolboy soccer player and his success with the Black Knights and his Dewsbury team of all stars. His own medals, sewn onto a black velvet cushioned cloth and displayed in a glass cabinet, were sometimes taken out for me to handle as a special treat.

During the war, Eddie brought the Rugby League Challenge Cup, which Dewsbury had won, to my school. Each proud pupil was allowed to take a drink of lemonade from it, through a straw. When I was a teenager, he supported my own rugby activities and sent telegrams of encouragement when I played in representative matches.

Uncle Eddie was a caring man who loved not only his family but anything he became involved with. Although he regarded his privacy as sacred, he was first in line if anyone – his fellow journalists included – needed help. On duty, he was the most approachable individual. Off it, there were only a select few who could get near him. Eddie's home was his castle and Mary defended their domain with ruthless efficiency.

An enthusiast by nature, Eddie had the ability to spark enthusiasm in others, whatever the cause. He was a gentleman who aimed to conduct himself on television as he would if entering anyone's home. This humility, together with a great deal of hard work, lay, I believe, at the root of his success.

By the force of his own personality and charm, from humble beginnings, Eddie created a unique place in the media world. He took whatever opportunities came his way, and if none were available, he had the acumen and ability to create them.

Although Eddie had his critics and opponents in the media business, he handled them with a Nelson-esque philosophy and got on with the job in hand. His loyalty to his media employers never wavered and they reciprocated in full.

In his later life, my wife and I took holidays with Eddie and Mary and we were there when he was first taken ill in France. His long demise and confinement with Alzheimer's was a terrible time for Mary and Tony. It was heartbreaking, too, that in its early stages Eddie himself could see his bleak future.

Overall, my enduring memory of Uncle Eddie is a saying of his with biblical overtones that he stuck to throughout his life: 'Those who drink the water should remember those who dug the well.' Thank you, Uncle Eddie, for what you gave us. May your own well never run dry.

Harry Waring
August 2007

NOTES

INTRODUCTION

1   Quoted in 'The Talking Trilby', feature written by David Howes, in *The Official Rugby League Centenary Magazine* (1995).
2   *Up and Over*, p. 58 (Dave Hadfield, Mainstream Publishing, 2004).

ONE – HE AIN'T HEAVY . . .

1   Rose George, for the *London Review of Books*, quoting *The Official Guide to Dewsbury*, 1957.
2   Unless otherwise attributed, this and future Harry Jepson quotes, in conversation with the author, March 2007.
3   Biographical detail from *Dewsbury Men of Science*, a *Dewsbury Reporter* special publication written by Margaret Watson, 2006.
4   Information from *The Dewsbury Greats*, a *Dewsbury Reporter* special publication written by Margaret Watson, November 1992.
5   'A Fond Farewell to TV's Most Tortured Tonsils', *Daily Express*, 2 May 1981.
6   Unless otherwise attributed, this and future Margaret Watson quotes, in conversation with the author, April 2007.
7   Unless otherwise attributed, this and future Harry Waring quotes, in conversation with the author, April 2007.
8   *Be My Guest*, BBC Radio 2, transmitted 12 March 1980.
9   *Desert Island Discs*, BBC Radio 4, transmitted Saturday, 23 and Monday, 25 February 1974, produced by Ronald Cook.
10   *Be My Guest*, BBC Radio 2, transmitted 12 March 1980.
11   Ibid.
12   More thrillingly modern cultural delights were on offer too. On 10 April 1923, for example, Tolson wrote that 224 boys attended the Picture House to view the film *Southward on the Quest*, a documentary about the explorer Ernest Shackleton's 1914–16 expedition to the Antarctic.
13   Biographical football details, *Dewsbury District News*, 4 July 1936.
14   The trip to London went ahead as outlined. In the school logbook, dated 22–23 May 1924, J.E. Tolson reveals that school was closed 'on account

of visit of top-class boys to London and the Wembley Exhibition'. Three days later, Tolson describes the excursion as having been 'a great success', adding that: 'The boys behaved splendidly throughout.'

TWO – THEATRE OF DREAMS

1 As confirmed by West Yorkshire Archive Service (Wakefield) search.

2 Stealing school property seems to have been most frowned upon, a crime that resulted in 'two strokes to the hand and three to the buttocks'. The all-time beatings record, however, must go to master W. Chappell, who, in 1933, received an alarming '25 strokes on rear' for 'talking after receiving repeated warning'. This, though, was the most extreme recorded punishment by far.

3 The *Sunday Times*, 3 May 1981. Previously, in that same newspaper's colour magazine supplement, Arthur Hopcraft had dated Waring's time at secretarial college as 'a year'.

4 The UK driving test officially came into force in 1935, just five years after a minimum driving age of seventeen had been introduced.

5 Alas, we have insufficient room here to do this seismic and fascinating event anything like the justice it deserves. Readers seeking more detail are directed to the three volumes in which this subject is far and away best dealt with: Robert Gate's *Rugby League: An Illustrated History* (Weidenfeld & Nicolson, 1989), Geoffrey Moorhouse's elegantly crafted *A People's Game: The Official History of Rugby League* (Hodder & Stoughton, 1995, updated 1996) and Tony Collins' quite magnificent *Rugby's Great Split: Class, Culture and the Origins of Rugby League Football* (Frank Cass, 1998).

6 Quoted in a *Daily Express* feature written by the Manchester-based journalist Gordon Burnett, date unknown.

7 *The Guardian*, 3 May 1979.

8 *The Eddie Waring Book of Rugby League* (Frederick Muller Ltd, 1966).

9 Original letter, BBC Written Archive Centre, Caversham Park, Reading.

10 Intriguingly, the internal memo to which Eddie's letter was attached – dated 11 December – refers to a mystery second correspondent who was also offering his services.

11 Alas, the arrival of the Black Knights came too late to keep Ernest Ward in the town. Ward, whose father, also called Ernest, had been capped for England once and acted as Dewsbury's trainer for a spell, had been expected to sign forms at Crown Flatt. As Waring would later write in his smashing little book *The Great Ones* (Pelham Books, 1969, p. 68): 'It seemed obvious that on his sixteenth birthday Ernest Ward would sign for Dewsbury. His father left the Dewsbury club and, to the great disappointment of the club, young Ernest signed professional forms, not at Crown Flatt but at Odsal for Bradford. His fee was a mere £150.'

12 Arthur Waring died aged 65 in 1941.

13 Recollections upon the death of Eddie Waring, *Dewsbury Reporter*, 29 October 1986.

THREE – CENTRE OF ATTENTION

1   Arthur Hopcraft, *Sunday Times Magazine*, 24 November 1968.

2   As its former deputy editor, Margaret Watson, explains: 'The *Dewsbury Reporter* sold far more papers than the *District News* in Dewsbury. But the *Batley News* sold more papers in Batley than the *Batley Reporter*. The *District News* never took a great hold in Dewsbury, just as the *Batley Reporter* was not the main paper in Batley.' Eventually, in 1959, a merger (i.e. takeover) was completed, one year after the centenary of the organisation that owned the *Dewsbury Reporter* and its stablemates the *Batley Reporter*, the *Mirfield Reporter* and the *Heckmondwike Reporter*. According to the deal, the 'Reporter' title would continue in Dewsbury, whilst the 'News' title remained in Batley. Within the past 15 years, this same organisation has also acquired ownership of the *Spenborough Guardian*.

3   Historical background information from 'Professional Baseball in Dewsbury', Ian Smyth, the Society for American Baseball Research (UK Chapter) website – www.sabruk.org.

4   Information from Tony Collins' *Rugby League in Twentieth Century Britain*, pp. 74–86 (Routledge, 2006).

5   In which St Helens, incidentally, were beaten 19–3.

6   Though the rest of the game tended to refer to Crown Flatt in the singular, Dewsbury locals often used the plural, 'Flatts'.

7   'Dewsbury (R.L.) Football Club, Season 1941–42 Report and Balance Sheet', for which the author is indebted to Tony Waring.

8   *Rugby League in Twentieth Century Britain*, Tony Collins, p. 78 (Routledge, 2006).

9   Undated report in the *Dewsbury Reporter*, 1943. Thanks are due to Salford historian Graham Morris for the quote.

10   In his thesis 'Up and Under: Eddie Waring, Television and the Image of Rugby League', published in *The Sports Historian* (May 2002), Dr Jack Williams, acknowledging the 29 May and 31 August 1943 editions of the *Dewsbury Reporter*, writes: 'In 1942–43 the highest attendance at any rugby league match had been 16,000 to see Dewsbury play Leeds at Leeds but the total number of paying spectators at all of Dewsbury's matches had been 200,000.'

11   Jack Williams, ibid.

12   Like a number of Black Knights, Frank Thurman was also a Springfield Chapel-goer.

13   Henry Rose, *Daily Express*, circa 1944.

14   BBC internal memo, held at the BBC Written Archives Centre, Caversham Park, Reading.

FOUR – EXPANDING HORIZONS

1   *Daily Express* feature written by Gordon Burnett, date unknown.

2   Although the national team played its Test matches under the name Northern Union or England before a name change to Great Britain in 1947, it has since become standard practice for statisticians to apply the name

Great Britain to those teams retrospectively. That said, partly in response to the development of amateur competitions in Ireland, Scotland and Wales, at the time of writing England seems set once again to become the favoured moniker of UK rugby league's highest-ranking national side.

3   *England to Australia and New Zealand* (Eddie Waring, F. Youngman Ltd, Leeds, 1947). Henceforth in this chapter, all personal quotes attributed to Waring are from here, unless stated otherwise.

4   'Australasian Tour 1946', business report by Wilf Gabbatt, held at the Rugby Football League archives, Red Hall, Leeds.

5   As an aside, Wilson, whose service as RFL secretary ran from 1920–46, can't resist an intriguing little dig at one of Waring's early throwaway lines, re the split from rugby union a half century before. 'The opening pages on the formation of the Northern Union Rugby Football Union 52 years ago are just introductory and not really part of the story,' he writes. 'This is a "foreword" and not a criticism, but the writer joins issue with the Author when he says that the breakaway from the Rugby Union is "so well known". The history of the great breakaway is, to-day, well known to probably less than 20 persons and as, of course, Eddie Waring is not one of them – he is too young – he shows wisdom in "leaving it at that".' Those keen to learn more should consult Tony Collins's *Rugby's Great Split: Class, Culture and the Origins of Rugby League Football* (Frank Cass, 1998).

6   As reheated by Geoffrey Moorhouse in his entertaining collection of essays *At The George*, p. 123 (Hodder & Stoughton, 1989).

7   *Rugby League: In Its Own Words*, p. 182 (Tim Wilkinson and Ray Gent, Impress Sport, 2004).

8   *Desert Island Discs*, BBC Radio 4, transmitted Saturday, 23 and Monday, 25 February 1974, produced by Ronald Cook.

9   'Leagues Across the Sea', *The Listener*, 9 August 1946.

10   *Be My Guest*, BBC Radio 2, transmitted 12 March 1980.

FIVE – A MAN OF VISION

1   The author is indebted to RFL historian Tony Collins for this information.

2   *England to Australia and New Zealand* (Eddie Waring, F. Youngman Ltd, Leeds, 1947). Brian Aherne was an English film actor who became a big name in Hollywood, eventually immortalised on the Hollywood Walk of Fame in Los Angeles. Among his best-known roles – as Black Knight fan Eddie would no doubt notice – he twice played King Arthur, in *Prince Valiant* (1954) and *Lancelot and Guinevere* (1963).

3   Unless otherwise attributed, this and future Eric Ashton quotes, in conversation with the author, April 2007.

4   Billy Boston, in conversation with the author, April 2007.

5   Unless otherwise attributed, this and future Alex Murphy quotes, in conversation with the author, April 2007.

6   Without Tom Mitchell's input, it is doubtful whether BARLA would ever have taken flight at all. The proposed new organisation lost an initial vote for official recognition 29–1 in 1972. That looked like being that until

Mitchell, as concerned as anyone at how a once-thriving amateur scene was now reduced to fewer than 150 clubs and a mere 30 youth teams, instigated a complete turnaround and a unanimous vote in favour some 12 months later.

7   *The Memoirs and Sporting Life of Tom Mitchell* (Tom Mitchell, Echotime Inc, 1998), an entertaining if hugely idiosyncratic account of the life of a man who numbered among his many acquaintances Nikita Krushchev, King Farouk and Picasso. Of the latter, Mitchell once told *Open Rugby* editor Harry Edgar that: 'We had a mutual interest in ceramics.' Among Tom Mitchell's other claims to fame were the founding of Edinburgh's Traverse Theatre, two unsuccessful attempts at standing for Parliament and the climbing of the Matterhorn. On his frequent visits to Cambridge University in the early 1930s whilst he was an agriculture student at Armstrong College, Newcastle, he is said also to have rubbed shoulders with Soviet spies Guy Burgess, Kim Philby and Donald Maclean.

8   Quoted by David Howes in 'The Talking Trilby', in *The Official Rugby League Centenary Magazine* (1995).

9   *England to Australia and New Zealand* (Eddie Waring, F. Youngman Ltd., Leeds, 1947).

10   *Eddie Waring on Rugby League*, p. 109 (Frederick Muller Ltd, 1981).

11   Unless otherwise attributed, this and future Douglas Hird quotes, in conversation with the author, March 2007.

12   'Introduction by Eddie Waring, BBC TV and *Sunday Mirror*', 'Shaw Cross Boys Club: 21 Years Reaching Forward 1947–1968', commemorative brochure (price 2s 6d).

13   *Rugby League Review: The Monthly Journal of Rugby League Football*, September 1947, Vol. 2 No. 13.

14   Tony Collins, *Rugby League in Twentieth Century Britain*, pp. 64–65 (Routledge, 2006).

15   *Rugby League Review*, October 1947, Vol. 2 No. 14.

16   Ibid, December 1947, Vol. 2 No. 16.

17   Ibid, March 1948, Vol. 2 No. 19.

18   Ibid.

19   This was a man who published a complete list of the names of Huddersfield's football committee after the Fartown club had knocked back his application for a free press ticket for a game against Hull.

20   Quoted by Geoffrey Moorhouse, *At The George*, p. 72 (Hodder & Stoughton, 1989).

21   This letter, along with all correspondence to and from the BBC quoted in this chapter, is held at the BBC Written Archives Centre, Caversham Park, Reading.

22   *Rugby League Review*, 25 October 1951.

23   *Sunday Pictorial*, 27 August 1950, reprinted in *Rugby League Journal*, Vol. 1 No. 1, 2002. Not surprisingly, the local Dewsbury papers took plenty of notice of this illustrious meeting too, especially when Eddie sent them a photograph. Harry Waring junior vividly recalls being dispatched by the family to buy 25 copies.

24   'About the North', Brian Finch, *Radio Times*, 26 September 1968.

25   *Rugby League Review*, 25 October 1951.

26   Statistical information from *A People's Game: The Official History of Rugby League* (Geoffrey Moorhouse, Hodder & Stoughton, 1995) and *Rugby League in Twentieth Century Britain,* Tony Collins (Routledge, 2006).

27   Peter Black, quoting anonymous BBC writer in annual reviews, *The Biggest Aspidistra in the World*, pp. 81–2 (BBC, 1972).

28   Tony Collins, *Rugby League in Twentieth Century Britain*, p. 93 (Routledge, 2006).

29   Ibid.

SIX – THE COURT OF KING EDDIE

1   The Los Angeles Rams, incidentally, were at that time part-owned by Bob Hope.

2   *Rugby League Gazette,* Vol. 2 No. 3, 16 September 1950.

3   Gus Risman, *Rugby Renegade* (Stanley Paul, 1958).

4   The Keighley-born Don Mosey was later rechristened 'the Alderman' by legendary cricket commentator Brian Johnson after joining the BBC's *Test Match Special* team in 1974.

5   Unless otherwise attributed, this and future Brian Batty quotes, in conversation with the author, March 2007.

6   Unless otherwise attributed, this and future Harry Edgar quotes, in conversation with the author, March 2007.

7   Unless otherwise attributed, this and future Tony Waring quotes, in conversation with the author, April 2007.

8   If he had been scouting, Eddie would have arrived 11 years too soon. Later Rossall School pupils would include the future England rugby union captain Peter Winterbottom. Older Rossallian pupils, meanwhile, included the composer Sir Thomas Beecham, *The Saint* creator Leslie Charteris and Walter Clopton Wingfield, the fabled inventor of lawn tennis.

9   Referred to by Eddie Waring in his article, 'The Trials of a Television Commentator' (*The John Player Rugby League Yearbook 1973–74*, edited by Jack Winstanley, Queen Anne Press, 1973).

10   Unless otherwise attributed, this and future David Howes quotes, in conversation with the author, April 2007.

11   Stella Hirst, in conversation with the author, March 2007.

12   Unless otherwise attributed, this and future Raymond Fletcher quotes, in conversation with the author, March 2007.

13   Unless otherwise attributed, this and future Dave Parker quotes, in conversation with the author, March 2007.

14   'Around Town in Eddie's Town', Michael Wale, *Radio Times*, 6 March 1971.

15   *Daily Mail*, 30 December 1967.

16   This and previous Arthur Hopcraft quote, *Sunday Times Magazine*, 24 November 1968.

SEVEN – MAKING A SPLASH

1   Arthur Hopcraft, *Sunday Times Magazine*, 24 November 1968.

2   Interview with Albert Hunt, *Radio Times*, 2 May 1981.

3   Copy of letter held at BBC Written Archives Centre, Caversham Park, Reading.

4   Quoted by David Howes, 'The Talking Trilby', in *The Official Rugby League Centenary Magazine* (1995).

5   Arthur Hopcraft, *Sunday Times Magazine*, 24 November 1968.

6   Copy of memo held at BBC Written Archives Centre, Caversham Park, Reading.

7   Along with Ray Lakeland, another producer on *Sport in the North* was the future *Morecambe and Wise* producer John Ammonds.

8   The Manchester-produced version of *Look North* was eventually rebranded *Look North West* in 1980, before progressing, via *News Northwest*, to its present title *North West Tonight*. In Yorkshire, meanwhile, *Look North* has remained *Look North*.

9   Unless otherwise attributed, this and future Ray Lakeland quotes, in conversation with the author, July 2007.

10   For which, according to his personal files at the BBC Written Archives Centre in Reading, he received £12 12s 0d plus third-class return rail fare.

11   Unless otherwise attributed, this and future Keith Macklin quotes, in conversation with the author, July 2007.

12   Correspondence held at BBC Written Archives Centre, Reading.

13   Keith Macklin went on to front the ITV northern region's rugby league show *RL Action*, in tandem with Elton Welsby and Richard Madeley – yes, that Richard Madeley. Later in the 1980s, Yorkshire produced its own Sunday-night highlights show, *Scrumdown*, with commentary provided by Macklin's fellow Northern commentating doyen John Helm. Granada, meanwhile, showed a full game every Saturday afternoon under the title *Rugby League Live*, hosted by current Sky Sports man Rob McCaffery and commentated on by Clive Tyldesley. Since the arrival of satellite television, rugby league coverage on ITV has dwindled to virtually nothing.

14   Correspondence held at BBC Written Archives Centre, Caversham Park, Reading.

15   Ibid.

16   Ibid.

17   Ibid.

18   Ibid.

19   Ibid.

20   The formidable Bagenal Harvey must surely be worthy of a biography in his own right. Born in Dublin and having been a promising cricketer in his youth, after an early career in publishing he went on to spend some 40 years as agent to many of the biggest sports and television personalities in Britain. In later years, he became closely involved with the All England tennis club at Wimbledon. He died in November 1987.

21   'On the Television', Harry Edgar, *Rugby League Journal*, Issue No. 12, Autumn 2005.

22   Figures as quoted in 'Up and Under: Eddie Waring, Television and the Image of Rugby League', Dr Jack Williams, thesis published in *The Sports Historian* (May 2002).

23   All quotes, 'The Trials of a Television Commentator', Eddie Waring, *The John Player Rugby League Yearbook 1973–74*, edited by Jack Winstanley (Queen Anne Press, 1973).

24   Chris Sandeman, in conversation with the author, March 2007.

25   Unless otherwise attributed, this and future Martyn Sadler quotes, in conversation with the author, March 2007.

26   'The Trials of a Television Commentator', Eddie Waring, *The John Player Rugby League Yearbook 1973–74*, edited by Jack Winstanley (Queen Anne Press, 1973).

27   'Around Town in Eddie's Town', Michael Wale, *Radio Times*, 6 March 1971.

28   As quoted by David Howes, 'The Talking Trilby', in *The Official Rugby League Centenary Magazine* (1995).

29   Gerry Anderson, *Express & Star*, 9 February 1978.

30   Jack Waterman, 'Eddie Waring: The Patter of Grimy Feet', *The Listener*, 3 November 1975. The Argyll, Birkenhead, was an old music-hall theatre.

31   *Roger: The Autobiography*, Roger Millward with Mike Sterriker (Riverhead Publishing, May 2005).

32   Allan Agar, in conversation with the author, March 2007.

33   Jack Waterman, 'Eddie Waring: The Patter of Grimy Feet', *The Listener*, 3 November 1975.

34   Geoffrey Mather, 'A Fond Farewell to TV's Most Tortured Tonsils', *Daily Express*, 2 May 1981.

35   'About the North', Brian Finch, *Radio Times*, 26 September 1968.

36   Eddie Waring, *England to Australia and New Zealand* (County Press, 1947).

37   Eddie Waring, *The Great Ones* (Pelham Books Ltd, 1969).

EIGHT – SEND IN THE CLOWNS

1   All quotes, *Yorkshire Post*, Monday, 13 February 1978.

2   Quoted in Dr Jack Williams, 'Up and Under: Eddie Waring, Television and the Image of Rugby League', thesis published in *The Sports Historian* (May 2002).

3   'The Voice of Rugby League Answers Back', *The Times*, 14 October 1971.

4   Dr Jack Williams, quoting *Rugby Leaguer*, 20 October 1971 edition, in 'Up and Under: Eddie Waring, Television and the Image of Rugby League', thesis published in *The Sports Historian* (May 2002).

5   Dr Jack Williams, 'Up and Under: Eddie Waring, Television and the Image of Rugby League', thesis published in *The Sports Historian* (May 2002).

6   Unless otherwise attributed, this and future Ray French quotes, in conversation with the author, March 2007.

7   Unless otherwise attributed, this and future Dave Woods quotes, in conversation with the author, March 2007.

8   Jack Dearden in conversation with the author, March 2007.

9   Unless otherwise attributed, this and future Eddie Hemmings quotes, in conversation with the author, March 2007.

10   Unless otherwise attributed, this and future Mike Stephenson quotes, in conversation with the author, March 2007.

11   Quoted by Norman Smithson, *Today*, 12 May 1962.

12   Unless otherwise attributed, this and future David Watkins quotes, in conversation with the author, April 2007.

13   Eddie Waring's roadshows were also a big influence on David Howes. In looking to stage a rugby league-based benefit concert in aid of the Hull KR player Paul Rose in 1979, Howes and the *Daily Mirror* journalist John Huxley came up with the idea of a *Daily Mirror* roadshow. 'It was a direct copy,' Howes admits. 'I had never seen the Eddie Waring show, but I was chatting with Dave Parker about it and it followed the same format: films, interviews and a lot of humour, in our case thanks to the involvement of Mick Morgan. We did around 100 shows in the end and raised a quarter of a million quid. But we made no secret of the fact that it was a new and probably more sophisticated version of Eddie's.' The *Daily Mirror* Rugby League Roadshow ran until around 1989, with ten shows a year.

14   Unless otherwise attributed, this and future Tony Collins quotes, in conversation with the author, April 2007.

15   'Ironies of League's National Exposure', Stephen Bowes, *Rugby League Journal*, Issue No. 17, Winter 2006.

16   Cec Thompson, *Born on the Wrong Side*, p. 142 (Arcadia Books Ltd, 2006).

17   Ibid, p. 36.

18   'I was not a success,' Bailey told *The Guardian* in 2000. 'They threw me straight in with no time to learn even the fundamentals. I thought I was dead a couple of times when the man with the ball ran straight at me and ploughed his knees into my chest. But I enjoyed the experience all right; by jove, those young guys in the north had a terrific sporting attitude, and what guts.'

19   Interested readers can discover more such detailed *Jeux Sans Frontières* facts at the meticulously assembled website devoted to the show, www.jsfnet.co.uk.

20   Quoted by David Howes, 'The Talking Trilby', in *The Official Rugby League Centenary Magazine* (1995).

21   Unless otherwise attributed, this and future Stuart Hall quotes, in conversation with the author, July 2007. Not that Hall would let anything as trivial as petty bureaucracy stop him, incidentally: having bought the rights to the show from the BBC some 25 years ago, he continues to front live *It's a Knockout* shows around the world even now.

22   Quoted at www.jsfnet.co.uk.

23   'Eddie Waring Communicates', Clive James, *The Observer*, 17 June 1973, reprinted in *Visions Before Midnight* (Cape, 1977).

24   Quoted by David Howes, 'The Talking Trilby', in *The Official Rugby League Centenary Magazine* (1995).

25   *Star Town* was essentially a rejigged version of Barney Colehan's *Top Town*, broadcast in 1978. Unlike in the earlier version, each competing town had its own celebrity supporter. Eddie Waring represented Leeds, and, for the final, Tessie O'Shea took over from Les Dawson as the representative of Blackpool. Others in the heats included Thora Hird (Morecambe), Mike Yarwood's mate Janet Brown (Edinburgh), Stan Stennett (Cardiff), Leslie Crowther (Bristol) and the outstandifold Stanley Unwin (Coventry) – deep joy, oh yes.
26   Letter in Harry Waring's private collection.
27   *The Independent*, 21 September 1999.
28   Help Yourself also had a tune in their repertoire called 'Frank Bough'.
29   Letter in Harry Waring's private collection.
30   Ibid.

NINE – BE NOT AFRAID

1   John Huxley, in conversation with the author, June 2007.
2   www.alzheimers.org.uk.
3   'The Man in a League of His Own Is to Retire', John Groser, *The Times*, 30 January 1981.
4   'Eddie Waring to End His Commentaries', Roger Heywood, *Daily Telegraph*, 30 January 1981.
5   'An Early Bath for the Voice of Rugby League', Paul Keel, *The Guardian*, 30 January 1981.
6   'Unfair', according to Reverend Regan, because 'he [Welland] criticises BBC policy towards rugby league and then blames Eddie Waring for it'. And 'ungracious' because 'retirement is a time to register appreciation or keep silent. When the man is gone, then is the time for policy changes.' Letter to *The Guardian*, 4 February 1981.
7   'The Waring Voice of League Past', Colin Welland, *The Guardian*, 31 January 1981.
8   'League of Friends Leave Eddie Waring Just a Little Touched', *Yorkshire Post*, 9 February 1981.
9   'A Fond Farewell to TV's Most Tortured Tonsils', Geoffrey Mather, *Daily Express*, 2 May 1981.
10   'Mimics' Idol Heads for Late Bath', David May, *Sunday Times*, 3 May 1981.
11   'A World of Sport at Buckingham Palace', *Evening Standard*, 23 March 1982.
12   'Eddie "Very Ill" in Hospital', *Daily Star*, 29 December 1983.
13   'Sports Diary', Simon Barnes, *The Times*, 1 November 1986.
14   'Voice of Rugby Could Do with Laryngitis', Huw Richards, playtheball.com, 5 May 2003.
15   *Mail on Sunday*, 1 February 1987.

INDEX

ABC (independent TV company) 191
ABC radio (Australian Broadcasting Corporation) 89
'Abide with Me' 31, 263
Acton and Willesden RLFC 70
Adams, Ken. J. 155
Adelaide 97–8
Aden 92, 94–5
Agar, Allan 205
Aherne, Brian 114
Alexandra Palace 134
All Blacks 149
All Golds 45, 149
Allbutt, Sir Clifford 25
Allis, Peter 237
Alzheimer's Society 260–1
Ampol Ltd 116
Anderson, Gerry 202, 227
Anderton, Bob 113, 283
Antibes 271
Arlott, John 14, 191, 236
Armstrong, Louis 234
Ashington 246
Ashton, Eric 115–16, 205
Ashton, Ken 214
Aspel, Michael 248
Associated Rediffusion Trophy 180
Athenium Hotel (London) 268
Atkinson, John 175–6
Attenborough, David 193, 195
Attlee, Clement 130
Auckland 78, 106–7, 110–11, 118
Australia RL team 45, 90, 92–3, 100, 101, 102, 104–5, 118, 141, 147, 190, 276
Australian Board of Control 90, 105, 119

Bailey, McDonald 238
Baker, 'Bunny' 205
Baker, Gordon 205
Baker, Hylda 240
Baker, Richard 12, 248
Ballance, Ernest 59–60, 64–5, 70
Bapty, John 156, 283
Barnes 264
Barnes, Allan 117
Barnes, Simon 277
Barnsley 125
Barnsley FC 36
Barriere, Paul 127
Barrow-in-Furness 114, 207, 213–14
Barrow RLFC 79, 93, 103, 140, 200
Barwick, Brian 256
Basingstoke 203
Baskerville, Albert Henry 45, 148
Bass, Alfie 255
Bassey, Shirley 12
Bath, Harry 159
Bath Hotel (Dewsbury) 23
Batley 20, 28, 53, 71, 120–1, 249
Batley Corporation 64
Batley Grammar School 24
Batley RLFC 48, 81, 215, 282
Batley Variety Club 182
Batten, Eric 95, 110
Batty, Brian 150–2
Battye, Ken 175
BBC see British Broadcasting Corporation
BBC Dance Orchestra 73
BBC-3 253
Be My Guest 31–2, 110, 268
Beanland, Arthur 151
Beatles, the 86, 253

Bedford RFC 135
Beecroft, Alfred 150
Belle Vue (Wakefield) 186
Bennett, Alan 203
Bentley, Jack 150, 166
Betty's (Harrogate) 203
Bevan, Aneurin 130
Biggest Aspidistra in the World, The 142–3
Bird, John 253
Birmingham 134
Black, Cilla 251
Black, Peter 142–3, 169, 203, 238–9, 275
Black Dyke Mills Band 31
Black Knights (aka Dewsbury Boys) 52–8, 61–2, 67, 83, 105, 119, 122, 158, 271, 285
Blackburn Rovers FC 49
Blackheath RFC 134–5
Blackpool 125, 159–60, 214, 241, 253, 255, 269
Blackwell, E.G. 141
Blankety Blank 251
Blein, Maurice 127
Blue Mountains 100
Blue Peter 251
Boddy, Agnes see Waring, Agnes
Bohemians RFC 68
Bolan, Marc 251
Bolton 125
Bolton Abbey 34
Bolton Wanderers FC 49
Boothroyd, Betty 25, 32
Bordeaux 127
Born on the Wrong Side 237–8
Boro' Football Weekly 37–9
Boston, Billy 115, 238
Bough, Frank 12, 185, 191, 248, 269

Bould, Beckett 71
Bould, Frank 52, 56, 58
Bowes, Stephen 235–6
Boyle, Katie 242
Braben, Eddie 247
Bradford 20, 31, 62, 73, 79, 95, 150, 240, 252
Bradford City Sox 61–2
Bradford Northern RLFC 53, 59, 68, 79, 81, 83, 95, 103, 131, 133, 140–1, 195, 199
Bradshaw railway timetable 97
Bramhope 161–3, 178, 194, 252, 271–5
Bramley RLFC 68–9, 82, 141, 155, 164
Bridlington 34, 241
Brief Encounter 95
Brighton 203, 242
Brisbane 90, 103–4
Brisbane Courier 96
British Amateur Rugby League Association (BARLA) 117
British Broadcasting Corporation (BBC) 11, 13, 30–1, 51–2, 54, 84–6, 103, 116–18, 131–7, 140–5, 147, 149, 152, 160, 162–4, 169, 173, 178–96, 198, 200, 204, 210–21, 224, 226, 228–30, 232–3, 236, 239–41, 245, 248, 250–2, 254–6, 258, 260–2, 264–5, 267–70, 272–5, 283
    BBC1 191, 246, 251
    BBC2 166, 193, 195–6, 201, 215, 226, 251
British Railways Board 276
British Transport Hotels 276
Brock, Thomas 54
Brontë, Anne 25
Brontë, Charlotte 25
Brontë, Rev. Patrick 25
Brook, Arthur (A.T.) 52, 56, 58
Brooke, Ian 175
Brooke-Taylor, Tim 254–5
Brown, George 250
Brown, Lou 118
Brown, Tom 127
Brussels 168
Buckingham Palace 268
Bundaberg 103
Burke, Mick 267
Burrell-Davies, Derek 213–14
Bygraves, Max 252

Caine Report 124, 212–15, 228

'Calan Lan' 102
Calloway, Tony 258
Cambridge University 124
Canberra 100
Cannon and Ball 263
Card, Harry 160
Carlaw Park 110
Carnforth 200
Castleford RLFC 47–8, 68, 81, 204–5, 214, 235, 251
Catalans Dragons 282
Caulms Woods 79
Cave, Allan 150
Cawthorne, Ernest 91
Central Park (Wigan) 80, 115, 141
Chadwick, Stanley 123–5, 129–30, 154
Challenge Cup 26, 46–8, 63, 72, 79–80, 83, 118, 131, 140, 142, 148, 170, 173–4, 184, 188–9, 205, 209, 217–18, 221, 252, 263, 266–8, 281–2, 285
Chamberlain, Neville 75
Channel M 220
Chapeltown Road (Leeds) 227
Chaplin, Charlie 249, 268
Charlton, Bobby 191, 246
Charlton, Jackie 246
Cheltenham 242
Chester, Charlie 241
Chicago 130, 148
Chifley, Joseph 100
Chivers, Alan 189
Christchurch 89, 107–9
Christmas Night with the Stars 250
Chumbawamba 256
Cilla 251
City Varieties (Leeds) 240, 251
Clarke, Alan 145, 179
Clarke, Phil 15
Clay, Eric 204
Cleaver, Millicent 214
Cleese, John 255
Clegg, Herbert 64
Clifton, Bernie 263
Clifton House Prep School 158
Clues, Arthur 276
Coetzer, Gert 175
Colehan, Barney 181–2, 240–1, 253, 257, 276
Coleman, David 14, 185, 191, 263, 269
Collins, Bobby 160
Collins, Professor Tony 49, 80–1, 144, 234, 236

Colombo (Ceylon/Sri Lanka) 92, 95
Colwyn Bay 242
Compton, Dennis 160
Congregationalist Church 23–4, 30–1, 162, 234
Cooper, Henry 258
Cooper, Lionel 119
Coventry 128, 255
Cowdrey, Colin 191
Cowgill, Bryan 178, 184, 192, 193, 269, 275
Crabtree, Eorl 79
Crabtree, Shirley 79
Craven Park (Barrow) 93
Craven Park (Hull) 266
'Creation', The' 239
Crigglestone 44
Crockford, Walter 91, 127
Cromwell, Oliver 129
Crosby, Bing 137
Crossley, Tom 216
Crown Flatt (Dewsbury) 21, 23, 28, 44, 46, 48, 51–2, 55, 57, 59–63, 65–70, 75, 77, 79–81, 83, 106, 119, 283
Crystal Palace 49
Cudbertson, Andrew 238
Cudlipp, Hugh 161
Curran, George 101
Cushing, Peter 12
'Cym Rhondda' 102

Daily Express 26, 60, 77, 83–4, 89, 131, 135, 150, 178, 202, 266–7
Daily Herald 150
Daily Mail 142, 150, 169, 203, 217–18, 238–9, 275
Daily Mirror 116, 150, 155, 255–6
Daily Sketch 150
Daily Star 273
Daily Telegraph 264
Daily Telegraph (Sydney) 89, 96, 100, 105
Dallas 130
Darlington 227
Davies, Lynn 160
Davies, Willie 103
Dawson, Anna 251
Dawson, Les 188
Dawson, Peter 110, 268
Day, Robin 12, 249–50
'Day We Went to Bangor', The' 268
Dearden, Jack 220–1
'Deep Harmony' 31, 268

'Delilah' 31, 268
Derby Baths (Blackpool) 269
Desert Island Discs 30–1, 38, 237, 256, 268
Devlin, Bruce 160
Dewsbury 7, 12, 19, 20–1, 23–5, 27, 34, 36, 38, 41–2, 44–6, 51–2, 54, 59, 63, 66, 70–1, 74–5, 77, 109, 122, 151, 159, 161, 165, 203, 221–3, 250, 273, 278, 283
Dewsbury, Batley and District Schools Football Association 35
Dewsbury Boys *see* Black Knights
Dewsbury District News 44, 55–8, 59, 61–2, 64–5, 67, 68–9, 71–4, 123
Dewsbury Empire 71, 240
Dewsbury Junior Technical and Commercial School 43
Dewsbury Moorend FC 36
Dewsbury Reporter 26, 27, 44, 54, 61, 68, 83, 221
Dewsbury RLFC 21–2, 30, 35, 44–8, 50, 52–3, 55–61, 63–5, 67–72, 75, 77–85, 114, 118, 128, 158, 235, 240, 282–3, 285
Dewsbury Royals 61–2
Dewsbury Town Hall 24, 81, 1 20
Dibnah, Fred 263
Dimmock, Peter 131–2, 134–5, 178–9, 185, 189, 193
Dixon, Alan 145, 179, 186
Doctor Who 210
Dodd, Ken 240
Doncaster 125, 128, 245
Dotrice, Roy 253
Dougall, Robert 248
Dowson, George 259
Drewry, Alfred 91, 156
Duckham, David 225
Duckworth, George 132
Duke of Gloucester 100

Earlsheaton 19
East View (Dewsbury) 59, 66
Eastborough Council School 32–3, 35–8, 42–3
Eastmoor Dragons ARLFC 121
Ebbw Vale 128
Ed Sullivan Show, The 139
Eddie Waring Appreciation Society 255–6

Eddie Waring Book of Rugby League, The 44
Eddie Waring Memorial Coin 283
Eddie Waring on Rugby League 47, 119, 205
Eddie Waring Rugby League Annual 154
Eden, Sir Anthony 139
Edgar, Harry 153, 159, 194
Edinburgh 159
Edward VIII 49
Edwards, Gareth 225
Egan, Joe 105
1895 Club 216–17, 226, 260
'Elijah' 261
Elizabeth II 160, 269
Elland Road (Leeds) 251
Elliott, John 214
Ellis, Arthur 240, 276
'Els Segadors' 282
Elvin, Sir Arthur 49–50
Empire Stadium *see* Wembley Stadium
England RL team *see* Great Britain RL Lions
England to Australia and New Zealand 91, 99–100
'Entente Cordiale' 268
'Eternally' 268
Evatt, Dr H.V. 90
Evening Standard 269
Exhibition Ground (Brisbane) 104
Express & Star 202, 227

Fallowfield, Bill 124–5, 129–30, 144, 154, 186, 191–2, 211–12, 228–9, 231–2
Fartown (Huddersfield) 47, 119
Featherstone Rovers RLFC 22, 48, 68, 140, 174, 180, 205
Felgen, Camillo 243
Fenton, Eileen 32, 35
Festival of Britain 139
Fiddler's Dram 268
Field, Shirley Anne 251
'Fight the Good Fight' 207, 267
Fiji 130, 148, 238
Filey 34
Finch, Brian 167–9
First Return 182–3
Flamborough Head 157
Fleetwood 159, 261
Fletcher, Raymond 165, 183, 209–11, 276

Floodlit Trophy 166, 195–6, 199, 201, 204, 215, 220, 226, 251, 268, 271
Formby, George 255
Forsyth, Bruce 11, 251
Fortescue, Harry 59–60, 64–5, 68
Fortune, John 253
Foster, Mr (headteacher, Eastborough School) 33–4, 42
Foster, Trevor 95, 110
Fox, Don 174–7
Fox, Sir Marcus 32
Fox, Neil 174, 176–7, 283
Fox, Sir Paul 180–1, 187, 189–91, 276
Fox, Peter 174
Fraiche, G. 127
France RL team 141, 179, 187
Francis, Roy 79, 231
Fraser, Peter 110
Fremantle 96–7
French, Ray 198, 218–20
Freud, Clement 250
Freyberg, Sir Bernard 110

Gabbatt, Wilf 92, 97
Galashiels 242
Gamble, Jack 204
Game That Got Away, The 233
Garden, Graeme 254–5
Garrick Club 227
Gee, Ken 95
Generation Game, The 11, 251
George, Mick 267
George Hotel (Huddersfield) 44–5, 223
Gibraltar 94
Gilbert and Sullivan 32, 268
Gillette Rugby League Heritage Centre 222–3
Gilmour, Lee 120
Giltinan, James J. 106
Go with Noakes 251
Gone North 233
Good Old Days, The 240
Goodies and the Beanstalk, The 254
Goodies Rule – O.K? 255
Grandstand 26, 164, 168, 173, 184–6, 188–9, 193, 195–6, 198, 210, 231, 235, 248, 263, 267, 275
Grange Moor 19
Graveson, Norman 200
Grayson, Larry 250–1
Great Australian Bight 96, 99

Great Britain RL Lions 15, 92,
99, 103, 116–17, 120, 135,
141, 152, 155, 174, 176, 179,
185, 187, 190, 221–2, 228,
238; *as England* 90, 101, 104–
5, 109, 111, 118, 140, 150
Great Northern Hotel
(London) 169
Great Ones, The 208, 238
Green, Hughie 250
Green Final 166
Green Wing 155
Greenfield Giants 61
Gregory, Andy 267, 283
Greymouth 109
Groser, John 264
Groves, Michael 215
Guardian, The 13, 167,
213, 264–5, 282; *see also*
Manchester Guardian

Haddock, Arthur 156, 183
Haddock, Neville 150
Hadfield, Dave 15
Hadfield, Stuart 117
Halifax 79, 143
Halifax Courier 166
Halifax RLFC 46, 81, 85, 133,
166, 204–5, 209, 211
Hall, Gordon 276
Hall, Stuart 240, 241, 242–5,
246–7, 269–70, 274
Halstead, Ivor 70–1, 74
Hanley, Ellery 283
Hardaker, Alan 186
Hardman, George 103
Hardwicke, Tom 165
Hargreaves, George 127
Harlequins RFC 134
Harris, Ted 116
Harrogate 158, 203, 228
Hart, Alan 265, 269, 275
Harvey, Bagenal 191, 192, 193
Haworth Baptist Harmonium
31
Headingley (Leeds) 46, 48, 79,
82–4, 93, 158, 165–6, 185–7,
199–201, 209, 212, 220, 230,
266–7, 272, 282
Healey 120
Healey, Denis 11, 249
Heath, Edward 250
Heavy Woollen District 19
Hebblethwaite, J. 175
Heckmondwike 20, 45
Help Yourself 256
Hemmings, Eddie 198, 219,
221, 224

Henderson, Dickie 252
Henderson, Michael 132, 134
Hepworth, Keith 204
Hevey, Michael 217
Hey, Vic 79
Heywood, Roger 264
Hi-De-Hi! 269
High Royds Hospital
(Menston) 273–5
Hill, Cliff 220
Hird, Douglas 120–1
Hirst, George 164–5
Hirst, Ken 175–6
Hirst, Stella 164–5
Hirst and Hellawell 42–3, 55
HMS Pinafore 32, 268
HMS *Indomitable* 90, 93–4,
96–7
HMS *Victorious* 96
Hobley, McDonald 241
Hollinroyd Road (Dewsbury)
28–9, 32, 44, 51, 59, 66, 82,
119, 131
Hollywood 130, 249
Holme Moss 135
Honolulu 130, 148
Hopcraft, Arthur 60, 168–9,
177, 180, 202–3, 216
Hope, Bob 130, 137, 148, 152
Horne, Willie 103
Hornsea 34
Howard, Trevor 95
Howerd, Frankie 250
Howes, David 84, 164, 165,
211–12, 227–31, 232, 259
Hudd, Roy 251
Huddart, Dick 283
Huddersfield 20, 44, 123, 222
Huddersfield RLFC 45–7, 69,
79, 119, 143, 180
Hudson, Barney 81
Hughes, Bill 166
Hull 20, 58, 63, 98, 150, 207,
227, 234
Hull Baseball Club 61
Hull Daily Mail 227
Hull Kingston Rovers RLFC
69, 78, 201, 204, 205, 227,
254, 263, 266
Hull RLFC 47, 68, 185, 194,
205, 263
Humphreys, Joe 150, 155, 166
Hunslet 22, 24, 150
Hunslet RLFC 45, 85, 139,
164, 180, 186, 207, 214, 220,
237, 254
Hunter, John 119
Hunter, Nick 195, 263, 270, 275

Huntly (NZ) 110
Huxley, John 260

'I See Stars' 160
Idle, Eric 253
'Ilkla Moor B'aht 'At' 48, 110,
263
Ilkley 107, 203, 273–6
I'm Sorry, I'll Read That Again
254
Imperial Hotel (Blackpool) 160
Independent, The 14, 256
Independent Labour Party 124
Independent Television (ITV)
79, 180–1, 182, 191–2, 193,
194, 205, 248, 251, 256
International Board of Rugby
League Football 127
Irvine, Andy 225
It's a Knockout 26, 177, 239–47,
251–2, 254, 257, 264, 269–70,
274, 276

Jackson, Glenda 12, 248
James, Clive 245–6
James, Jimmy 250
Jenkins, Dai 103
Jenkinson, Philip 248
Jenolan Caves (NSW) 100
Jepson, Harry 22, 84–5, 139,
150–1, 154, 164, 183, 266, 274
Jeux Sans Frontières 239, 241,
269; *see also It's a Knockout*
Jim'll Fix It 257–8
John, Barry 225
John, Elton 12
John Player Trophy 232
John Player Yearbook 196
Johnson, Celia 95
Jones, Ronnie 268
Jones, Tom 31
Joyce, Ramon *see* Fletcher,
Raymond
Junee (Australia) 100
Junior Showtime 205

K-9 210, 230
Kaiser Chiefs 276
Kalgoorlie 97
Kane, John 83
Karalius, Vince 231
Kaye, Bernard G. 54, 55
Keel, Paul 264
Kelner, Martin 13
Kilburn, Professor Tom 25
King, Phil 152, 155
Kinnear, Roy, senior 50
Kipling, Rudyard 25

Kitching, Jack 133
Knowsley Road (St Helens) 77, 166

Lake District 160
Lakeland, Muriel 194, 269
Lakeland, Ray 182, 184, 186, 193–4, 195, 196–7, 204, 250, 269, 272
Lance Todd Trophy 174, 267, 283
Lanchester Polytechnic 255
Langside (Bramhope) 161, 163, 271, 273
Laurel and Hardy 251
Lawler, Darcy 118
League Express 198, 234
League of Gentlemen 279
League Weekly 166
Ledgard, Jim 276
Leech, Joe 151
Leeds 14, 20, 54, 79, 156, 158, 161, 165, 167–9, 183, 192, 202, 216, 227–8, 240, 253, 256–7, 263, 268, 270, 273, 276
Leeds Assizes 129
Leeds Bradford Airport 161, 271
Leeds General Infirmary 187
Leeds Grammar School 276
Leeds Mercury 151
Leeds Oaks 61
Leeds RLFC 53, 72–4, 79, 82–4, 89, 103, 118, 128, 139, 141, 155, 164, 173–6, 186, 201, 209, 211, 217, 220, 228, 235, 253, 266–7, 271
Leicester 128
Leigh RLFC 47, 68–9, 180, 195, 238, 251
Leitch, Sam 218
Leonard, Deke 256
Levula, Joe 238
Listener, The 108–9, 202, 245
Liverpool 63
Liverpool FC 221
Liverpool Stanley RLFC 55, 67–8, 82
Liverpool University 255
Lloyd, Selwyn 252
Lockwood, Baroness Betty 25, 32
Lockwood, Richard 'Dicky' 44–5, 46, 72
Lockwood Brass Band 251
Loftus Road (London) 180
London 49, 63, 70–4, 96, 125–6, 128, 131, 134, 139, 142, 147, 150, 161, 169, 173, 178, 180, 182, 191, 217–18, 223, 227–8, 233, 252, 254, 264, 274, 277, 282
London Palladium 47
Lonsborough, Anita 160
Look – Mike Yarwood! 249
Look North 161, 165, 183
Los Angeles 130, 148
Los Angeles Rams 148
Lowe, Arthur 12
Luton 269
Lydon, Joe 283
Lyman, Joe 48
Lyttelton (NZ) 108

McCarthy, Winston 108
McDermott, Barrie 224
McGill, David 257
McLaren, Bill 236
MacNamara, Brendon 67–8
McNamara, Jack 167
Macklin, Keith 186–8
Macklin, Margaret 134–5
Madoc, Ruth 269
Maine Road (Manchester) 185
Malkin, Joe 48
Malta 93–4
Manchester 20, 52, 56, 90, 135, 150, 156, 161, 164, 169, 182, 184, 189, 212–15, 220, 240, 252
Manchester Evening News 91, 167
Manchester Guardian 52, 91; see also *Guardian, The*
Manchester United FC 198
Manning, Louis 258
Mansfield RLFC 128
'Maori Poi Song' 110, 268
Marsden, Florence Harriet 'Florrie' see Waring, Florence
Marsden, Mr and Mrs William Henry 28
Martin, Jonathan 229, 275
Martyn, Nicky 255
Maskell, Dan 237
Maslen, Steve 276
Mather, Geoffrey 26, 202, 203, 207, 266–7
Mather, Harold 213
Maxin, Ernest 248
May, David 267
Mekons, the 256
Melbourne 96, 98
Mendelssohn, Felix 261
Menuhin, Yehudi 12
Merchant of Venice, The 35

Messiah 168, 239
Metcalfe, Ashley 183
Metcalfe, Tony 183, 232
Methodist Sevens 162
Michell, John 25
Michelmore, Cliff 248
Middleton, Harry 192
Mike Yarwood Christmas Show, The 250
Millward, Roger 204
Mitchell, Tom 117, 228, 231–2
Modley, Albert 252
Montague, Dennis 200
Monty Python's Flying Circus 253–4
Moore, Patrick 248
Moores, John 61
Moorhouse, Geoffrey 130
Moorlands prep school 158
Morecambe 241, 251
Morecambe, Eric 12, 13, 240, 247–9, 250, 252, 253
Morecambe and Wise Show, The 247, 251
Morecambe and Wise Christmas Show, The 12, 247–9, 254, 259
Morecambe Bay 93
Morgan, Cliff 225, 229, 269, 275
Morgan, John 276
Morley, Robert 12
Morris, Oliver 85
Mosey, Don 150
Motson, John 237
Mouskouri, Nana 12
Mudie, James 190
Muggeridge, Malcolm 250
Murdoch, Rupert 283
Murphy, Alex 116–17, 205–6, 263, 283
Myerscough, Jack 164, 211, 253, 266, 271, 274
Myler, Frank 150

Nationwide 256
National Baseball Association 61
New College, London 24
New South Wales RL team 99, 101
New York 130, 136, 148
New Zealand Broadcasting Company 107
New Zealand Maori RL team 109, 110
New Zealand Rugby League (NZRL) 106

New Zealand RL team 76–7, 110, 135, 185
Newcastle (Australia) 101, 207
Newcastle RLFC (UK) 68, 128
Newcastle United FC 49
Newley, Anthony 268
Newlyn 126
Newport RFC 224
Newsome, Mark 45–6
Nice 271
Noakes, John 251
Noble, Ronnie 192, 273
'Non, Je Ne Regrette Rien' 268
Norman, Barry 12, 248
Northern Union 45–6, 48–9, 91, 127
Northern Union News 123
Nottingham Forest FC 36
Nou Camp (Barcelona) 282
Nova Scotia 111
Nullabor Plain (Australia) 92, 97
Nureyev, Rudolf 12

Oakwell (Barnsley) 36
Oaten, Jack 191–2
Observer, The 245
O'Connor, Terry 224
Oddie, Bill 254–5
Odsal Stadium (Bradford) 60, 64, 69, 73, 75, 81, 166, 200
Offiah, Martin 283
Old Trafford 93, 283
Oldham RLFC 46, 48, 142, 180, 186
Oldroyd, George 64
Oldroyd, Sir Mark 24, 27, 74
Olympic Hotel (Sydney) 99
Open Rugby 153
Orford, Sandy 81
O'Shea, Tessie 253
Ossett 20, 64
O'Sullevan, Peter 253
Otley 271
Owen, Ray 175
Owens, Ike 101
Owl Lane (Dewsbury) 21
Oxenhope 31
Oxford University 153, 185
Oxley, David 211, 227, 228, 229, 232, 259, 263, 276

Packer, Frank 102, 252
Packer, Kerry 252
Paddington (Sydney) 99
Palace Hotel (Colombo)
Palin, Michael 254

Panama Canal 111
Panorama 181
Parc des Princes (Paris) 179
Paris 127, 141, 148, 179, 253
Parker, Dave 166–7, 183, 199–200, 203–5, 218, 231–2, 251, 257, 265
Parker, Handel 31
Parkinson, Michael 14, 248
Parsons, Nicholas 251
Peasholm Park (Scarborough) 241
Peel, Harry 66
Peilot, Monsieur 127
Pennington, Phil 217
Penrith RLFC 222
People, The 150, 155, 258, 276; see also Sunday People
Perpignan 282
Perth (Australia) 96
Phillips, Keith 275
Piaf, Edith 268
Pickard, James Arthur 72
Pickering, Ron 236
Pickles, Wilfred 143
'Pie Jesu' 276
Pike, Magnus 13
Plomley, Roy 30, 38, 237, 256
Plymouth 90, 94, 96
Pollard, Su 269
Pontypridd RFC 85, 128
Pooley, Margaret 257
Port Pirie (Australia) 97
Port Said (Egypt) 94
Port Vale FC 35
Post Office Road (Featherstone) 174
Powell, Roy 119
Presley, Elvis 139
Preston, Charles 59
Previn, André 12
Princess Margaret 251
Pullin, A.W. 151

Quakers 272
Queens Hotel (Leeds) 14–15, 54, 156, 161, 163–5, 167–9, 189, 192, 201–2, 213, 223, 253, 268, 276
Queens Park Rangers FC 180
Queensland RL team 99, 103

Radio Times 11, 142, 167–8, 169, 177, 201, 241, 257
Randwick (Sydney) 100
Rawson, Hector 164, 183
Ray, Ted 241
Rectory Field (Blackheath) 135

Redfearn, Alan 119
Redfearn, David 119
Redgrave, Michael 12
Redwood, Jack 106, 127
Regan, Rev. John 264
Reid, Beryl 251
Reith, Lord John 142, 143, 144, 162
Reynolds, S.E. 132
Rhodes, Billy 48
Rhodes, Trevor 35
Richards, Huw 277
Richardson, 'Cosh' 72
Rigg, Diana 12
Riley, Tom 150
Ripping Yarns 254
Rippon, Angela 12
Riscoe, Johnnie 194
Risman, Bev 175–6, 228
Risman, Gus 79, 93, 96, 99, 101, 149
Roberts, Charlie 71
Robinson, John 276
Rochdale Hornets RLFC 48, 50, 70, 82, 207, 215, 238
Rockhampton (Australia) 103
Roger 204
Rogers, Keith 133
Rose, Henry 83
Rossall School 159
Rothman's Rugby League Yearbook 165
Rotorua 110
Rowans, The (Bramhope) 161, 178
Royal Albert Hall 162
Rugby Football League (RFL) 49, 77, 80–1, 84, 127, 129–30, 136–7, 140–2, 144, 148, 154, 164–5, 179, 182, 189, 191, 194, 211, 227–30, 234, 259–60, 268, 271, 274, 283
Rugby Football Union (RFU) 45–6
Rugby League Chairmen's Association 117
Rugby League Council 52, 90, 92, 125, 129, 213, 228, 230
Rugby League Extra 182
Rugby League Gazette 148
Rugby League Hour 220
Rugby League in Twentieth Century Britain 49, 80–1, 144
Rugby League Journal 153, 194, 235
Rugby League Review 123, 126–30, 136–7, 147–8, 153

Rugby League World Cup 141, 179
Rugby League Writers' Association 174
Rugby Leaguer 144, 165, 167, 214, 276
Rugby Renegade 149
rugby union 13, 45, 68, 74, 107–8, 117, 124, 127, 134, 142, 144, 158–9, 196, 219, 225–6, 236, 277, 282
Ryde 126

Sadler, Martyn 198, 234
St Bede's Grammar School 240
St Giles' Church (Bramhope) 275–6
St Helens 233, 264
St Helens Recs RLFC 47
St Helens RLFC 48, 52, 76, 115, 120, 154, 166, 186–7, 195, 207, 211, 216, 218, 228, 282
St John Ambulance Brigade 270
Salford 214
Salford and District League 61
Salford RLFC 57, 79, 81, 101, 149, 185, 207, 224–6, 228, 233
San Francisco 130
Sandeman, Chris 197–8
Savile, Jimmy 257–8
Saville and Shaw Cross colliery 21
Scarborough Seagulls 61
Scarlet Street 95
Schofield, Garry 119
Seabourne, Barry 175
Selby 98
Selby Town FC 36
Seeling, Charlie, junior 30, 76, 276
Shane, Paul 269
Sharlston 174
Shaw, Frank 144
Shaw, Peter 276
Shaw Cross Boys Club (aka Sharks) 119–22
'She's a Lassie from Lancashire' 263
Sheffield 125, 256
Sheffield Dons 61–2
Sheffield United FC 49
Shelley, Professor 107
Shipley Glen 31
Short, Back and Sides 251

Sicily landings 93
Simon Dee Show, The 169
Sky Sports 197–8, 219, 221, 222, 223, 224, 283
Sky Sports magazine 222
Smith, Bill 199–200
Smith, Frank 81
Smith, George 81
Smith, G.W. 148
Smith, Harry 72
Smith, Harvey 160
Smith, Tony 276
Smithson, Norman 216, 237, 250
Smythe, V. 85
Snape, Brian 228
Songs of Praise 11, 256–7, 261
'Sos Pan Fach' 102
South Pacific 248
South View (Dewsbury) 28–9, 66
Southwood, David 191
Southampton 157
Spencer, Ken 210
Sport in the North 182, 190
Sports Special 182
Sportsnight with Coleman 196
Sportsview 179, 184–5, 190, 192
Springfield, Dusty 253
Springfield Congregational Chapel 23–4, 27–8, 31–2, 36–7, 41, 52, 65
SS *Rangitiki* 78, 111
Stade Pershing (Paris) 148
Staincliffe 121
Star Town 252
Starmer-Smith, Nigel 236
Station Road (Swinton) 135, 139
Stephenson, Mike 15, 120, 221–4
Stewart, Rod 253
Stockport Express 185
Stokes, Richard 130
Streatham and Mitcham RLFC 70
Success Story 268
Suez Canal 94
Sullivan, Clive 278
Sullivan, Jim 50, 80–1
Sullivan, Mick 115, 119
Sun, The 213–14, 216, 270
Sunday Mirror 89, 116, 123, 154, 160, 163, 166–7, 183, 189, 257, 259–60, 272, 276
Sunday People 152; *see also People, The*

Sunday Pictorial 89, 92, 101, 113, 123, 125, 130–1, 136, 151, 154, 161, 165, 179, 183, 189, 218, 238
Sunday Telegraph (Sydney) 89
Sunday Telegraph Sports Parade 102, 113
Sunday Times 168, 177, 202, 216, 267
Sunderland (Tyne and Wear) 269
Sunderland, Harry 128, 145, 147–50, 186, 231, 283
Sutton Coldfield 131, 134
Swinton RLFC 47, 135, 140, 142, 145, 167, 178, 213
Sydney 90, 93, 97–100, 102, 105, 117, 119
Sydney Cricket Ground 93, 99–100, 118–19
Sydney Morning Herald 96
Sydney Opera House 100
Sydney Sun 96

Tamworth (Australia) 103
Tattersals Club (Sydney) 105
Teeman, Ronnie 164, 213
Tehidy Hospital (Camborne) 258
Telegraph & Argus 200
'There Is Nothing Like a Dame' 248
This Is Your Life 162
This Sporting Life 224
Thompson, Cec 237–8
Thornhill 19, 52
Thornton Cleveleys 256, 261
3YA radio 89
Thrum Hall (Halifax) 166, 205
Thurman, Frank 83
Thurrock 243
Tilbury Docks 111
Times, The 264, 277
Today 216, 237, 250
Todd, Lance 149, 283
Tolson, John Edwin 33, 34–6, 37–8, 42–3
Top Town 241
'Top Try' Trophy 283
Topliss, David 283
Toshack, John 268
Townsville (Australia) 103–4
Trueman, Fred 181, 191
Turner, Derek 188
Twickenham 134–5
Two Ronnies, The 13
2UW radio 102

Ukulele Man, The 255

Vaudetti, Rosanna 243
Vickers-Armstrong 93
Vine, David 242, 253
Vigo, Green 220
Vollenhoven, Tom Van 154

Wagstaff, Harold 45
Wakefield 20, 44, 121, 233, 249
Wakefield Cubs 61
Wakefield Trinity RLFC 45, 67, 140, 173–5, 180, 186, 188, 257
Wakeman, Rick 268
Wale, Michael 169, 201, 257
Walker, Murray 236
Ward, David 119
Ward, Ernest 53, 61, 105, 276
Ward, Rev. John Raymond 276
Ward, Phyllis 64
Waring, Agnes 65–6, 156, 162
Waring, Arthur 24, 28, 31, 36, 44, 54, 63, 65
Waring, Florence Harriet ('Florrie') 24, 28, 30, 157
Waring, Harry 27–8, 29, 31, 36–7, 38, 42, 44, 54, 63, 66, 70, 76, 114–15, 119, 158, 164, 218, 240, 249, 252–3, 267, 271–2, 285–6
Waring, Henry Arthur ('Harry') 24, 26, 28–9, 36, 114, 119, 122
Waring, Mary 157, 161, 190, 194, 265, 271–7, 283, 285–6
Waring, Tony 157–62, 163, 181–2, 185, 238, 242, 249–53, 254–5, 268–9, 272, 273–4, 283, 286
Warrington RLFC 47, 53, 72–4, 113, 128, 131, 141, 180, 210, 219, 283
Washington, Edward 25
Washington Redskins 148
Waterman, Jack 202, 207, 245
Watersplash final 173–7, 209, 220, 228, 263
Watkins, David 205, 224–6

Watson, Bernard 175
Watson, Margaret 26, 165, 221
Watson, Trevor 165, 211
'We Sail the Ocean Blue' 32, 268
Welland, Colin 264–5
Wellington 106, 108–10
Wembley Stadium 15, 38, 47, 49–51, 72–4, 80, 124, 126, 133, 137, 140, 142, 148, 154, 173, 175–6, 184, 188, 205, 225, 233, 257, 263–4, 267–8, 281–3
Wesley, Rev. John 23, 27
Westminster Palace Hotel (London) 45
Wharfedale General Hospital (Otley) 271
What's My Line? 242
Wheelwright Grammar School 41
'When the Saints Go Marching In' 251
Whitcombe, Frank 95
White City 49
Whitehaven 114, 153
Whitehaven RLFC 187
Whitmore, Richard 248
Who, The 253
Wide Bay (Australia) 103
Widnes RLFC 131, 207, 263
Wigan Examiner 151
Wigan RLFC 30, 47–8, 50, 80–3, 95, 105, 115, 118, 131, 139–42, 147, 149, 151, 180, 185–6, 194, 206, 219–20, 238, 254, 282
Wilderspool 141
Williams, Dickie 276
Williams, Dr Jack 214–15
Willis, Bob 268
Wilson, Geoff 258, 276
Wilson, Glyn 276
Wilson, Harold 11, 249–50
Wilson, James 276
Wilson, John 49, 92, 124
Wilson, Peter 131
Wilson, Ricky 276
Windsor, Jim 155

Windsors Rugby League Annual 155
Wise, Ernie 12, 13, 240, 247–9, 252, 253
Wogan, Terry 253
Wolstenholme, Kenneth 177, 237
Womersley, Harry 141, 210
Woods, Dave 220, 278
Woods, Peter 248
Wooldridge, Ian 217–18, 226–7, 229
Wooler, Margaret 25
Wooller, William 181
Workington Town RLFC 117, 140, 231, 235, 237, 282
World of Sport 182

Yarwood, Mike 11, 26, 249–50
Yates, Jess 250
Yates, John 276
York 175, 272
York Maroons 61
York RLFC 82, 141
Yorkshire Association of Boys Clubs 120
Yorkshire Baseball League 61–2
Yorkshire Boys Montague Burton Cup 53
Yorkshire Cup 46, 79, 85, 141, 235
Yorkshire Evening News 54, 89, 156, 229
Yorkshire Evening Post 156, 183, 215, 276
Yorkshire Federation of Supporters Clubs 53
Yorkshire-Lancashire Major League 62
Yorkshire Post 92, 151, 156, 165, 183, 209–12, 230, 266, 276
Yorkshire Rugby Football Union 46
Yorkshire Schools Shield 36
Yorkshire Sport 150
Yorkshire Television 186, 191–2, 194, 276
'You Were Never Lovelier' 248